THE
ROUGHEST
RIDERS

THE
ROUGHEST
RIDERS

THE UNTOLD STORY OF THE BLACK SOLDIERS
IN THE SPANISH-AMERICAN WAR

JEROME TUCCILLE

CHICAGO
REVIEW
PRESS

Copyright © 2015 by Jerome Tuccille
All rights reserved
First edition
Published by Chicago Review Press Incorporated
814 North Franklin Street
Chicago, Illinois 60610
ISBN 978-1-61373-046-1

Library of Congress Cataloging-in-Publication Data
Tuccille, Jerome.
  The roughest riders : the untold story of the Black soldiers in the Spanish-
American War / Jerome Tuccille. — First edition.
     pages cm
  Includes bibliographical references and index.
  ISBN 978-1-61373-046-1 (cloth)
  1. Spanish-American War, 1898—Participation, African American. 2. Spanish-
American War, 1898—Campaigns. 3. African American soldiers—History—
19th century. I. Title.

  E725.5.N3T83 2015
  973.8'9—dc23

                    2015001414

Interior design: PerfecType, Nashville, TN

Printed in the United States of America
5 4 3 2 1

To my grandsons, Jasper, Hugo, and Anthony

The powerful purpose of this monument is to motivate us. To motivate us to keep struggling until all Americans have an equal seat at our national table, until all Americans enjoy every opportunity to excel, every chance to achieve their dream.

—General Colin L. Powell, July 25, 1992,
dedicating the Buffalo Soldier Monument
at Fort Leavenworth, Kansas

Contents

Cast of Main Characters

Emilio Aguinaldo, also known as Aquino, the fiery leader of the revolutionary forces in the Philippines.

Joseph B. Batchelor, a captain who led contingents of Buffalo Soldiers and white troops in the Philippines.

Horace Bivins, a sergeant with the all-black Tenth Cavalry in charge of their Hotchkiss guns.

Charles Boyd, a captain reporting to Major Young in Mexico, where Boyd was killed in action.

Allyn Capron Sr., a captain and the father of the young Rough Rider killed at Las Guasimas.

Allyn Capron Jr., a captain with the Rough Riders who was killed in action in Cuba.

Venustiano Carranza, a former ally of Pancho Villa during efforts to overthrow the Mexican government, before the two men turned on each other.

Herschel V. Cashin, the only reporter covering the Buffalo Soldiers with Wheeler's and Young's forces in Cuba.

Pascual Cervera, vice admiral of the Spanish fleet stationed in Cuba.

Adna Chaffee, a general reporting to Lawton who came to the aid of the Rough Riders on several occasions.

Stephen Crane, the well-known author of *The Red Badge of Courage* and a reporter for the *World* who helped carry fellow reporter Edward Marshall to safety after he was shot.

Benjamin O. Davis, a black volunteer who would go on to become the first African American general in the US Army on October 25, 1940.

Richard Harding Davis, a noted reporter of the period who covered the war in Cuba for the *New York Herald*.

George Dewey, a naval commodore and commander of the US Asiatic Fleet dispatched by Roosevelt to the Philippines during Secretary Long's absence from Washington, DC.

David Fagen, a Buffalo Soldier who became a legend after he switched sides and joined the rebels in the Philippines.

Hamilton Fish, the grandson of President Ulysses S. Grant's secretary of state of the same name, and a Rough Rider volunteer killed in battle in Cuba.

Henry Flipper, the first black graduate of West Point.

Calixto García, the general in command of the Cuban rebel forces around Santiago de Cuba.

George A. Garretson, the general who commanded American forces, including Buffalo Soldiers, heading north from Guánica to Yauco in Puerto Rico.

Benjamin Grierson, the first commander of the Tenth Cavalry.

Edward Hatch, the first commander of the Ninth Cavalry.

Hamilton Hawkins, a general who came to the assistance of Lawton and some of his Buffalo Soldiers on San Juan Hill.

Jacob Kent, a general in command of the all-black Twenty-Fourth Infantry in Cuba.

C. D. Kirby, a first sergeant who wrote about the action he saw with the black Ninth Cavalry in Cuba.

Henry LaMotte, the aging surgeon and medical officer who served as a major attached to the Rough Riders.

Henry Lawton, a general in command of Buffalo Soldiers and white units in Cuba and, later, in the Philippines, where he was killed in action.

Arsenio Linares, the commanding general of the Spanish forces defending Santiago de Cuba.

John D. Long, secretary of the navy and Theodore Roosevelt's boss at the time the USS *Maine* was sunk in Havana Harbor.

William Ludlow, a general who directed some of the key assaults on El Caney.

Edward Marshall, a correspondent for the *New York Journal* who was seriously wounded while covering the war in Cuba.

Edward J. McClernand, the lieutenant colonel who served as a top aide to General Shafter.

William McKinley, president of the United States during the Spanish-American War.

Enrique Méndez López, the lieutenant commanding a Puerto Rican militia unit in the coastal town of Guánica.

Evan Miles, a colonel engaged in much of the action around El Caney.

Nelson A. Miles, the commanding general of the US Army during the Spanish-American War.

Albert L. Mills, a captain who delivered Shafter's message that Generals Wheeler and Young were being replaced in the field by Colonel Wood and General Samuel S. Sumner, the result of which was putting Roosevelt in sole command of the Rough Riders.

James A. Moss, a lieutenant who had experimented with the use of bicycles in warfare and fought with the Buffalo Soldiers at El Caney.

William Owen "Buckey" O'Neill, former mayor of Prescott, Arizona, and a captain with the Rough Riders who was killed in action in Cuba.

George S. Patton, the future World War II general who was a lieutenant reporting to Captain Pershing during the Villa expedition.

John "Black Jack" Pershing, the captain who led the Buffalo Soldiers of the Tenth Cavalry in Cuba before he became a legendary general during World War I.

Colin L. Powell, the general who was the first black chairman of the Joint Chiefs of Staff and who later became secretary of state during the first Bush administration. Powell brought the Buffalo Soldiers into the national consciousness by dedicating the memorial in their honor at Fort Leavenworth, Kansas, in 1992.

Francisco Puig, the lieutenant colonel in command of the Cazador Patria Battalion in Yauco, Puerto Rico, who committed suicide when the Americans overran his defenses.

Robustiano Rivera, the lighthouse keeper in Guánica.

Theodore Roosevelt, the assistant secretary of the navy during the McKinley administration who later became the leader of the Rough Riders and president of the United States.

William T. Sampson, the naval captain who led the first inquiry into the sinking of the USS *Maine* and was afterward promoted to rear admiral in command of the United States' North Atlantic Squadron.

William R. Shafter, the elderly commanding general of US forces in Cuba who had himself fought for the North during the Civil War.

Theophilus Gould Steward, the chaplain and only black officer with the Twenty-Fifth Infantry Regiment, the first troop ordered to war in Cuba.

José Toral, the Spanish general who replaced General Linares after the latter was wounded in battle.

Harry S. Truman, the president of the United States whose executive order integrated the US armed forces in 1948.

Joaquín Vara del Rey y Rubio, a Spanish general who was killed in action while defending the village of El Caney against the American assault.

Pancho Villa, the Mexican revolutionary who eluded attempts by the US government to capture him after he and his men raided a New Mexico border town.

Joseph "Fighting Joe" Wheeler, an aging Confederate veteran of the Civil War who served as a general in command of Buffalo Soldiers in Cuba.

Charles A. Wikoff, the colonel who led a unit of Buffalo Soldiers up San Juan Hill and there became the most senior-ranking American officer killed in action to that date.

Woodrow Wilson, president of the United States during World War I and openly hostile toward racial equality in the military.

Leonard Wood, a colonel and medical doctor, the head of the First Volunteer Cavalry, and the original leader of the Rough Riders.

Charles Young, the third African American graduate of West Point, who was also a captain during the war in the Philippines and a major during the search for Pancho Villa in Mexico.

Samuel B. M. Young, a general who was the second-in-command to General Wheeler.

Prologue

L ieutenant Colonel Theodore Roosevelt was worried about the condition of some of his men. They were cavalrymen, not foot soldiers, and this narrow path through rugged terrain required special stamina. Most of his Rough Riders were volunteers, cowboys used to making their way on horseback over flat western desert and prairie land, yet here they were, on hilly trails sometimes facing brush so thick they had to pass through it single file. Roosevelt, on horseback himself, led his men along the rugged wagon road following the coast. The day before, several hundred white and black soldiers had bushwhacked the trail under nearly impossible conditions.

Another column of soldiers, consisting of both all-white and all-black regiments, had blazed its own route through thick foliage a few hours before Roosevelt's Rough Riders started out. The grueling path wound precipitously along the coast, causing some of the troops to stretch out like an accordion behind the men plowing on before them. One soldier later said, "They advanced as blind men would through the dense underbrush." They continued their sluggish pace for five arduous miles toward Siboney, their first stop along the shoreline. The combined US forces that had landed so far totaled about a thousand.

Roosevelt urged his men to follow him as closely as possible as he rode ahead to catch up with the others in Siboney. The Cuban summer heat was unbearable, even as twilight approached; it had taken them all afternoon to navigate less than five miles under the worst conditions imaginable. The heavy loads the men carried on their backs made the temperature and humidity almost unendurable.

Roosevelt and his Rough Riders finally arrived the evening after the first column of soldiers had made camp. He ordered the men to rest as much as possible, in preparation for launching an assault on the well-fortified Spanish positions up in the hills. They bivouacked in a torrential downpour that lasted for hours near the dismal coastal village of Siboney, at the edge of the Caribbean just east of Santiago de Cuba. When the rain let up, the men fried pork and hardtack and washed it down with bitter coffee. Roosevelt had orders to set off at daybreak with the other regiments and make their way uphill toward Las Guasimas, a settlement located at the junction of two mountain passes. The Spanish had fifteen hundred or more regular army troops in place, with orders from General Arsenio Linares to hold off the Americans.

The Spanish soldiers had superior weaponry at their disposal. Most were armed with 7mm Mauser rifles with repeating bolt action, high-velocity cartridges, and smokeless powder. Supporting them from behind was an impressive array of artillery that could cut through trees and bring an avalanche of fallen timber down on the Americans' heads. The Rough Riders and the other American troops carried more outdated equipment—smaller .30 caliber Krag-Jørgensen rifles and carbines, and Springfield rifles with carbon-powder charges that emitted black smoke and revealed the troops' positions. Their artillery consisted of a four-gun detachment of older hand-cranked Gatling and Hotchkiss guns. Roosevelt moved forward and the American soldiers followed in his wake.

The Americans opened fire first, and the Spaniards responded with their rapid-fire rifles and artillery. The US guns filled the air with billowing dark smoke, while the Spanish weapons gave off no smoke of their own, making their emplacements hard to pinpoint. The Americans advanced blindly into the face of the whizzing bullets and cannonades raining down on them. Their noses filled with acrid smoke, their eyes burned like fire, and their ears rang with the deafening pounding.

Then tree limbs came crashing down and the American troops started to drop around Roosevelt, who continued his upward advance. Men were tumbling like bowling pins, some struck in the head, others in the groin and legs. Roosevelt was hit indirectly himself when a bullet smashed through a palm tree and showered him with splinters and wood dust. The sounds, smells, and taste of war smothered everything. The fighting raged for a couple of hours, and Roosevelt's Rough Riders were struck especially hard, as they were in the lead now and were in danger of being completely cut down in their tracks.

Despite the chaos, US troops eventually prevailed against the Spanish defenses at Las Guasimas, the first battle in Cuba, thanks mostly to the intervention of black troops who prevented the Rough Riders from being wiped out. It would not be the last time black soldiers would come to the rescue. The Spaniards, meanwhile, pulled back and formed new perimeters a few miles farther uphill. One line of defense was at Kettle Hill, a second was strung along San Juan Hill, a bit to the south. Both positions would eventually be taken, but first came the major struggle in the miserable village of El Caney, a mountain town to the north.

◀■▶

A week after the Battle of Las Guasimas, the order came for the Americans to capture El Caney and the two major hills in the cradle of land known as the San Juan Heights. After a bloody day-long battle, American forces eventually overran El Caney thanks largely to the all-black Twenty-Fifth Infantry Regiment. Roosevelt was assigned to focus the Rough Riders on Kettle Hill, situated between San Juan and El Caney. There, Roosevelt's troops came under heavy fire from the Spaniards, who were laid out along the crest, ensconced in hand-dug trenches that kept them shielded from—yet gave them a somewhat truncated view of—approaching hostile forces. Other Spanish troops were well hidden behind stone barricades and inside blockhouses that provided good protection against the advancing Americans.

Roosevelt attempted to put his Rough Riders in the lead, but he and his men had trouble keeping up with the regulars of the all-black Tenth Cavalry, under the command of Captain John "Black Jack" Pershing. Together, they pushed on through blistering enemy fire, taking heavy losses as they slogged uphill. In general, the Spaniards occupied well-concealed positions, although they were not entrenched in what the Americans would have considered the most advantageous locations. Had it been them defending the hill, they would have placed most of their troops along a lower promontory on Kettle Hill—the "military crest"—a hundred yards or so below the geographical peak. That would have given the defenders a more commanding view of the downward slope, providing them a clear, unobstructed line of fire. Still, there was little question that the enemy had the advantage, lying in trenches as the Americans climbed under great duress.

The Spanish continued to unleash all their firepower, inflicting mounting losses on the Americans. Near the brink of disaster, the attackers managed to maintain their forward momentum and suddenly became invigorated by the sight of the Spanish flag on the crest. The all-black regiments, including Pershing's Tenth and the black Ninth to their left, charged past the Rough Riders toward the clearing near the top, lacing the air with chilling battle cries they had learned in earlier wars. They ran ahead furiously and courageously, seemingly without regard for their own lives and safety. The specter they created took the Spaniards by surprise and shocked them with the sheer ferocity of the attack. The Spanish gave way, some throwing down their weapons while others broke and ran down the paths leading southward toward San Juan Hill.

Roosevelt's Rough Riders followed the black soldiers to the peak as the Spaniards streamed down the far side of the hill. But Roosevelt had been delayed a moment earlier when his horse became ensnared in a barbed wire barricade, halting his progress and forcing him to climb the rest of the way on foot with his remaining men struggling up behind him. Once there, the Americans stormed together over the abandoned Spanish fortifications, unable to believe that they had prevailed in the face of what looked like certain annihilation just minutes before. Kettle Hill was theirs now, totally vacated by enemy troops except for the dead and wounded.

The Spanish fled as fast as they could toward San Juan Hill, occasionally turning to attempt resistance, showering their pursuers with a fusillade of bullets and shells, but there was no reversal of their broad retreat. The Americans, meanwhile, were too exhausted after the arduous climb to follow them. With rifles that had been thrown aside by deserting Spaniards or retrieved from the wounded enemy soldiers left behind, they fired with relish at the retreating troops, now in open disarray.

But the battle for San Juan Hill itself was still in progress, with five thousand American troops engaged in the action, including the Buffalo Soldiers of the Twenty-Fourth Infantry, who had made the climb from Siboney and another hill called El Pozo. Black and white soldiers from three different brigades launched their own attack on

San Juan Hill, with the Twenty-Fourth leading the way. There, too, they overcame enemy resistance after hours of bloody combat. As they swarmed over San Juan Hill, they could see the Spaniards running as fast as they could down every path available to them. It was all over now, except for the final mopping up, which would include the conquest of the main Spanish fortifications around the city of Santiago de Cuba.

The air stank with blood, burned flesh, and spent shells. Roosevelt strode among the wreckage and counted the dead and wounded. The army's official tally of those who fell in battle was far smaller than the number of casualties reported by eyewitnesses to the action; the pantheon of black and white men who lost their lives or were wounded fighting with Roosevelt's Rough Riders was much larger than first reported. The popular press also perpetuated inaccuracies regarding the battle itself, claiming Roosevelt and his volunteers chased the Spanish from San Juan Hill virtually unaided, when the reality was that they did not even make it into the thick of battle until most of the heavy fighting was over.

A major omission by the press was the role the black soldiers played in these campaigns. To understand how the black troops came to be here, in this hellhole on a hill, we must go back to the beginning, when freedom was no more than an empty promise.

PART ONE

The Landing

1

They knew all too well how it felt to be freed but not yet free. Following the Civil War, the shackles of slavery had been undone, but the reality of the master-slave relationship still reigned across the land. Black Americans had little or no access to the mainstream economic system of their country, yet there was always room for them in the military. All nations need fodder for the battlefield, for their ongoing campaigns to slaughter other human beings in war, and the US government was no exception. Of the two million men who put their lives at risk to preserve the Union, 10 percent of them were African Americans.

Massachusetts governor John A. Andrew commissioned one of the first black units in March 1863, with the encouragement of Northern abolitionists including Ralph Waldo Emerson and the two younger brothers of Henry and William James, Wilkinson and Robertson. The "all-colored" Fifty-Fourth Massachusetts Volunteer Infantry Regiment trained at Camp Meigs outside of Boston and then was sent south on May 28 of the same year. After arriving in Beaufort, South Carolina, it joined up with the white Second South Carolina Volunteers and fought Confederate forces with them on

James Island on July 16, stopping a Southern assault and losing forty-two men in the skirmish. Sergeant William H. Carney with the Fifty-Fourth later received the Medal of Honor for carrying the Union flag up to the enemy ramparts, singing, "Boys, the old flag never touched the ground!"

Two days later, the Fifty-Fourth led an attack with fixed bayonets against Fort Wagner near Charleston, the birthplace and bastion of the Southern rebellion, which was defended by Confederate soldiers under the command of General Pierre Gustave Toutant Beauregard, the "Little Napoleon of the South." The black troops surged over the sharpened wooden stakes ringing the fort and continued into a water-filled ditch. Two of their captains were killed immediately, and Sergeant Major Lewis Douglass, the son of abolitionist Frederick Douglass, was wounded when his sword was ripped from his side by a canister shell. "Men fell all around me," Douglass wrote later. "A shell would explode and clear a space of twenty feet." The vicious battle cost the Fifty-Fourth dearly, with a loss of 281 men in all.

Major-General James G. Blunt, who led the First Kansas Colored Regiment in combat, described the fighting skill of the units under his command in a letter to Congress: "The Negroes (First Colored Regiment) were too much for the enemy, and let me say here that I never saw such fighting as was done by that Negro regiment. They fought like veterans, with a coolness and valor that is unsurpassed. They preserved their line perfect throughout the whole engagement, and although in the hottest of the fight, they never once faltered. Too much praise cannot be awarded them for their gallantry. The question that Negroes will fight is settled; besides, they make better soldiers in every respect than any troops I have ever had under my command."

They took up arms to win their own rights as free and equal citizens of the rapidly growing country, but the effort succeeded only in keeping the states together without attaining the main goal of abolishing slavery. Of the nearly 200,000 African American men who fought in one of the bloodiest wars in American history, 36,847 lost their lives. The cost to the nation was heavy, and the country remained as racially divided as it had been at the start.

And then the War Between the States was over, and the question of what to do with the discharged soldiers—how to employ them, how to keep them economically viable—rose from the stink and wreckage as it does after every war. The question was all the more pertinent for black soldiers being mustered out of uniform, since their options were more limited. The whites in the South considered them an inferior species, and those in the North didn't welcome the competition for available peacetime jobs.

Future president James A. Garfield, a staunch abolitionist, was ahead of his time with regard to civil rights. Is freedom "the bare privilege of not being chained?" he asked in a speech delivered right after the war, when he was serving as a congressman. "If this is all, then freedom is a bitter mockery, a cruel delusion. . . . Let us not commit ourselves to the absurd and senseless dogma that the color of the skin shall be the basis of suffrage, the talisman of liberty."

What was the answer to the nation's dilemma?

Again, war came to the rescue as the country looked for new territories to conquer, more enemies to fight. Greater numbers of strong young bodies were needed on the frontier as the government looked westward to push its boundaries into uncharted regions. But the Native Americans, who had occupied much of that land almost since time had begun, had other ideas. This was their land, they believed. They lived, hunted, fished, and practiced their spiritual rituals there, a situation that the US government had considered problematic for decades. As the expanding nation encroached farther onto those native lands, the inevitable clashes became more and more frequent. In this, African Americans had a new role to play, another military calling: to serve the cause of white America's dreams of empire.

"There is no greater civilizing agency for the Negro, whether we look upon the conservative or advancing side, than the army," wrote Theophilus Gould Steward, an ordained chaplain who founded the African Methodist Episcopal Church in South Carolina and Georgia. Steward believed that black Americans would eventually emerge from their parlous condition in American society and take their place alongside whites, in part by proving their mettle against the gore and strife of mortal combat in service of the country.

There is some disagreement about the origins of the term "buffalo soldiers." Some attribute it to the Cheyenne in the 1870s, who compared black men in combat to the wild buffaloes they fought on the plains. Others believe the phrase originated with the Comanche, who were intrigued by the black men's dark skin and tight curly hair. Possibly, the truth is a combination of the two accounts. One Cheyenne warrior said that this new type of soldier had "a thick and shaggy mane of hair" and "fought like a cornered buffalo." Also like a buffalo, he "suffered wound after wound, yet had not died." In truth, the African Americans who signed up for service during the Indian Wars of the late nineteenth century quickly earned a reputation as some of the fiercest fighters the Native Americans had ever encountered.

After the Civil War, the United States Colored Troops were organized into two regiments of black cavalry—the Ninth and Tenth—and four regiments of black infantry—the Thirty-Eighth, Thirty-Ninth, Fortieth, and Forty-First. The Tenth was the original, activated at Fort Leavenworth, Kansas, in 1867. In April 1869, the Thirty-Ninth and Fortieth were regrouped as the Twenty-Fourth

Infantry Regiment, based in Fort Clark, Texas, which they regarded as a soldier's paradise. "Beautiful rivers, grass and grassy plains, teemed with game," wrote Captain William G. Muller, with the Twenty-Fourth. "The buffalo overran the plains in the autumn; immense herds of antelope, thousands of deer, wild turkeys, quail, duck, and geese were everywhere—not to speak of cattle run wild, by the thousands, free to everyone."

Seven months later, the Thirty-Eighth and Forty-First were combined into the Twenty-Fifth Infantry Regiment, stationed at Jackson Barracks in New Orleans. They were led mostly by white officers, although a handful of blacks were promoted into the officer ranks, among them Benjamin Grierson, first commander of the Tenth Cavalry; Edward Hatch, first commander of the Ninth; and Henry Flipper, the first black graduate of West Point. Flipper was the seventh African American to enter the military academy, where he encountered a measure of public racism from some white cadets who otherwise treated him with respect in private. "In short, there is a fearful lack of backbone," he wrote home. The whites for the most part were afraid to befriend him in front of other whites and ostracized him from their clubs. "There was no society for me to enjoy—no friends, male or female, for me to visit, or with whom I could have any social intercourse, so absolute was my isolation." He was simply "the colored cadet."

In July 1875, sections of the Tenth Cavalry and the Twenty-Fourth and Twenty-Fifth Infantries were put under the command of Colonel William R. Shafter, a future general who directed them on a famous expedition across the plains through Comanche territory and who would later lead them into war in Cuba.

Various wars raged on for the better part of three decades, with black soldiers fighting alongside their white brothers in combat throughout the southwestern United States and up through the endless expanses of the Great Plains region. Over the course

After the Civil War, the US Colored Troops were eventually organized into two cavalry and two infantry regiments, including the Twenty-Fifth Infantry, which was given the name Buffalo Soldiers by the Indians they fought out west.
Library of Congress Prints and Photographs Division (LC-DIG-ppmsca-11406)

of innumerable campaigns, thirteen black enlisted men and six black officers earned the Medal of Honor, and countless other African Americans pitched in to support their nation with grunt labor that included developing roads, constructing buildings, and delivering mail.

In 1892, President Benjamin Harrison dispatched black troops to Wyoming during the storied Johnson County War, which climaxed in a shootout between large, wealthy, settled ranchers and small farmers more recent to the area. A band of Buffalo Soldiers headquartered in Fort Robinson, Nebraska, rode northwest by train to Gillette, in the northeastern corner of Wyoming, and from there marched farther northwest to Suggs, a railroad town, where they constructed Camp Bettens in mid-June, despite hostility from the local populace. Once entrenched near the center of the battle, they teamed up with white troops and a sheriff's posse to help quell the violence and capture a gang of killers hired by the ranchers. The white locals were not overly enamored of armed black soldiers intervening in what they regarded as a regional dispute. Nevertheless, the black troops stayed on for nearly a year before the issue was resolved and law and order was restored to the satisfaction of the federal government. One black soldier lost his life and two were wounded during the infamous clash that has come down through history known as the Battle of Suggs. A year following the conflict, Suggs was abandoned in favor of the new town of Arvada, on the opposite bank of the Powder River.

2

The Indian Wars, too, staggered to an end, most of the Native American tribes having been subdued and relocated to one of several Indian reservations that had come into existence since 1851. The United States had defeated another enemy in battle and shuttled its people onto vast parcels of mostly arid land where they came under the tutelage of religious leaders, many of them Quakers in the earlier years, whose job it was to "civilize" them and force them to adapt to a new way of life.

The end of military hostilities once again left thousands of Buffalo Soldiers without the means to earn a living, unless they were willing to return to their old jobs, which, while not exactly slave labor this time, was not far from it. For many, the only option was once again subservient labor at low pay for white employers who could afford their services. Once again, white America was unsettled by the prospect of so many black warriors returning from the wilderness, and many voiced concerns about potential uprisings similar to the slave revolts in ancient Rome.

The black soldiers who had served their country well in combat thought they had earned a proper place in American society, and when they found the sentiment was not shared by the majority of the population, they felt the range of emotions from disappointment to outrage, just as they had so many times before. Yet, although the "civilized" society they returned to was anything but open and welcoming, there had been some gains since Reconstruction ended in 1877. During the next thirteen years, real estate owned by black Americans tripled, and school enrollment and literacy rates improved more than 40 percent. In New York City, about thirteen thousand black residents paid taxes on $1.5 million worth of property they owned, and they had deposited a quarter of a million dollars in the banks. The numbers were even more impressive in Philadelphia, where the black population was double that of New York.

African Americans voted in greater numbers, with many elected to public office. Black colleges and universities including Howard, Morehouse, Fisk, and Tuskegee, sprung up during this time, propelling their students into the professional ranks as doctors, lawyers, and teachers. Yet all of this occurred within an apartheid environment, where separate never amounted to equal, and "uppity" blacks who didn't know their place were treated with scorn and often brutalized.

The African American writer Charles W. Chesnutt described the feelings of a black nurse in his 1901 novel *The Marrow of Tradition*: "These old-time Negroes made her sick with their slavering over the white folks, who, she supposed, favored them and made much of them because they had once belonged to them—much the same reason why they fondled their cats and dogs. For her part, they gave her nothing but her wages, and small wages at that, and she owed them nothing more than equivalent service. It was purely a matter of business; she sold her time for their money. There was no question of love between them."

By this time, a generation had passed since the official end of slavery, and younger African Americans—both former soldiers and the offspring of former slaves—were eager to shuck off the trappings of their ancestors' servile past. Their forefathers had put their lives on the line for their country, and in some cases either died or were mangled by war for their efforts. They had absorbed the dazzling rhetoric of Frederick Douglass and the lessons taught by his oratorical successor, Booker T. Washington, the first head of Alabama's Tuskegee Institute. In 1895, Washington urged new generations of black Americans to work hard, save money, buy property, and rise into the middle class. And while all that advice was well and good if they were allowed to play on a level field, with no insurmountable obstacles strewn in their paths, that was not the reality, not for African Americans in general, and not for the soldiers returning from the wild frontier. What they found instead was a hostile environment, as mean-spirited and un-Christian as the one that had put them under the lash since their forebears arrived on slave ships. In 1901, President Theodore Roosevelt invited Washington to dinner at the White House. It was the first such invitation of its kind, but the backlash was so vicious that Roosevelt never made another. The potential political cost was not worth the risk.

To keep black citizens from climbing further up the tottering ladder of equality, white America had launched a three-pronged assault designed to obliterate the type of progress that had occurred during Reconstruction. The all-out war against equal rights started with disenfranchisement in the voting booth. Beginning in 1890, while the Buffalo Soldiers were still in uniform dodging bullets and arrows out west, every southern state enacted laws that effectively prevented black people from voting, depriving them of the most essential democratic right of all. The second prong was segregation under the so-called Jim Crow laws, which took their name from an old minstrel routine, "Jumping Jim Crow," and came to be used as a derogatory stereotype of black Americans. No sooner had the federal government abolished slavery than states passed legislation that created separate racial treatment in housing, banking, the workplace, restaurants, unions, transportation, restrooms, drinking fountains, schools, and other facilities. In 1896, "separate but equal" became the law of the land in the South, and it was a *de facto* practice in the North as well.

Schools set aside for black students were notably inferior to white schools. A journalist of the period described the situation in Pennsylvania as similar to that in other areas of the country: "The interest manifested for the colored man is more for political effect, and those who prate the loudest about the moral elevation and political advancement of the colored man are the first to turn against him when he wants a friend." He claimed that teachers hired for black schools were totally incompetent, evidence that perpetuating ignorance was a way of keeping black Americans in chains.

Modern civil rights advocates recognized the true inequality of the period. "With white supremacy challenged throughout the South, many whites sought to protect their former status by threatening African Americans who exercised their new rights," wrote black educator Henry Louis Gates.

Florida led the way along the path of infamy with laws mandating the separation of races on trains. Mississippi, Texas, Louisiana, Alabama, Arkansas, and other southern states followed quickly in Florida's wake. These states singled out the idea of integrated train travel as particularly offensive since it forced people of different races to come into physical contact with one another, the men and women of both races given no option but to mingle with one another in close quarters, black skin rubbing up against white skin.

Laws enforcing segregation did much to damage the push for equality, but the most vicious prong in the overall attack was vigilante justice in the form of lynching, primarily of black males. During the

1890s, an average of 187 lynchings occurred every year—between three and four murders a week for more than a decade. The familiar picture was that of bigoted rednecks implementing their savage form of retribution under the cover of night, but the truth was even more horrifying. Lynchings of black Americans had become a spectator sport, as eager onlookers, fueled by gallons of alcohol, reveled in the violence in broad daylight. It was more or less an official pastime, a latter-day version of the public games held at the Colosseum in Rome. And as in those ancient ceremonies, the lynchings themselves were not always a quick deliverance of the victim into eternity, since an unspeakable ritual of torture often preceded the actual execution. The police did not intervene.

Ida B. Wells-Barnett, an African American journalist of the period writing for a newspaper called *Free Speech*, compiled a list of reasons why black citizens might readily find themselves with nooses around their necks: "insubordination; talking disrespectfully; striking a white man; slapping a white boy; writing an insulting letter; a personal debt of fifty cents; a funeral bill of ten dollars; organizing sharecroppers; being too prosperous," and the list goes on. More often than not, raping a white woman was also included, and an accusation of such was often punished without a semblance of proof.

There was only one thing left for African Americans to do, claimed Wells-Barnett, and that was to save their money and move to a part of the country that recognized their rights as free and equal human beings. She encouraged black citizens to look for places that would provide them with fair trials when they were accused of crimes, instead of murdering them in cold blood whenever they were targeted by racist whites.

The larger problem, of course, was there was no place to go that offered blacks that much more protection than they had in the deeper regions of the South. The North was hardly more receptive, although the hostility was less overt. The landed classes in New York, Boston, and other northern cities were busy vilifying the new immigrants from Ireland, Germany, Poland, Russia, Italy, and China, and actively fighting for legislation to limit the foreign hordes that came swarming onto American soil in increasing numbers during the later decades of the nineteenth century. These xenophobic Northerners were not about to champion the cause of oppressed black people, whom most of them regarded as genetically inferior in the first place.

That great compendium of knowledge, the *Encyclopædia Britannica*, contained the following entry under the heading *negro* in its 1903 edition: "By the nearly unanimous consent of anthropologists[,] this type occupies the lowest position in the evolutionary scale, thus affording the best material for the comparative study of the highest anthropoids and the human species. . . . The fundamental equality [desired for African Americans] by ignorant philanthropists is belied by the whole history of the race."

On May 18, 1896, the highest court in the land, the US Supreme Court, rendered a notorious 7–1 decision on segregation in the case of *Plessy v. Ferguson*: "We consider the underlying fallacy of the plaintiff's argument to consist in the assumption that the enforced separation of the two races stamps the colored race with a badge of inferiority. Legislation is powerless to eradicate racial instincts or to abolish distinctions based upon physical differences, and the attempt to do so can only result in accentuating the difficulties of the present situation."

In other words, racial separation was the best policy for the nation.

Except on the battlefield! While black and white combat units were themselves segregated, there was no distinction between the two in the line of fire. Arrows, bullets, and cannonballs discriminated against no one; they hit their mark where they fell, obliterating lives and crippling soldiers without regard to race. They struck down white and black alike.

This, then, was the world the Buffalo Soldiers came home to after their years in the wilderness fighting for their country. Many of those who survived wore the scars of their injuries proudly, only to find that they couldn't work at the same places, attend the same schools, eat at the same lunch counters, or drink from the same water fountains as the white people they had fought alongside. Those who tried were likely to be brutalized and hanged.

Then something came along to change the status quo: America went to war again. Naturally enough, the nation had a new need for strong, healthy, young bodies to serve in combat against the country's latest enemy, and black soldiers, who had fought so well in earlier battles, were the obvious choice.

3

At 9:40 on Tuesday evening, February 15, 1898, deliverance of sorts arrived when a horrific explosion shattered the tropical stillness in the harbor off Havana, Cuba. "*Maine* blown up in Havana Harbor at 9:40 tonight, and destroyed," read the dispatch sent to Secretary of the Navy John D. Long by the ship's captain, Charles Dwight Sigsbee. "Many wounded and doubtless more killed or drowned," continued the report. Long received the news at 1:40 in the morning of February 16 and directly sent Commander D. W. Dickens to the White House to awaken President William McKinley.

"The president came out in his dressing gown," Dickens recalled later. "I handed him the dispatch, which he read with great gravity. He seemed to be very deeply impressed with the news," reading it over two or three times before replying.

The American battleship the USS *Maine* had been anchored facing the harbor, five hundred yards from the arsenal and two hundred yards from the floating dock there. It was an intensely dark night, with low-hanging rainclouds that drenched the area immediately after the explosion. The detonation ripped through the bowels of the vessel, with its 355-man crew aboard, including 290 sailors, 39 marines, and 26 officers. The eruption obliterated the first third of the ship, where most of the men were sleeping or resting, and the remaining wreckage quickly sank to the bottom of the harbor. Two hundred and fifty-three men were killed instantly, and eight others succumbed to their injuries shortly afterward. Of the ninety-four survivors, only sixteen escaped unscathed. Black sailors were among the dead and wounded. The explosion rocked the Havana waterfront, knocked out the harbor's electrical power, toppled a long network of telegraph and telephone poles, and ignited fires for blocks around. The noise and concussion roused the entire city and swamped many smaller boats in the harbor.

Tensions between the United States and Spain had been mounting for some time, particularly in response to the situation in Cuba. The Spanish colony had been struggling to free itself from Spain's oppression for more than thirty years, and in 1868 the citizens had risen up against their overlords and persisted in that struggle for a decade. The United States, which had strong economic ties and real estate interests on the island, sided with the revolutionaries, lending them moral and financial support. America also nearly stepped in with military force in 1873 when the Spanish captured the American munitions and personnel ship *Virginius*, executing fifty-three men, including US citizens. The incident ultimately passed without America declaring war on Spain, and US support for the Cubans remained strong, especially when the islanders rebelled again in April 1895.

Spain responded by dispatching General Valeriano Weyler y Nicolau to suppress the insurgents. Weyler soon earned the sobriquet "The Butcher" when he adopted a Pol Pot–style solution of sorts, relocating innumerable Cubans to concentration camps near Spanish military headquarters. His brutal policies resulted in the starvation of more than one hundred thousand Cubans and incited war fever in the United States. The so-called yellow press of the era demanded that President McKinley take forceful action to protect American interests on the island.

US minister to Spain Stewart L. Woodford told the Spanish government to "take Weyler out of Cuba or we will do it for you." Spain recalled Weyler on October 2, 1897, but it was too late to have much effect. Although Spain replaced Weyler with a more conciliatory officer, General Ramón Blanco, the Cubans were not about to be mollified. They had long since reached the tipping point under Spanish domination. Cuba's economy lay in tatters, with unemployment soaring and Spain still maintaining a tight rein on the citizens themselves. On January 24, 1898, McKinley gave in to the pressure and ordered the USS *Maine* to sail from Key West, Florida, to Havana. It departed from Florida at 11:00 PM that night and arrived in Cuba at 9:30 the following morning, anchoring at Buoy Number 4 in thirty-six feet of water, between the *Alfonso XII*, a Spanish battle cruiser, and the *Gneisenau*, a German training steamer.

Spain reluctantly accepted the presence of the American ship in Cuban waters, as long as the crew remained on board and did not try to stir up trouble on land. Consequently, all crewmembers were confined to the vessel from the time it arrived until it was destroyed, with only officers permitted to go ashore when necessary. The American battleship was indeed impressive. It was originally designed as an armored cruiser with more than seven thousand square feet of canvas, and was later redesigned as a second-class battleship.

The *Maine* measured 324 feet and 4 inches in length. It had a beam of 57 feet, a draft of 22 feet, 6 inches, and was divided into 214 watertight compartments. It displaced 6,650 tons of water and was propelled by twin screws that generated a horsepower of more than 9,000, with a maximum speed of 17 knots. The vessel was fitted out with a ramming bow, giving it the appearance of a gargantuan waterborne battering ram. It was also designed for effective naval combat; two main winged or "sponsoned" gun turrets containing four ten-inch guns pointed menacingly over the sides, with the ability to fire fore and aft in any kind of ship-to-ship confrontation. Six six-inch guns, seven rapid-fire six-pounders, and torpedoes that could be launched through four tubes fleshed out the ship's military might. Spain cast a wary eye on the US battleship but took no action to expel it from Havana Harbor.

And then the ship exploded, prompting the US government to establish a naval court of inquiry to investigate the incident on February 17. The delegation, headed by Captain William T. Sampson of

The explosion aboard the USS *Maine* on February 15, 1898, obliterated the first third of the ship, where most of the men were sleeping or resting, and the remaining wreckage quickly sank to the bottom of the harbor. Two hundred and fifty-three men were killed instantly.

Library of Congress Prints and Photographs Division (LC-DIG-det-4a14340)

the battleship *Iowa*, traveled to Havana to determine exactly what had happened. Sampson and his team began their investigation on February 21. The inquiry dragged on for more than four long weeks, with the investigation hampered by the absence of any floating debris. The entire wreck lay submerged at the bottom of the harbor, preventing close and detailed examination. The board concluded that the *Maine* had been sunk by an external device, most likely a mine floating in the water. The team returned to the States without fixing the blame directly on Spain, but the American public was not satisfied by such an ambiguous outcome. Spain, many decided, was guilty by implication if not by actual fact. War fever mounted, and the drums of impending war grew louder in the distance, fanned by newspapers demanding that Spain be held accountable, even without definitive proof.

The *New York Journal*, owned by William Randolph Hearst, offered a $50,000 reward for "the conviction of the criminals who sent 258 American sailors to their deaths." That figure was revised later. Joseph Pulitzer's *New York World* was not quite as shrill yet also insisted that a Spanish mine had caused the destruction. Privately, however, Pulitzer admitted that "nobody outside a lunatic asylum" really believed Spain would trigger such an event. The *Chicago Tribune* took a different tack, opining that "the people want no disgraceful negotiations with Spain" and that "should the president plunge his administration into that morass, he and his party would be swept out of power in 1900 by a fine burst of popular indignation. An administration which stains the national honor will never be forgiven."

President McKinley wavered briefly, still hoping for a diplomatic solution, but the pressure proved impossible to ignore. He had already been labeled as "weak, and catering to the rabble, and, besides, a low politician," by the Spanish minister in Washington, Dupuy de Lôme, in a letter de Lôme wrote to an editor in Madrid.

McKinley was still seething because of the attack on his character, and on April 21 he accelerated military preparations and imposed a naval blockade of Cuba. At the same time, he ordered Spain to withdraw from Cuba immediately. The Spanish, who had denied all along any involvement in the incident, were incensed. Their own position hardened. They declared war on the United States two days later. On April 25, McKinley issued his first call for 125,000 volunteers, along with a war appropriations bill, which sailed through Congress without a single dissenting vote.

A second board of inquiry conducted in 1911 proved more detailed, but no more decisive. When Congress approved funds to salvage the wreckage, US army engineers built a cofferdam around the battleship and floated it to the surface, finally allowing a panel of naval technicians the opportunity to view the damage firsthand. Finding the bottom hull plates bent backward and inward, they declared that a mine had detonated under the magazine and destroyed the ship. Still, the matter was not concluded to everyone's satisfaction.

A book published in 1976 by Admiral Hyman G. Rickover, *How the Battleship* Maine *Was Destroyed*, backed the conclusion reached by the 1911 board of inquiry. Rickover, wondering if scientific advances over the decades would be more decisive on the matter, commissioned two experts on explosions to examine the documents generated by the first two inquiries, plus information on the construction and ammunition of the *Maine*. His panel concluded that the damage caused to the ship was inconsistent with the external explosion of a mine. The most likely cause, they speculated, was spontaneous combustion of coal in the bunker next to the magazine. To this day, the true cause of the detonation remains a mystery—one of those great riddles of history that will likely never be resolved.

The bottom line for McKinley, however, was that the American public was in an uproar, demanding that Spain be held to account for the explosion, lack of definitive proof notwithstanding. By this point, a diplomatic solution was politically out of the question. War with Spain had become increasingly inevitable, thrummed into the public consciousness by the energy of war fever, a jingoistic press, and homegrown political warlords longing to propel the United States more deeply into world affairs.

4

In any event, America was at war again. Assistant Secretary of the Navy Theodore Roosevelt had been champing at the bit to take on Spain and other foreign powers for some time. He admitted that he was a quietly rampant *Cuba Libre* man who couldn't wait to go to war with Spain: "I had preached, with all the fervor and zeal I possessed, our duty to intervene in Cuba, and to take this opportunity of driving the Spaniard from the Western World."

His imperialistic impulses were no secret to anyone. A year before becoming assistant secretary of the navy, Roosevelt wrote a letter stating that, if he had his own way, the United States would annex the Hawaiian Islands the very next day. If that proved impossible, he at least wanted to establish a protectorate over them. Roosevelt also advocated immediately building a canal across Nicaragua and commissioning a dozen new battleships, half of which would be anchored off the Pacific Coast to protect America from dangers presented by the Japanese. He considered Japan to have nothing but ill will toward the United States, and it behooved the government to take preemptive action against the hostile country.

As it happened, Roosevelt got his wish, thanks to an explosion ninety miles off the coast of the United States. He wrote in a letter to a friend before the explosion that he desired a war with Spain for several reasons: he believed the United States should act on behalf of the Cubans from a place of both humanity and self-interest; he thought the war would be a giant step forward in freeing America from European domination; and he said the American people would benefit from the exercise by having something to think about other than the quest for material gain. Roosevelt believed a justifiable war would prepare US military forces for the kind of empire he envisioned, by testing the army and navy in challenging battle conditions. He added that he would be extremely sorry if the experiment was not attempted.

Roosevelt's warlike inclinations intensified in the wake of the *Maine* disaster. He called the incident an act of treachery on the part of the Spaniards and said he would give anything "if President McKinley would order the fleet to Havana tomorrow." He took advantage of his boss's brief absence from Washington to confer with Henry Cabot Lodge, a senator from Massachusetts and fellow imperialist. The two crafted a war strategy based on the presumption that Roosevelt was in charge when Long, the secretary of the navy, was out of town. Roosevelt dispatched three squadrons of ships on different routes to Cuba, an action that stunned Long when he returned to the nation's capital the next day.

"I find that Roosevelt, in his precipitate way, has come very near causing more of an explosion than happened to the *Maine*," Long stated publicly. "The very devil seemed to possess him yesterday afternoon. He has gone at things like a bull in a china shop."

Mark Twain had an even more poignant take on Roosevelt. The man is "clearly insane," wrote the great satirist, "and insanest upon war and its supreme glories."

Roosevelt compounded his misappropriation of authority by firing off a confidential telegram to Commodore George Dewey, commander of the US Asiatic Fleet, telling him to order his squadron, except for the *Monocacy*, to Hong Kong. He advised Dewey to keep his boilers full of coal and, in the event of a declaration of war with Spain, to see that the Spanish squadron does not leave the Asiatic coast. Roosevelt told Dewey to then commence "offensive operations in Philippine Islands" and to stand by for further orders.

For whatever reason, Long failed to rescind Roosevelt's orders. He seemed to feel that more harm would be done to the United States' reputation by ordering an about-face in reaction to Roosevelt's insubordination. Roosevelt had clearly usurped his boss's authority, positioned himself as the man in charge of the navy, and forced McKinley's hand by unequivocally launching America on a path to war. Long had little choice but to rubber-stamp his assistant's directive after Spain officially declared war on the United States on April 23.

"War has commenced between the United States and Spain," Long telegraphed Dewey on April 25. "Proceed at once to Philippine Islands. Commence operations particularly against the Spanish fleet. You must capture vessels or destroy. Use utmost endeavor."

It took Dewey's squadron six hours, firing at ranges from two thousand to five thousand yards, to destroy Spain's naval forces in the Philippines. The islands now effectively belonged to the United States—although it would take a prolonged ground campaign to effectively assume total control—earning Dewey a place in history as a result of the engagement. Puerto Rico and other Spanish colonies would also be sucked into the US orbit in the aftermath.

Cuba was next on Roosevelt's hit list. After receiving word of Dewey's decisive victory, Roosevelt promptly resigned his post and joined the army, organizing his own quasi-private cowboy militia that also included an odd assortment of Ivy League types. No one was more stunned by Roosevelt's latest move than Long. Why on earth would Roosevelt quit an important job in Washington to "brush mosquitoes from his neck in the Florida sands?" he asked.

John Hay, Lincoln's former secretary, a writer and a future secretary of state, was more than a little amused by Roosevelt's temperament and decision: "Theodore Roosevelt, that *wilder verwegener*, has left the Navy Department, where he had the chance of his life, and has joined a cowboy regiment."

Roosevelt now had an opportunity to test his own mettle in combat as assistant to Colonel Leonard Wood, head of the First Volunteer Cavalry. Wood was a medical doctor, and it was during his tenure as personal physician to Presidents Grover Cleveland and William McKinley that he developed a friendship with Roosevelt. He had taken part in the last campaign against the Native American chieftain Geronimo in 1886, and in that same year he was awarded the Medal of Honor for carrying dispatches across a hundred miles of hostile territory and for leading an infantry unit in combat against the Apaches. Still, he had no experience as an officer in the field against a modern, well-armed enemy.

It wouldn't be long before Roosevelt would be joining the assemblage of volunteers as they stormed into the inferno of battle under Wood's command. The flamboyant crew of soldiers were known as "Teddy's Terrors" at first, and later "Roosevelt's Rough Riders." Roosevelt himself was nothing if not good copy. The newspapers loved him for the color he provided, particularly in the form of audacious words that poured out of his mouth. Wood resented the attention given to his subordinate; but Wood's Terrors or Wood's Rough Riders didn't have the same alliterative ring as the other names, and newspaper reporters knew a good headline when they saw one. Far be it from them to abandon a catchy title for the sake of accuracy.

Roosevelt had been in love with the cowboy lifestyle since his days on the American plains, and in forming his troop, he recruited a raunchy band of individualists, men who did not look at life with the spirit of decorum and conventionality that prevailed on the East Coast. Out of an estimated 25,000 enlisted men who volunteered, he selected 1,241 young soldiers—plus 54 officers—all of them expert marksmen and seasoned cavalrymen. In addition to the cowboys and the Western gunmen, Roosevelt also attracted a claque of Eastern bluebloods, bored and wealthy Ivy Leaguers cast more or less in his own mold who were looking for adventure and thought that a popular war against ethnic inferiors—the "Garlics," some of them called the Spaniards—would be a jolly way to find it.

On his way to Cuba, however, Roosevelt would meet up with another type of soldier who was not cut from the common cloth. These were the black soldiers who had already proven themselves in war. They were the Buffalo Soldiers, and within months they would join Roosevelt and his Rough Riders on their charge up a remote hill in the torrid heat and humidity of the Cuban jungle.

5

Theodore Roosevelt, freshly out from under the dubious supervision of Secretary of the Navy John D. Long, lost no time inciting the wrath of his new commanding officer, Colonel Leonard Wood. San Antonio, Texas, was hot in May, and after an intense day of drilling under the scorching sun, Roosevelt, getting overly friendly with his band of ragtag volunteers, announced, "The men can go in and drink all the beer they want, which I will pay for!" To the dismay of his superiors, he hopped in a van and led his troops to the nearest saloon, where they spent the evening drowning their thirst thanks to their leader's generosity.

Wood reprimanded Roosevelt for his flagrant breach of military discipline. It hardly instilled respect, Wood scolded, for officers to go out drinking with their men. Roosevelt absorbed the rebuke, saluted Wood, and promptly vanished into the night. A while later, he returned to Wood's tent and told the colonel, "Sir, I consider myself the damnedest ass within ten miles of this camp. Good night, sir."

The soldiers in training remained in San Antonio for a few weeks, earning the respect and gratitude of the locals, who admired the men's spirit and appreciated their patronage—even without

Roosevelt's companionship in the barrooms. When it was time to leave for war a month later, the townspeople treated them to a farewell party, complete with a band led by the son of German immigrants who composed a tune called "Cavalry Charge." The piece culminated with drums, cymbals, and live cannon fire. With the sound of cannons roaring in the night, some of the men thought the town was under attack and began firing their own weapons randomly into the air. Men, women, and children dove under picnic tables or ran into the woods. The electricity failed, apparently the result of an overload on the grid, cloaking the town in darkness except for the flashes from guns and cannons.

"I was in the Franco-Prussian War and saw some hot times," the German American composer said the next day, "but I was about as uneasy last night as I ever was in battle."

San Antonio, Texas, was blistering hot in May 1898, when Teddy Roosevelt arrived to assemble the Rough Riders under the command of Colonel Leonard Wood.
Library of Congress Prints and Photographs Division (LC-DIG-ppmsca-37599)

In contrast, Roosevelt and his Rough Riders found the whole incident highly amusing, a good preparation for the real battle ahead. They departed from San Antonio by train laughing, heading for Tampa, Florida, the final stop before embarking for Cuba. The only one who was not amused was Roosevelt's commander, Colonel Wood.

Preceding Roosevelt and his entourage to Tampa by two months was the all-black Twenty-Fifth Infantry, the first troops ordered into war by President McKinley. "The Negro is better able to withstand the Cuban climate than the white man," reasoned the commanding general of the US Army, Nelson A. Miles. The Buffalo Soldiers had last seen action in the Johnson County War of 1892, from which they emerged as heroes. On their way southeast in March through the Great Plains region, the veteran Indian-fighters passed through a long string of towns in which they were greeted with waves and cheers by supportive locals. The black soldiers waved back, distinctive in their dark blue shirts, khaki breeches, and ten-gallon hats. American flags adorned their train as it pulled into St. Paul, Minnesota, where a gathering of white settlers clamored for tunic buttons to keep as souvenirs. The Buffalo Soldiers accommodated the townspeople by pulling buttons off their uniforms and tossing them into the crowd. "We had to pin our clothes on with sundry nails and sharpened bits of wood," one of the soldiers commented afterward.

It was the first time the entire regiment had met together since 1870, and the journey was "a marked event, attracting the attention of the daily and illustrated press," wrote Chaplain Theophilus G. Steward, the only black officer in the infantry unit. No sooner were they reunited, however, than they were ordered to separate.

Commander of the US Army, Major-General Nelson A. Miles, believed that black soldiers were better equipped genetically to withstand the torrid weather of the tropics than their white counterparts.

Library of Congress Prints and Photographs Division (LC-USZ62-122405)

At the Union Depot at St. Paul, two companies were told to proceed directly to Key West, and six other companies were directed to Chickamauga in Georgia. Those six, accompanied by the regimental band, were the first troops to arrive in the park at Chickamauga, where they joined with a large contingent of white troops.

"The streets were jammed, the people wild with enthusiasm," wrote scholar William G. Muller in his history of the event. And then the mood of jubilation turned to one of hostility and hatred.

The trainload of black infantrymen crossed an invisible but real divide, the Mason-Dixon Line; they had made the transition from the North to the South.

"It is needless to attempt a description of patriotism displayed by the liberty loving people of the country along our line of travel until reaching the South," wrote Herschel V. Cashin, a white historian of the era who rode with the troops. In the South, he said, "cool receptions told the tale of race prejudice even though these brave men were rushing to the front in the very face of grim death to defend the flag and preserve the country's honor and dignity."

As the Twenty-Fifth headed deeper into the South, the War Department activated four new regiments of black soldiers to join them—the Seventh through the Tenth US Volunteer Infantries, led mostly by white officers. The Eighth had been stationed at Fort Thomas, Kentucky, where there had been three officers' messes: one for white captains and higher-ranking white officers, a second for black lieutenants, and a third for mostly white field and staff officers. Two black staff officers—the chaplain and the assistant surgeon—dined with the lieutenants.

Even as the black infantrymen traveled through the hostile South on the way to war, some military voices came forward with concern. Writing to the editor of the *Cleveland Gazette*, Chaplain George Washington Proileau of the Ninth Cavalry wrote, "Talk about fighting and freeing poor Cuba and of Spain's brutality. . . . Is America any better than Spain? Has she not subjects in her very midst who are murdered daily without a trial of judge or jury? Has she not subjects in her borders whose children are half-fed and half-clothed, because their father's skin is black?" The chaplain, himself a former slave, continued, "Yet the Negro is loyal to his country's flag. O! He is a noble creature, loyal and true. . . . Forgetting that he is ostracized, his race considered as dumb as driven cattle, yet, as loyal and true men, he answers the call to arms and with blinding tears in his eyes and sobs he goes forth: he sings 'My Country 'Tis of Thee, Sweet Land of Liberty,' and though the word 'liberty' chokes him, he swallowed it and finished the stanza 'of Thee I sing.' "

Yet, the majority of African American civilians endorsed the war, some on the grounds that it was the patriotic thing to do, and others with the opinion that it would bring their people in contact with other "colored" cultures. "Will Cuba be a Negro republic?" asked an article in the *Afro-American Sentinel*, out of Omaha, Nebraska. "Decidedly so, because the greater portion of the insurgents are Negroes and they are politically ambitious. In Cuba the colored man may engage in business and make a great success. Puerto Rico is another field for Negro colonization and they should not fail to grasp this great opportunity."

It also helped that no army regiments had a better reputation than the colored regiments, and, claimed Steward, none performed better in combat. He hoped that black soldiers, or American soldiers of any color, would never have to fight another war, but he said that if black troops were called on to serve their country again, he had no doubt they would do their unenviable duty as patriotic Americans.

So, while some African Americans believed that black troops should take no part in a war of white imperialism, a larger part thought it was worth the effort to secure a foothold in a predominantly black culture where there were greater opportunities for advancement. As for the soldiers themselves, many of them reasoned, logically enough, that their patriotism during this new war would finally earn them the respect they deserved. So they soldiered on, at first thinking they were headed into a warzone on a tropical island south of Florida, but soon realizing they were already traveling through enemy territory within US borders.

The Twenty-Fifth Infantry was the first to arrive in Chickamauga Park, Georgia, where it was soon joined by the other black contingents. One of the volunteers with the Eighth was eighteen-year-old Benjamin O. Davis, who would go on to become the first African American general in the US Army four decades later, on October 25, 1940. Their instructions changed from day to day; some heard they would eventually be departing for Tampa, Florida, others that they were headed for the Dry Tortugas, a remote outpost situated due west of the Florida Keys and north of Havana, Cuba. Other units had orders to go to New Orleans, Louisiana. Their final destination was never in question, however; they would all eventually be risking their necks in the hellhole of wartime Cuba.

The Spanish troops stationed in Cuba included 150,000 regulars and more than 40,000 volunteers, all there in opposition to only about 50,000 Cuban revolutionaries. The US Army originally counted a little more than 27,000 men and 2,000 officers, only a handful of whom were black. On April 22, Congress had passed the Mobilization Act, allowing for an increase in wartime army strength up to 200,000, plus a regular standing army of 65,000. Three days later, McKinley issued his call for 125,000 volunteers to man the campaign in Cuba.

The black soldiers stayed in Chickamauga Park for a few weeks in March and April, pitching tents, chopping wood, lighting campfires, cleaning equipment, drilling under the punishing sun, and losing a baseball game against a team of white soldiers before five thousand spectators. In the beginning, the sojourn in Georgia passed well, according to Theophilus G. Steward, chaplain of the Twenty-Fifth, who said he was pleased to see the fraternity that characterized the relationship between white and black servicemen. He noted in particular that an atmosphere close to friendship prevailed between the black Twenty-Fifth and the white Twelfth.

"Our camp life at Chickamauga Park was one round of pleasure," wrote John E. Lewis, a trooper with the Tenth. He reported that although white Southerners often tried to stir up trouble between the white and black soldiers, sometimes it backfired, as in one case when a white soldier objected to the verbal abuse being showered on one of his black comrades by a local white, and he responded by punching out the white civilian. The fight became ferocious and ended in the death of the white Southerner, an act that went unpunished by local authorities. Up to that time, this was one of few instances in the history of American race relations when blacks and whites stood together as one against white racism at large. Before Chickamauga, many of the black soldiers had never been befriended or treated as equals by white men in uniform.

The white press, however, proved less generous. The southern newspapers launched a campaign of malicious abuse against the armed black troops in their community and complained almost daily about their uncivilized conduct. The black soldiers in Chickamauga withstood the insults, backed for the most part by their fellow soldiers, who attributed the hostility to the "well-known prejudices of the Southern people." As a result, the onslaught of press abuse carried little weight with the men, and in short order, the brouhaha subsided and the black contingents in Georgia were ordered to pack up and get ready to assemble in Tampa, Florida, the next step along the path that would take them to the killing zones in Cuba.

At the end of April, the black troops sent their heavy luggage into storage, shipping off to war with only the equipment deemed essential for combat. They assembled on the Chickamauga and Chattanooga National Military Park, established by Congress in 1890 to commemorate a Civil War battle, and then headed deeper into the South, toward the even greater swampland of racial animosity around Tampa.

6

ampa at the time was "a BUM place," according to a white volunteer, First Sergeant Henry A. Dobson, who left a cache of
letters describing his experience there. Two railroads linked
Tampa—described by one reporter at the time as "a desolate village
filled with derelict wooden houses drifting on an ocean of sand"—
to Georgia, Louisiana, and other states to the north. The major edi-
fice in town was the Tampa Bay Hotel, grotesquely out of place with
its silver minarets and wide porches set amid an arid wasteland of
sand, pines, palmettoes, industrial plants, and squalid houses. A
few substantial homes for a handful of richer residents, who were a
tiny minority of the town's fourteen thousand citizens, stood apart
from the others. During the first two weeks of May 1898, more than
four thousand black troops descended on this military staging area
of "congestion and confusion," which had been chosen as the one
best suited for embarkation to Cuba, wrote historian Karl Grimser.

The words *chaos* and *confusion* inadequately described the prevailing atmosphere in the region. Commanding General William R.
Shafter and his sizable staff of officers were hard-pressed to instill
discipline and order over the troops pouring into town. Soldiers of

the Twenty-Fourth and Twenty-Fifth pitched their tents in Tampa Heights, west of Ybor City on the banks of the Hillsborough River, and the Ninth found space nearby. By the time the Tenth arrived, the campsites were so crowded that the unit had to set up in Lakeland, east of Tampa, alongside a few white units. With the tent poles barely in place, the sight of so many armed black men in town sent shockwaves rippling throughout the community.

The *Tampa Morning Tribune* was quick to fan the fires of hatred and resentment. "The colored infantrymen stationed in Tampa and vicinity have made themselves very offensive to the people of the city," the newspaper reported. "The men insist upon being treated as white men are treated[,] and the citizens will not make any distinction between the colored troops and the colored civilians." The press gave front-page coverage to every incident involving black soldiers, reporting daily about "rackets" and "riots" caused by "these black ruffians in uniform."

"Here in Lakeland we struck the hotbed of the rebels," wrote John E. Lewis. He described Lakeland as a beautiful little town with a population of about fifteen hundred residents, mostly farmers and country people. The town was surrounded by beautiful lakes, but they stood in counterpoint to the viciousness of the locals, who terrorized the black troops as soon as they arrived, turning the weeks before the war into a hell at home for them. The soldiers encamped there had to watch over their shoulders at all times and be constantly on the lookout for signs of mob violence. Every time a black soldier crossed the line or committed so much as a minor crime, local whites were ready to inflict summary justice on them. Any African American would suffice for a victim, whether or not he was the guilty party.

After making camp, one party of black soldiers entered a drugstore to buy some soda and was subjected to a torrent of abuse from the druggist, who refused to serve them, telling them to take their money elsewhere. The men were enraged, and the heated emotions were further inflamed when a white barber named Abe Collins came into the store, called them one racial epithet after another, and told them to get the hell out of there or he'd have them strung up. The barber turned on his heels, went back to his barbershop, got his pistols, and returned to the drugstore waving the guns. The soldiers never gave Collins a chance to use them. They pulled their own pistols, and five shots rang out. One of them struck the barber, who fell dead to the floor. The cops showed up quickly after that, arresting two of the soldiers and disarming the rest. Fortunately, that was the end of the action, as the black troops had put the local whites on notice that here was a different breed of men than they had seen before.

But the newspapers would not let the matter die completely. They continued to play on the fears of racist locals, who demanded greater police protection against these armed invaders with "criminal proclivities." At the same time, they largely ignored the fights and wild behavior by the white soldiers camped throughout the area. "Prejudice reigns supreme here against the colored troops," a black infantryman wrote to a friend in Baltimore. Everything the African American soldiers did was chronicled disproportionately, attributed in some cases to black brazenness and criminality. White drunkenness scarcely rated a mention in the dailies, but the press excoriated black men who dared look for a drink in white-only saloons. They were also accused of trying to foment riots among law-abiding citizens, who appealed to General Shafter to protect "respectable white citizens" from the black outlaws.

Soon, fistfights erupted between black and white soldiers, who would shortly be fighting side by side against America's common enemy. Reports of dissention among the troops traveled into the North, and Philadelphia sent a committee to Tampa to investigate. Almost predictably, the team of officials blamed the outbreaks of violence on "the insolence of the Negroes" who were trying "to run Tampa." Black frustration became incendiary when more and more saloons and cafés refused to serve them. "We don't deal with colored people," one merchant was quoted. "We don't sell to damned niggers."

Captain John Bigelow, a sympathetic white officer in a black regiment, came to his soldiers' defense, writing later that if whites had treated the black soldiers with more civility, however much they might discriminate against them, the violence could have been averted.

It all came to a boil on the very eve of the troops' departure for Cuba. Fired up with alcohol, a white Ohio volunteer thought it would be great fun to snatch a two-year-old black child from his mother, hang him upside down with one hand, and spank him with the other. His comrades joined in on the evening's entertainment by demonstrating their marksmanship. With the boy's mother wailing helplessly, the soldiers took turns firing their pistols at the boy to see who could wing a bullet closest to him without actually hitting him. The winner was a white soldier who ripped a hole in a sleeve of the boy's shirt, missing his skin by less than an inch. At the end of the contest, the Ohioans handed the child back to his weeping mother and headed back toward their tents.

Word of the outrage flared like wildfire through the black campsites. Totally fed up with the hostility they had faced in Tampa, the troops of the Twenty-Fourth and Twenty-Fifth stormed through town, firing their weapons into the air and charging through the white-only saloons and brothels, tearing the establishments apart as they took on all comers, civilians and soldiers alike. The combined forces of the camp guards and Tampa police were unable to quell the riot. Finally, the commanding general assigned the job of restoring peace to the all-white Second Georgia Volunteer Infantry. They waded in with fixed bayonets, loaded guns, and heavy truncheons, and battled with the black troops through the wee hours of the morning. Near daybreak on the morning of June 7, the Georgia volunteers had accomplished their mission.

In an attempt to cover up the extent of the mayhem, the official report stated that no one had been killed in the incident. Local newspapers claimed that twenty-seven black soldiers and a handful of whites had sustained serious enough injuries for them to be transported to Fort McPherson, in East Point, Georgia, on the southwest edge of Atlanta. The black press, however, viewed the melee differently, reporting that the streets of Tampa "ran red with Negro blood" and "many Afro-Americans were killed and scores wounded." Howard Zinn wondered in his 1980 book *A People's History of the United States* why the black troops maintained their loyalty to their country in the face of such rampant racism. Many black American soldiers began to question that sort of lopsided loyalty themselves. In the four years between 1889 and 1902, black troops wrote 114 letters to black newspapers complaining about the way they were treated by their fellow countrymen.

For once, the *Tampa Morning Tribune* played down the publicity given to the black soldiers involved in the riot, believing that if the true facts got out, they would reflect adversely on the city. The newspaper's chamber-of-commerce mentality won out over snarling racial bigotry, for the moment at least.

7

eddy Roosevelt and the First United States Volunteer Cavalry left San Antonio bound for Tampa on May 29. His seven trainloads of troops, mules, horses, and a mountain lion cub—with up to eighteen cars in each train—made great fodder for the press as they passed almost twelve hundred miles through the heart of the South. Cheering multitudes greeted them at almost every stop, where they restocked their supplies, sometimes roping chickens, pigs, and virtually everything else that was edible, hauling them up through the train windows and cooking them on the floors. Roosevelt had gathered around him an eccentric collection of men who were accustomed to the use of firearms and to fending for themselves in nature, he said. The future president wrote that the men he picked were "intelligent and self-reliant; they possessed hardihood and endurance and physical prowess."

When they arrived in Tampa on June 3 to what was described as "an appalling spectacle of congestion and confusion," the only people surprised that there was no one on hand to meet them and tell them where to camp were Roosevelt and his men. Worst of all, there was no food set aside for them. Roosevelt and his officers made the rounds of local merchants and used their own money to restock their supplies. Then they confiscated some abandoned wagons to transport their food and luggage to a campground a little more than a mile west of the Tampa Bay Hotel, near the present-day intersection of Armenia Avenue and Kennedy Boulevard. By noon, they had pitched their tents in long, straight rows alongside those of the Second, Third, and Fifth Cavalry divisions, with the officers' quarters on one end and a kitchen on the opposite end. Roosevelt lost no time ordering his men onto an open field to begin marching

Tampa was chaotic in May 1898 when the Rough Riders finally arrived after their long journey from San Antonio. Roosevelt and his fellow officers had to spend their own money to buy food and supplies for the troops.

Library of Congress Prints and Photographs Division (LC-DIG-stereo-1s01904)

drills, followed by cavalry drills a day later when their horses were sufficiently rested.

With his men hunkered down awaiting orders to debark for Cuba, Roosevelt set up his headquarters at the Tampa Bay Hotel, where his friend Colonel Wood allowed him to spend the night, from the dinner hour until breakfast the following morning. General Shafter dispensed $175,000 to pay the men the money due to them for their service, and they immediately set out for Ybor City and other areas in the middle of town for a night of carousing. The Rough Riders in their brown canvas uniforms and wide-brimmed gray hats stood out from their fellow soldiers dressed in traditional dark blue shirts and trousers.

Shafter and the other senior officers debated strategy at the hotel before sailing for Cuba. One of the first orders of business was deciding where to land on the Cuban coast. Shafter at first believed they would go ashore somewhere around Matanzas or Cardenas, east of Havana on the northern side of the island. Shafter insisted that an American victory would require upward of five thousand American troops, who would join forces with twenty-five thousand Cuban rebels to battle the Spanish soldiers, which he was convinced numbered no more than fifty thousand scattered throughout the island. With that number of troops under his command, plus a concentrated naval bombardment on the city of Havana, Shafter thought the conquest of Cuba would be a simple affair.

In retrospect, the general's assessment of the challenges he faced proved to be ludicrous. What he thought would be accomplished in a few months with so few soldiers—to say nothing of the dangers incurred by striking directly at Havana—fell far short of the terrible reality.

General William R. Shafter, well past his prime and hobbled by obesity and gout, is generally believed to have
botched the disembarkation from Tampa, which was a
bedlam of chaos and confusion.

Commons.Wikimedia.Org

The soldiers jammed into the bars, brothels, and gambling houses
with pockets full of cash to spend. Fights broke out among Roosevelt's troops and regular army soldiers, and when they got tired of
pounding on one another, they ransacked local homes, beat up the
town cops, invaded a British ship in the harbor, and stole bananas,
coconuts, and booze. Children followed the Rough Riders through
the streets as they drank, laughed, fought, and rampaged at will.
Some of the local youth made cardboard spurs, which they taped

onto their shoes in imitation of Roosevelt's curious collection of cowboys, ranchers, former sheriffs, gunfighters, some Eastern blue-bloods, and a handful of Native Americans. The Easterners were mostly wealthy university kids looking for adventure, among them Hamilton Fish, grandson of President Ulysses S. Grant's secretary of state. More typical were the rough-and-tumble Westerners like former Dodge City marshal Benjamin Daniels, who had had half his ear chewed off during a barroom brawl. Most of them had never seen so much water before, let alone saltwater, and were disappointed to learn they couldn't drink it.

Their sojourn in Tampa lasted only a few days. President McKinley, feverishly following developments in Cuba from his war room on the second floor of the White House, surrounded by an array of maps and fifteen telephones, sent word that the troops should prepare to depart toward the eastern coastline of Cuba—not the northern coast—where the rebels maintained a strong presence. He assembled a fleet of transport ships beyond a narrow stretch of land bordering the dredged canal in Port Tampa. He then ordered General Shafter to begin shifting men and material along the single nine-mile track connecting the campsites around the city to the ships in the harbor—an ordeal that lasted almost two weeks.

Roosevelt's Rough Riders were devastated when they learned that they would have to leave their beloved horses behind, except for six horses per regiment for the officers. On the first sailing, there was only enough room aboard the fleet for essential supplies, pack mules, the small number of horses, and eight troops of seventy men. The allowance for the officers' baggage was reduced from 250 to 80 pounds. Navy secretary Long, however, convinced the president that such a small armada would easily be destroyed by the Spanish fleet under the command of Vice Admiral Pascual Cervera, which could intercept them before they reached Cuba. Cervera was said to be heading toward Cuba with fresh troops, arms, and supplies.

The United States' North Atlantic Squadron, commanded by William T. Sampson, by then promoted to Rear Admiral, was entrusted with blockading the Cuban ports. McKinley counter-manded his original instructions and dispatched orders to board the entire expedition simultaneously, triggering a frantic twenty-four-hour rush to get everyone ready to leave as quickly as possible. As it turned out, the transport ships could carry only about sixteen thousand men, rather than the twenty-five thousand authorized for service in Cuba, and Roosevelt was informed he could take with him only 560 of his Rough Riders, roughly half of the men who had signed up. The rest had to remain behind in Tampa. The American fleet was to depart at daybreak on June 8. Anyone not aboard by then would be left behind.

Roosevelt was furious at the bungled operation, mismanaged from the start before they even got under way. He and his entire group of Rough Riders were in danger of missing out on the action altogether when a train scheduled to pick them up at midnight failed to arrive.

"We were ordered to be at a certain track with all our bag-gage at midnight," Roosevelt wrote, "there to take a train for Port Tampa." The Rough Riders were there at midnight, but the train never showed up. The men crashed along the sides of the tracks, trying to get some sleep, while Wood, Roosevelt, and a few other officers looked for someone—anyone—with information about what they should do. Every so often they came across a general or two, none of whom knew any more than they did. Other regiments had already boarded trains, only to remain stationary on the tracks when the cars failed to get moving.

At three o'clock in the morning, Wood got a message telling him to hike his men over to a different set of tracks, where a train would be waiting for them. Again, no such train was in evidence. Finally, at six in the morning, Roosevelt and the Rough Riders decided to take matters into their own hands. They commandeered an empty coal train with long flatcars and ordered the engineer to get them on their way to Port Tampa. They simply stopped the train and hopped on board, startling the unsuspecting engineer. Wood and Roosevelt convinced the befuddled gentleman to start backing down the track westward, until they reached the end of the line at the coast in Port Tampa, almost ten miles away.

Just as daylight was breaking over the eastern horizon, the train chugged into the so-called Last Chance Village, a makeshift town or staging area containing bars, brothels, and women cooking chicken on Cuban clay stoves. The locale was aptly named, as it was the last chance for the men to load up on a decent meal, beer, or whiskey, and a girl if time allowed. Roosevelt and his men were grimy with soot and coal dust, but their entire unit and equipment were intact. They stepped off the flatcars into the chaos of the harbor, staring in alarm at the thousands of men who had beaten them there and were struggling to scamper onto the ships in time.

More confusion ensued when they looked out at the flotilla of thirty-one ships and realized they had no instructions about which one was assigned to them. Roosevelt tracked down Colonel Charles Frederic Humphrey, the overwhelmed officer in charge of loading operations, who told Roosevelt to take a launch out to the *Yucatan*, which was anchored off the dock. Roosevelt mustered his men, and together they outmaneuvered two other regiments also anxious to board the ship, which was quickly filled to capacity. Roosevelt managed to get two of his horses, Rain in the Face and Texas, on board as well.

And there they remained for a week, the entire expedition that was supposed to leave at dawn, sweltering beneath the blistering Florida sun, chowing down on bad food—including so-called corned beef, which the men called "embalmed meat"—fuming inwardly over the hopelessly crowded conditions aboard ship and boiling to get into action as they waited for orders to sail. On the evening of June 13, they finally received word to get ready to depart from their US homeland the next morning and head down the coast of Florida toward war in Cuba.

When Roosevelt discovered that no ship had been assigned to the Rough Riders to transport them to Cuba, he outmaneuvered two other regiments to get his men on board the already overcrowded *Yucatan*.

Library of Congress Prints and Photographs Division (LC-USZ62-57122)

8

The black regiments, along with a small group of white soldiers, were assigned to six ships: the *Miami, Alamo, Comal, Concho, City of Washington,* and *Leona.* They were sent down to the lowest deck, where no light could penetrate the dark enclosure beyond the ten feet from the main hatch. The bunks were stacked in four tiers and lined up so closely together that the men could barely slip between them. They were constructed of raw timber, with rectangular rims four to six inches high. There was no bedding except for whatever the men could improvise for themselves, using blankets for mattresses and haversacks for pillows. The men were forced to stack their gear, including their clothes, shelter-halves, rifles, and ammunition, on their bunks, allowing them scarcely enough room to stretch out and sleep. Toilet and bathing facilities were all but nonexistent. The lowest deck of the *Concho* contained a single toilet for more than twelve hundred soldiers.

Adding insult to injury, the black troops were confined aboard ship during the time they were in port, while their white brethren were allowed to visit the bars, brothels, and cafés in Last Chance Village whenever they pleased. They crowded onto the upper decks to find sunlight and breathe fresh air as often as they could, but they seethed over the ongoing racism they were subjected to, even as they prepared to risk their lives in war on foreign soil.

Sergeant Major Frank W. Pullen of the Twenty-Fifth said that the black troops on board were not allowed to "intermingle" with the whites. "We were put on board," he said, "but it is simply because we cannot use the term *under board*. We were huddled together below two other regiments and under the water line, in the dirtiest, closest, most sickening place imaginable. For about fifteen days we were on the water in this dirty hole, but being soldiers we were compelled to accept this without a murmur." They ate corned beef, canned tomatoes, and hardtack until they were almost sickened by it, but it was the only food available for them.

Their anger reached a boiling point when their officers ordered them to let the white regiments make coffee and eat their meals first, before the black troops could assuage their own hunger. Pullen said it was a miracle they managed to live through those days aboard ship in the harbor under such horrendous conditions. They swallowed their pride and accepted their fate without exploding in violence, a tribute to the collective self-discipline they displayed.

The days passed with the men overwhelmed by acute boredom. There was little to do but fall in line for inspections, pull guard duty, exercise as best they could in the limited space, and gamble away the little money they had.

Finally, word came that it was time to raise anchor and set off toward Cuba. They left Port Tampa the morning of June 14 to great fanfare, with bands playing, flags flying, and the men clustered like ants on the rigging as the flotilla slowly steamed out to sea.

The transports presented a picturesque spectacle as they departed toward the open ocean. The ships sailed out in three columns, each column separated from the others by a thousand yards, with the ships about four hundred yards apart from one another. Smaller vessels escorted the American fleet from Port Tampa until it reached a point between the Dry Tortugas and Key West, where it was met by the battleship *Indiana* and thirteen other war vessels. When they passed around Key West, the *New York* was in the lead, followed by the *Iowa* and the *Indiana*. The official count was fifty-three ships in all, including thirty-five transports, four auxiliary vessels, and fourteen warships. The American armada presented an impressive sight for a fledgling empire about to expand its global reach.

"The passage to Santiago was generally smooth and uneventful," noted General Shafter in his official report. Colonel Wood described the passage from his own perspective with a bit more color: "Painted ships in a painted ocean—imagine three great long lines of steaming transports with a warship at the head of each line . . . on a sea of indigo blue as smooth as a millpond. The trade wind sweeping through the ship has made the voyage very comfortable."

It was not so comfortable for the men in the hold, however. Body lice had infested them and their clothing for weeks before they left, and without the ability to boil their uniforms and underwear aboard ship, they had to seize every opportunity to tie their belongings to ropes on deck and drag them in the water behind the moving ships to dislodge the parasites.

The weather was balmy until the fleet entered the Windward Passage between the western coast of Haiti and the eastern tip of Cuba, where high winds and rough seas buffeted the ships. Throughout the journey, the Americans avoided an encounter with Cervera and his Spanish armada, which had slipped past Sampson's North American Squadron on its voyage to Havana. After rounding the east coast of Cuba on the morning of June 20, the US ships headed west past Guantanamo Bay along the southern coastline toward the town of Daiquiri, about eighteen miles east of Santiago de Cuba.

Despite the cool breeze, a heavy mist obscured the shore as the men prepared to disembark once the order came. At about five o'clock the next morning, the heavy gray clouds began to evaporate, the wind picked up, and breaking daylight revealed the great flotilla of transports stretching as far as five miles out to sea, with the warships closer in. Towering rocky hills devoid of foliage dominated the coastline. The boats anchored about noon slightly west of the harbor, where Rear Admiral Sampson was anxiously waiting. He boarded General Shafter's vessel, the *Seguranca*, and together they debarked to confer with Cuban General Calixto García, who occupied the area with about four thousand well-armed, battle-hardened troops. That afternoon they met with the sixty-year-old Cuban leader in the town of Aserradero in Santiago Province.

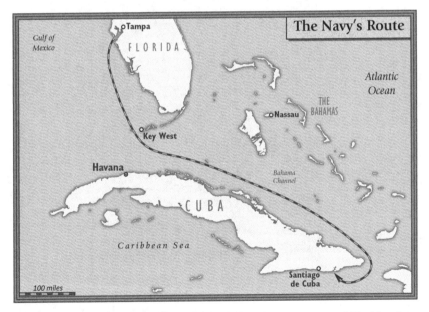

The US fleet followed a route southward along the west coast of Florida, then southeast across the Bahama Channel, and finally around the Windward Passage on its way to Daiquiri, near Santiago de Cuba on the island's southern shore.

Based on a map that appeared in *San Juan Hill 1898* by Angus Konstam, Osprey Publishing, 1998.

García had been anticipating their arrival ever since he received a letter from Major-General Nelson A. Miles dated June 2, 1898, which read in part: "It would be a very great assistance if you could have as large a force as possible in the vicinity of the harbor of Santiago de Cuba, and communicate any information[,] by signals which Colonel Hernandez will explain to you[,] either to our navy or to our army on its arrival, which we hope will be before many days."

Miles had also requested that García march his rebels to the coast and harass the Spanish troops in and around Santiago de Cuba. He advised the Cubans to attack the Spanish at all points and

Calixto García, the elderly leader of the Cuban rebels in the region around Santiago de Cuba, coordinated his efforts with the American invasion forces, which were in the process of disembarking after their voyage from Florida.

Library of Congress Prints and Photographs Division (LC-USZ62-91767)

prevent them from sending reinforcements to the region. He also asked him to try to seize any commanding positions to the east or west of Santiago de Cuba before the Americans arrived. Once there, American ships would begin to bombard the entire coastal area with the big guns on the battleships.

García took some umbrage at Miles's deprecating tone. Hadn't they, García and his rebels, already been shedding their own blood to free their land from Spanish rule for decades before the Americans entered the fray? Nevertheless, he needed American support to win the war, and he responded cordially, saying that he would "take measures at once to carry out your recommendations. . . . Will march without delay."

García performed his job well, attacking Spanish positions in and around the landing zone as the rebels burst out of the bush and fired volley after volley at the enemy. Although they could not see what was happening up in the hills, the Americans could hear from their ships the rebel shouts echoing in the air: "¡Viva Cuba Libra! ¡Viva los Americanos!"

Shafter, Sampson, and García devised a battle plan to attack the rear of the Spanish garrison in the vicinity, following the debarkation of the American troops on June 22. But the process of unloading thousands of soldiers, animals, and equipment onto shore proved to be a logistical nightmare. The fleet now lay anchored a mile and more offshore, and the men had to file onto small boats and make the crossing to land in heavy seas. The Spanish soldiers occupied the higher peaks and could use the men and boats for target practice as they struggled to navigate the choppy water. García's forces held the terrain on both sides of the Spanish garrison but were unable to move in for the kill without American help. To soften Spanish resistance, Sampson ordered a steady bombardment of the villages along the coast as Miles had promised, an effort that continued for two to three hours. The boom of the big guns on the *New Orleans, Detroit, Castine, Wasp, Suwanee,* and *Texas* echoed off the cliff walls, and shells exploded spectacularly in the jungle growth on the higher elevations.

"The first day[,] Sampson got all his gunboats together and fired shots all around the landing, tearing everything around there all to pieces," wrote C. D. Kirby, with the black Ninth, to his mother. "The following day we all landed and went about a mile before we struck camp."

The American shells exploded on Spanish forts, blockhouses, and various entrenchments in Daiquiri, Siboney, and other villages strewn for twenty miles along the coast, clearing the way for the Americans to come ashore. But the process of getting them there continued to be hazardous.

"We did the landing as we had done everything else—that is, in a scramble, each commander shifting for himself," Roosevelt wrote. They landed at the squalid port village of Daiquiri, where a railroad and ironworks factory was located. There were no landing facilities there, so the American transport ships were forced to remain offshore near the gunboats, while the men jumped down onto the few landing vessels they had and then rowed toward land in a heaving sea.

The larger boats carried ten or twelve men each, while the smaller craft had room for only six or seven. Making matters worse, the uniforms issued to the men were made of heavy canvas and wool, more suitable for winter in Montana than for summer in Cuba. The thickness of the Rough Riders' campaign hats alone could stop anything short of an axe, one of the men quipped. The clothing, along with their weapons, shelter-halves, and other equipment, weighed the men down unmercifully in the damp air and mounting heat. Slowly, the men inched toward shore and approached an abandoned and dilapidated railroad pier. To get from the boats onto land, the men had to leap from the water amid turbulent waves while in full possession of their gear. The pack mules and horses had to be pushed off the boats so they could swim ashore on their own.

Not everyone made it safely to land. A boat transporting black soldiers from the Tenth capsized, and two of the soldiers attempted to leap onto the dock but fell beneath the churning waters of the harbor and sank under the weight of their blanket rolls and other equipment. One of the Rough Riders, Captain William Owen "Buckey" O'Neill, a former mayor of Prescott, Arizona, plunged into the water in full uniform in an attempt to save them. His efforts, sadly, failed, and the men vanished from sight and lost their lives before they had a chance to fire a single shot at the enemy.

9

The troops of the black Twenty-Fifth were among the first to land a short distance from the pier. "We landed in rowboats, amid, and after the cessation of the bombardment of the little hamlet and coast by the men-of-war and battle-ships," wrote a soldier in the unit. "We then helped ourselves to cocoanuts [sic] which we found in abundance near the landing."

The first wave of troops had now landed on Cuban soil, and the veteran soldiers pitched right in and looked about for suitable campsites. Most of them, both black and white, had seen action in earlier wars, with battle scars to show for their combat experience, but some were young recruits no more than seventeen or eighteen years old and weren't yet familiar with the rigors of warfare. Some of the Rough Riders had also made it onto dry ground, if one could describe the wet Cuban coastline that way. These volunteers, although experienced adventurers and hunters from the West or thrill-seeking wealthy Easterners, were, like the teenage soldiers, as yet untested against live enemy fire.

The troops were wet and tired, and some of the animals were even worse off. Sadly, one of Roosevelt's mounts, Rain in the Face, swam the wrong way and drowned among the heaving waves. The other, Texas, made it to the beach with most of the other animals. Texas showed signs of wear and tear after having spent two weeks on the transport ship, and he was breathing heavily after his efforts to swim ashore, but Roosevelt was delighted that his horse perked up in short order and was able to carry his master.

About one-third of the men and equipment reached land by nightfall on June 22, but it would take another two days for the entire army to hit the beach. While the men were struggling toward land, a group of horsemen came galloping down from the hills waving a Cuban flag above their heads. They also carried a white flag, a prearranged signal that indicated the Spanish forces under General Arsenio Linares had abandoned Daiquiri and taken up defensive positions in the hills outside Santiago.

The troops pitched camp below the cliffs rising from the beach. They bivouacked on the beach outside Daiquiri where a railroad crossed a wagon road leading to the coastal town of Siboney, about six miles to the west. The Tenth, a black unit under the command of General Joseph "Fighting Joe" Wheeler—as were the Rough Riders—had also made it ashore earlier than most of the other troops. Already in his sixties, Wheeler had been a Confederate army general during the Civil War, and many of the men thought he had lost his grip on reality by this time. He seemed to have his wars mixed up when he exhorted his troops in Cuba to charge because "we've got the damn Yankees on the run again." A small, intense man and a graduate of West Point, he represented Alabama in Congress for seven terms after the Civil War and was second in command to Shafter in Cuba. Wheeler was the physical opposite of Shafter, who weighed in at well over three hundred pounds and was, at that moment, indisposed with an attack of gout aboard the *Seguranca*.

Shafter was also an old veteran, a year older than Wheeler at sixty-three. He accepted a commission in a Michigan volunteer unit during the Civil War and received the nation's highest decoration, the Medal of Honor, for his actions at the Battle of Fair Oaks, where he was wounded. He was taken prisoner at the Battle of Thompson's Station and spent three months in a Confederate

General Wheeler (left) was inclined to defy orders from his superior, General Shafter (right), whose tactics he regarded as too timid. They had fought on opposite sides during the Civil War, and Wheeler sometimes got his wars mixed up when he referred to the Spaniards as "damn Yankees."

Commons.Wikimedia.Org

jail. After his release, he was appointed colonel of the all-black Seventeenth Regiment and led it at the Battle of Nashville. By the time the war ended, he had risen to the rank of brigadier general. In the early 1890s, Shafter fought on the American frontier in the Indian Wars and earned the soubriquet "Pecos Bill" during his campaigns against the Cheyenne, Comanche, and other tribes.

Not only were Shafter and Wheeler physical opposites, but they had fought on opposing sides during the Civil War. The gargantuan, ailing Shafter was regarded as an unlikely candidate for his commanding role in Cuba. He was past his prime, as was Wheeler, and the two men resented each other.

The soldiers who camped that first night in Daiquiri immediately came under attack—not from enemy soldiers, as they'd feared, but from giant land crabs the size of small dogs that crawled into the two-man tents and skittered over the men while they attempted to sleep. The Americans had never seen anything like them before, not even the Westerners who were used to encountering snakes, scorpions, tarantulas, lizards, and all sorts of pinching and biting creatures in the desert. No one had ever seen crabs of this magnitude, and they fought them off throughout the night, unable to get much-needed rest during the ordeal. Fortunately, the crabs were scavengers that ate only carrion and weren't interested in live meat.

The crabs were gone by morning, and above the men and their campsites loomed the mountains with virtually impassable roads. Beyond them, eighteen miles of thick jungle teemed with venomous snakes and other reptiles, slithering and crawling over the hills between the troops and their primary objective: the town of Santiago de Cuba.

The Twenty-Fifth black infantry and some white units were under the command of General Henry Lawton. General Shafter devised a plan for Lawton's divisions to take the lead, trekking from the beach toward Siboney over rugged and swampy coastal terrain. Bringing up the rear would be a cavalry division composed of regulars and volunteers, including the black Ninth and Tenth, a few white units, and the Rough Riders, all dismounted except for Roosevelt, Wood, and some of the other officers. They were under the command of General Wheeler, who hated the idea of being in the rear, since he wanted to lead the charge against those Yankees up in the hills.

"That night about 7 o'clock the Captain asked the First Sergeant to send me to him," wrote C. D. Kirby with the black Ninth. "I reported to the Captain, who asked me if I was afraid of the Spaniards, and I replied that I was not afraid of anything, whereupon the Captain ordered me to take my gun and belt and report to him. I soon returned and he said, 'I want you to go to the dock and watch the grub, and if anyone comes around there kill him.'"

It was pitch black where Kirby was stationed, but at about 12:30 in the morning he made out two figures approaching in the dark through the brush. Kirby remained quiet until they drew closer. He admitted that he was shaking with fear, but he held his ground and commanded them to halt. They ignored his warning and kept on coming. Kirby called out twice more in a loud voice, but still the two figures kept approaching. Finally, Kirby stepped behind a rock, took aim, and shot one of the men, killing him on the spot. The dead soldier's companion shot back and missed, the bullet glancing off a rock and winging Kirby on the shoulder. Kirby shot him too, knocking him to the ground but not killing him. Kirby advanced and asked the man how he was feeling. "Pretty bad," the Spaniard said. Kirby slammed him across the head with the butt of his pistol, knocking him unconscious and temporarily putting him out of his misery. For this incident, as well as his action in combat later, the captain gave the black trooper the name "Brave Fighting Kirby."

Around dawn, the order came for the first column of men, including the Buffalo Soldiers of the Twenty-Fifth, to leave immediately and push along on the path to Siboney. The black Ninth and Tenth stayed behind with Wheeler's forces, also serving under his second-in-command, General Samuel B. M. Young. The Twenty-Fifth and some white units marched single file on the unpaved trail, with orders to hook up with the black Twenty-Fourth under General Jacob Kent after they landed. The Twenty-Fifth and their white compatriots left almost as soon as they hit the beach and made first camp around 8:30 that evening.

"We marched about four and a half miles through the mountains; then we made camp," a black soldier with the Twenty-Fifth wrote later. Another with the same outfit wrote, "A short distance ahead (from the shore) we bivouacked for the night. We were soon lying in dreamland, so far from friends and home, indeed, on a distant, distant shore."

A white staff officer described the movement similarly in his own account of the action: "General Lawton, with his Division, in obedience to this order, pushed forward from Daiquiri about five miles, when night overtook him and he bivouacked on the road." The campsite was a brush-covered flat with heavy jungle growth on one side and a shallow, stagnant pool on the other. The men dined on canned meat and beans heated on open fires; hardtack; and coconuts and chili peppers they found in the area, all washed down with coffee made from river water.

The rainy season had arrived, making the going more treacherous as the men slogged over muddy trails beneath dripping canopies of trees. The land crabs returned, their appetites for carrion intensified with the advent of the steady tropical downpours, turning them into even more formidable adversaries than the men had first thought. The Spanish proved to be less of a problem, offering only token resistance at Siboney, which the first column of Americans occupied on the morning of June 23. Shafter had instructed Lawton to remain there while the rest of the supplies were being unloaded onto the beach at Siboney, now that his troops were in control there.

Wheeler and Roosevelt fumed at being left behind at the Daiquiri campsite to guard against any possible Spanish rearguard assault. Each of them had trouble containing his urge to be in the middle of the fighting, one to enhance his military career and the other his political one. Fighting Joe decided to take action on his own, defying Shafter's orders. He left Daiquiri with a squad of scouts early on June 23, and Young followed closely behind with some white regulars and some black soldiers from the Ninth and Tenth. Wheeler infuriated Roosevelt all the more with his order for Roosevelt to stay behind with his band of Rough Riders.

Wheeler was surprised to see that the Spaniards had not defended the route to Siboney at several locations where they could have had a distinct advantage over the Americans grinding their way along the trail. Lawton was almost speechless when he saw Wheeler and his scouts tromping unannounced into his campsite. Wheeler informed Lawton that he had learned from Cuban rebels on the way that Spanish forces lay well entrenched at a fork in the trail three or four miles inland. Wheeler wanted to march uphill and assault the position directly, but Lawton viewed the situation differently. Lawton preferred to take a more circuitous route along the seacoast and attack the Spanish flank, forcing them toward Santiago at the risk of being cut off from their main line of defense. The two generals stood there at loggerheads, one obeying his commander's orders, the other in open defiance of them.

10

General Shafter sat hobbled by gout on his ship, observing the activity on the coast the best he could through field glasses. Richard Harding Davis, a reporter for the *New York Herald*, vividly captured the scene during the landing:

> It was one of the most weird and remarkable scenes of the war, probably of any war. An army was being landed on an enemy's coast at the dead of night, but with somewhat more of cheers and shrieks and laughter than rise from the bathers in the surf at Coney Island on a hot Sunday. It was a pandemonium of noises. The men still to be landed from the "prison hulks," as they called the transports, were singing in chorus, the men already on shore were dancing naked around the camp fires on the beach, or shouting with delight as they plunged into the first bath that had been offered in seven days, and those in the launches as they were pitched head-first at the soil of Cuba, signalized their arrival by howls of triumph. On either side rose black, overhanging ridges, in the lowland between were white tents and burning fires, and from the ocean came the blazing, dazzling eyes of the search-lights shaming the quiet moonlight.

For his part, Shafter sat immobilized by his throbbing foot and the oppressive heat and humidity bearing down on him. He tried to make what sense he could of the men milling about on the shore, but he couldn't be sure which troops were Lawton's and which were Wheeler's amid the chaos. His mood was soured all the more by the lack of communication from his men on land.

The place that lay a few miles uphill at the crossroads was called Las Guasimas, named for the fruit-bearing trees that adorned the hill. Before the Spanish had chased them out, the locals used to pluck the fruit and feed it to their pigs. Richard Harding Davis, one of the handful of writers who reported from the scene, depicted the site as "not even a village, nor even a collection of houses." Two trails came together there, forming the apex of a V. The site was located about three miles inland from Siboney. From the point where they met, the trails merged and continued along a single trail toward Santiago. General Wheeler took it upon himself to reconnoiter the area in the company of some Cuban rebels. He declared openly that he intended to attack Las Guasimas in the morning, whether Shafter authorized it or not.

While Lawton and Wheeler debated military strategy, Roosevelt sat stewing with his Rough Riders on the beach in Daiquiri. They glumly ate a lunch of bacon and beans while Roosevelt reined in his urge to get moving along the route Wheeler had taken earlier. Finally, at 1:30 in the afternoon of June 23, Colonel Wood told Roosevelt that he received an order from Wheeler for the Rough Riders to strike out along the coast toward Siboney. In addition to a supply of rations, they planned to carry with them an assortment of picks, shovels, and other equipment that would come in handy for digging trenches. Their mule train was reduced to 16 animals

The Ninth and Tenth black cavalry saved the Rough Riders from extermination at Las Guasimas, about three miles inland from the coast. Roosevelt was injured in the battle, and several of his top aides lost their lives.
Library of Congress Prints and Photographs Division (LC-USCZ4-508)

from the 189 they had started with in San Antonio; some had been left behind in Florida, and others never made the swim to shore. But before they got under way, Wood decided to leave the slimmed-down mule train with all the equipment in Daiquiri to speed up their journey. They compensated by taking with them some extra first-aid kits instead.

The men trudged awkwardly along the crude trail, except for Wood and Roosevelt, the latter furious that he had to ride his one remaining horse bareback "like an Indian." *New York Journal* correspondent Edward Marshall recalled that Roosevelt's "wrath was boiling and his grief was heart-breaking." Somehow, Marshall's saddle had made it to shore even though his own horse had remained behind, so he lent Roosevelt his saddle to relieve his distress.

After Wood, Roosevelt, and company got started, their aging surgeon and medical officer, Major Henry LaMotte, decided to disobey orders and follow them with the mules, which he had laden down with additional medical supplies. He led the pack riding bareback on one of the mules to ease the pain of an ankle he had sprained. The going was slow and difficult, but he was determined to make sure the troops had ample medical supplies, including surgical implements he would need in the event of inevitable injuries. The line of men and mules stretched farther out along the path as the various units moved ahead at an uneven pace, the better-conditioned pushing ahead to the front of the group while the cavalrymen, unused to long hikes, fell to the rear.

Well ahead of them all was Wheeler, who had lost patience with Lawton and took it upon himself to plan military strategy with his subordinate, General Young, and with Colonel Wood, once he arrived. Young would do Wheeler's bidding no matter what, and Wheeler felt that Wood—and Roosevelt in particular—would be more agreeable to an aggressive military action than the overly cautious Lawton. He also mistakenly included in his plans one of the Cuban rebel leaders whom he had encountered in the area: an unsavory character and possible turncoat who called himself General Castillo.

Each man with Wood and Roosevelt carried on his back a blanket roll, one hundred rounds of ammunition, and his weapons. They stuffed whatever rations they could into haversacks and the pockets of their uniforms, and a few others slung entrenching tools and axes on straps across their chests. The ground was rocky and soggy, making the footing all the more hazardous with the heavy loads. The path they traveled was sarcastically labeled El Camino Real—The Royal Road. Like the others who had passed before them, they pushed along in single file since the path was not wide enough for two men to walk abreast. It was rutted with wagon tracks that turned into streams of flowing mud during a torrential downpour, something that occurred every day this time of year. The heat and humidity were unbearable, and the men sweltered all the more beneath the weight of their heavy, sodden uniforms. The thick jungle growth pressed in on them from all sides, snagging their packs and rifles as they pressed on toward Siboney.

Before they reached the village, they came across a wide stream flowing with clear water up to their shins. Wood sent word back to the men straggling behind that they could stop and fill their canteens if they took care not to stir up the mud from the bottom. But no sooner had they topped off their canteens than they heard the sounds of laughter and splashing farther upstream. Young had arrived earlier with the other troops in Wheeler's command, including the black soldiers with the Ninth and Tenth, who were stripped down to their skivvies, some bathing, others pissing in the stream. The Rough Riders were so outraged by the sight of the cavorting black troops, who were apparently bearing up far better than they were under the ordeal, that they cursed them loudly and made a show of dumping the water back into the stream.

It wasn't long before they began to discard more than water. Men were falling by the wayside sick with exhaustion and heat prostration. Many tossed off their bedrolls, haversacks, cooking utensils, picks, and shovels in an effort to lighten their loads. Roosevelt, still on horseback, fell back through the ranks to urge his men forward. Some staggered to their feet in a heroic effort to reach their destination. As Roosevelt rode along, he saw that some of his troops had even abandoned their food rations—mostly heavy cans of meat, potatoes, and tomatoes. They all continued along the path, hoping to rendezvous as soon as possible with the black Twenty-Fifth and the white regulars, who had been the first to march to Siboney with Lawton. Wood rode ahead with a few of the men after urging

Roosevelt to do what was necessary to get the men into camp in good condition.

To his credit, Roosevelt admitted that the journey was easy for him since he was on horseback, while his men had to slog along on foot.

PART TWO

The Hills

11

Wood reached Siboney ahead of his troops, and there he encountered Fighting Joe Wheeler at 7:30 in the evening. Wheeler, with Young and Castillo by his side, informed Wood that there was a Spanish encampment on a hill a few miles inland and he intended to take it by force with or without Lawton's consent—or Shafter's, for that matter.

Lawton was still in denial, refusing to believe that Wheeler would flout his commanding general's orders and take such action on his own. Young, as Wheeler expected, rubber-stamped his boss's decision, saying, "General Wheeler, give me permission to go out there." Wood, too, offered no resistance to Wheeler's plan. Lawton finally got the message that Wheeler had stacked the deck against him and "was scheming to leave him in the lurch and have a fight." Roosevelt rode into camp about 9 PM, with most of his men trudging in after him. He ignored Lawton and immediately joined forces with Wheeler and the others, expressing his own desire to move against the Spaniards.

Lawton tried to get word of what was transpiring to Shafter, who was still incapacitated on the *Seguranca* and wondering what was happening on shore, but a storm had kicked up, roiling the seas and making it impossible for a lifeboat to traverse the three miles out to Shafter's vessel. So Shafter sat anchored in the dark, except for the bright searchlights that illuminated the shore, where the men danced on the beach around their campfires. Night had fallen like a shroud on the overhead cliffs.

Along the coast in Siboney, Lawton tried frantically to stop Wheeler from launching his unauthorized military operation. Wheeler planned to attack Las Guasimas early the next morning, June 24, but Roosevelt's men appeared incapable at the moment of making the grinding uphill climb with only one night's rest. They threw themselves onto the ground, making camp on a bluff over-looking the sea. Most of them were exhausted and dehydrated, suf-fering from blistered feet and painful insect bites. But their spirits rose when they realized that they were almost within shooting dis-tance of the enemy. They lit fires and broke out what rations they had left, mostly bacon and hardtack. Troops from the black Tenth had found some sweet Spanish wine alongside the path, which they willingly shared with Roosevelt's men. For the moment, all ani-mosity between the black and white soldiers had faded. They were soon to be comrades in arms, risking their lives in combat on for-eign soil.

While one batch of soldiers rested in camp awaiting orders for the next move, the transport ships managed to brave the churn-ing water and land additional troops on the beach at Daiquiri. Not all of them made it through the dangerous waters onto land, and the operation was halted when the fury of the storm intensified, blasting the entire coastline with howling winds and driving rain. The downpour doused the campfires and saturated the blanket rolls and equipment, turning the night into a vortex of water and wind. The men gave up all hope of staying dry. They wolfed down the remains of their soggy food and curled up on the muddy ground in a fruitless effort to get some sleep. The pounding rain lasted about an hour before it rolled farther inland, leaving the invaders wet and cold as the pitch-black night closed in around them.

Wheeler told Young and Wood to be ready to attack Las Guasimas before daybreak. But it would be a long, uncomfortable night before dawn tinted the sky. The men had difficulty falling asleep until after midnight. When the rain stopped, Roosevelt scouted the area with his close friend Sergeant Hamilton Fish and Captain Allyn Capron Jr., Wood's third-ranking officer after Roosevelt. Both Fish and Capron had intimations of their own mortality in the hours before the battle.

The layout of the land east and north of Santiago de Cuba, with the major hills and battle sites spread throughout the region.

Based on a map that appeared in *San Juan Hill 1898* by Angus Konstam, Osprey Publishing, 1998.

"It would be my luck to be put out now," Fish told Roosevelt.

"Well, by tomorrow at this time the long sleep will be on many of us," Capron muttered with a similar sentiment.

Major LaMotte rumbled into camp around 3:00 AM with his mule train and medical supplies, waking up most of the men, including Wood and Roosevelt. Wood had called for reveille at 4:00 AM, and he didn't appreciate having his rest disturbed by a lower-ranking officer, much less one who had disobeyed his orders to leave the mules in Daiquiri. He ordered LaMotte to unload his supplies, establish a base hospital, and stay put in Siboney. Wood was happy enough to have the mules available, however, and he ordered his men to rope their weapons around the sixteen mules LaMotte had brought into camp. Roosevelt's displeasure with LaMotte was more pronounced than Wood's; if LaMotte was going to disobey orders and bring the mules to Siboney, he should at least have had the foresight to carry dry bedding for him and the rain-soaked troops. LaMotte suffered Roosevelt's wrath in silence. "He seemed to think . . . that I should have selected his bedding," he said afterward, "but as I had not brought a stitch of bedding or clothing myself, I didn't think he had any right to complain."

Now that he was awake, Wood let Captain Capron in on the morning's plan of attack, and Capron volunteered to lead the Rough Riders up the trail. Wheeler intended to send Young up the main road with two squadrons of white and black troops, the First and Tenth regulars, and have Wood and Roosevelt march a column of Rough Riders up a steeper mountain path to their left. The combined American forces totaled approximately one thousand men—including about five hundred Rough Riders—taking on what proved to be less than half the number of the Spanish defenders they expected to encounter.

The men relit the fires and ate a breakfast of bacon, canned tomatoes, and hardtack fried in bacon grease a little after 4:00 AM.

Some had a handful of coffee beans, which they smashed with rocks and boiled in river water. Others discovered a cache of Cuban rum, which they poured into their canteens to fortify themselves before the onset of battle. The troops were ready for whatever came next.

Six leading reporters of the day, including Richard Harding Davis, Edward Marshall, and Stephen Crane, the author of *The Red Badge of Courage* who was writing for the *World*, had been chosen to cover the men as they charged before the Spanish guns. Others would join them later.

Crane was particularly taken with the spirit of Captain Buckey O'Neill, who had tried to save the two black soldiers from drowning during the beach landing. "He was going to take his men into any sort of holocaust," the great writer reported, "because—he loved it for itself—the thing itself—the whirl, the unknown."

It was still dark at 5:00 AM, the time Wheeler had chosen to set his battle plan in motion. But Wood, Roosevelt, and their men were not ready to get going until an hour later, when the first rays of sun illuminated the eastern horizon and revealed "a beautiful valley of grass between two ranges of hills bordering the Daiquiri River," a black soldier wrote. Roosevelt was displeased when some of the black soldiers needled his men about dragging their feet and holding them all back, implying that the white troops were afraid to face the Spaniards. Roosevelt shot back that he intended to hit Las Guasimas first, despite the arduous route that had been assigned to the volunteers, and he would send back some severed enemy heads for them to keep as trophies if they liked. Notwithstanding the banter, everyone's adrenalin was flowing. The competitive atmosphere that existed between the volunteers and regulars invigorated the men for the battle ahead.

The main path, the so-called El Camino Real, made a turn north-ward from the coast and climbed inland across the verdant valley described by the black trooper. Running parallel about a mile to the left was a steep mountain pass that rose in places as much as forty-five degrees until it joined with the main path at Las Guasimas. Wheeler had instructed Young to hit the Spanish entrenchments first with his white and black forces totaling just under five hundred men. As Young and his troops pushed the Spanish closer toward the mountain ridge, Wood and Roosevelt were to strike the Spanish soldiers on the western flank with their five hundred or so Rough Riders, trapping the Spaniards between the two attacking columns.

Such was the master strategy, although Wood and Roosevelt had forged their own private pact to reach Las Guasimas ahead of the others. What they hadn't taken into consideration, however, was the mule train that would be trailing along with them up the sharp mountain incline. The pass was narrow and treacherous, and the mules turned out to be more of a burden than a benefit. The ropes tying the weapons to the mules would not hold, and Wood was exasperated soon after they had started. In desperation, he called LaMotte back into action and ordered him to take charge of the mule train. LaMotte did as instructed, but once again in his own fashion, reloading thirteen of the mules with medical supplies and strapping three of them with some machine guns that he knew would be needed in battle.

The men crossed a stream and then a railroad track. At that point the two columns of soldiers separated onto their assigned routes: the Rough Riders on the mountain trail and the others tra-versing the valley to their right before beginning the climb up the hill. The Rough Riders, tanked up on Cuban rum, made their way merrily in the beginning, "babbling joyously, arguing, recounting, laughing, making more noise than a train going through a tunnel," wrote Stephen Crane.

The regular white and black troops led by Young proceeded in a more disciplined fashion, acting like seasoned professionals soon to be facing death. They had been in combat before and knew what it was like to engage well-armed enemies. As the sun rose higher in the cloudless blue sky, the heat and humidity built up with a tropical ferocity, and the spirits of the Rough Riders started to flag along with their stamina. Both Wood and Roosevelt knew that the men were not in the best shape for arduous hiking, and from their vantage atop their horses, they looked on in dismay as their troops faltered on the sides of the path and discarded their equipment. The incline grew steeper, taxing the group's ability to maintain a steady pace. Soon the path turned into a rocky scramble as the men were forced to claw their way up on their hands and feet. Wood and Roosevelt did all they could do to keep their mounts from sliding backward down the slope.

Not all of the Rough Riders made it to the top. Foot weary from the unaccustomed exertion, they were burdened by their winter-weight uniforms and drenched in sweat, their dehydration worsened by heavy consumption of rum instead of water. Behind them all, the elderly LaMotte lumbered uphill with his mules, stopping often to keep the rope hitches from coming undone when they got snagged in low-hanging branches. Wood and Roosevelt rode at the head of the pack, trying to preserve some semblance of order in their unraveling ranks. Before they reached Las Guasimas, the two leaders came across a wooden blockhouse that would have served as a good defensive fort for the Spanish, except that it was occupied by some of Lawton's troops, including members of the black Twenty-Fifth. When Lawton had realized that Wheeler could not be diverted, he had sent an advance party to head Wheeler off at the pass, so to speak, but instead they had intercepted the Rough Riders while Wheeler's men trekked across the valley.

The outer wall of the blockhouse measured twelve feet in height, with a few feet of dirt banked against the inner wall, allowing the defenders to fire on their stomachs through narrow slits. It struck Wood and Roosevelt immediately that had Lawton's troops not gotten there first to chase off the Spaniards, the Rough Riders would have stumbled into an ambush and taken heavy losses. The Spaniards had retreated to a hill a few miles farther along the pass, and Lawton's regulars said they would keep some guards at the blockhouse to prevent the Spaniards from circling back down while the Rough Riders continued their climb. Wood sent word to LaMotte to hurry along the mules that were carrying the weapons. LaMotte hung back with most of the mule train and sent the three bearing machine guns ahead.

12

The going got a bit easier when the Rough Riders crested a hill and reached more level ground. The jungle growth thinned out, allowing a refreshing ocean breeze to waft in over the cliff and cool them off. The troops in the lead could see their own ships in the harbor and the tents strung out along the beach. The sky was blue and clear, and the idyllic view stood in sharp contrast to the punishing terrain they had just endured. The area was "carpeted with grass almost as soft as the turf in the garden of an old English country house," reported Edward Marshall in the *New York Journal.* "The tropical growth on our right shot up rank and strong for ten or fifteen feet, and then arched over until our resting-place was almost embowered. On the left was a narrow, treeless slope on which tall Cuban grass waved lazily."

Every now and then they passed through glades and shoulders along the trail, from which they could see far out to the horizon. Roosevelt thought the area was strikingly beautiful and peaceful. It seemed to him and some of the Rough Riders from the West that they were off on a hunting excursion instead of tromping ahead into a gory battle.

After a bit, Wood and Roosevelt could see Young's column of men closing in on them from the right. There was no way the Rough Riders were going to reach Las Guasimas before the white and black troops in the valley, who had made better time across the open landscape. Unknown to both of them at that moment was that Wheeler was riding up on horseback to join Young and his men; Fighting Joe was just as anxious as Wood and Roosevelt to engage the "Yankee" Spaniards first.

General Young ordered a delay so that the attack could begin on both flanks at the same time. He moved to the front right, alongside the white and black regulars of the Twenty-Fifth. While Young held his ground, Wheeler caught up with him from behind. He took stock of the situation, considered their options, and then gave his approval for the next stage of the battle that would soon begin.

Scouts had reported enemy troops well entrenched where the paths came together in Las Guasimas. The Spanish troops had cut down trees and stacked their trunks and branches for a barricade where the roads met. The Spaniards were posted on a range of high hills in the form of a V, the opening being toward Siboney, according to Chaplain Steward.

Young's troops restarted their march across the valley as soon as the generals were sure that the Rough Riders were in position to renew their own advance and hit the Spanish flank simultaneously. Wheeler and Young spotted the enemy first, the sun glinting brightly off the Spanish guns and artillery.

To their left, Wood posted a Cherokee scout named Tom Isbell and two of Castillo's Cubans in the lead as they forged their way over spongy level ground. A couple hundred yards behind them were Hamilton Fish and other scouts, and to their rear was Captain Capron leading a platoon of sixty troops walking in single file. Roosevelt followed Capron and his group, although he quickly began to pick up his pace to move closer to the front. Marching with the main body of men, with the entire line stretched out for more than a mile, were Stephen Crane, Richard Harding Davis, and most of the other correspondents selected by Roosevelt and Wood. Only one journalist, Herschel V. Cashin, marched with Young's troops on the main path.

A burst of energy surged through the ranks as both columns inched toward the Spanish barricade. One soldier reported that the adrenalin took hold as they proceeded, the bulk of the men eager to "get into the real war business." The ground in front of them now was dotted with palm trees, tall grass, and cactus plants. Scurrying off to the sides was an assortment of huge spiders, lizards, and the ever-present land crabs with purple claws, orange legs, and black backs with yellow polka dots. Overhead flew tropical birds emitting a cacophony of ominous squawks.

The two columns of Americans temporarily lost sight of one another across the ridgeline dividing the Rough Riders from the regulars, and Wood called a halt to get his bearings. Coordinating the two-pronged attack took precedence over everything else, including the question of which column hit the enemy first. He judged the enemy to be no more than a quarter to a half mile ahead, and he feared an ambush more than anything else. The Rough Riders were making their usual racket as they plodded up the path. Wood fell back to confer with Roosevelt and Capron.

"Pass the word back to keep silence in the ranks," Wood said testily to the others.

"Stop that talkin', can't ye, damn it!" barked a sergeant, a former New York City cop.

LaMotte finally caught up to the officers at the front of the line and told Roosevelt that he had counted fifty-two men who had dropped out along the way, reducing their ranks by about 10 percent. Wood didn't want to hear any of it, however. When Roosevelt asked him to slow the pace and let the stragglers catch up, Wood replied, "I have no time for that now! We are in sight of the enemy, sir!"

The enemy was indeed close at hand, though not yet visible, as they lay protected behind their well-laid barricades. Roosevelt was not quite convinced of that until he stumbled across some strands of cut barbed wire that had previously crossed the path. He noticed that the wire had just recently been cut; the ends were bright, showing no signs of rust despite the heavy rains and high humidity.

Both Wood and Roosevelt concluded that they were being set up for another ambush—they later suspected that Castillo, the self-styled Cuban general, might have collaborated with the Spanish—and it was time to tone down the party atmosphere that had prevailed at times during the climb from Siboney. They had the men recheck their rifles to ensure they were fully loaded and tie down their loose equipment to prevent any more rattling than was necessary. At that moment, Capron, who had reconnoitered the pass ahead, reported back that their scouts had come across a dead Spaniard whose corpse had been picked almost to the bone by vultures, crabs, and a variety of nasty insects. The remains of the dead soldier lay ahead just before the pass veered back into the jungle.

Meanwhile, Young's scouts on the right had spotted the Spaniards at 7:20 in the morning and were almost in range of their guns. His men had dragged their three Hotchkiss artillery pieces across the flat, dry ground leading toward the enemy line. The Spaniards lay behind their felled-tree barricades, further protected by large boulders on top of a steep hill. Others lay in hand-dug trenches beside the barricades. Young told his men to stop again until he was sure that Wood and Roosevelt had drawn close enough to hit the Spaniards on the left flank. "Don't shoot until you see something to shoot at!" Young commanded. At eight o'clock, Wheeler took command of his forward unit.

The main line of defenders stretched across the junction of the two paths. Nearby, brick houses used for storing sugarcane stood in profile against the sky. The Spaniards, having positioned most of their sharpshooters in the tall grass to the west rather than on a steep slope on the east that dropped into the valley, posed a greater threat to the Rough Riders than to Wheeler's forces.

"General Young and myself examined the position of the enemy," Wheeler reported afterward. "The lines were deployed and I directed him to open fire with the Hotchkiss guns. The enemy replied and the firing immediately became general."

The Rough Riders were almost there when they heard the roaring of the guns. As they tried to step up their advance, a volley of bullets flew from the Spaniards' Mausers, although mostly whizzing above their heads. The shots ripped through the trees, emitting an unnerving noise like the humming of telegraph wires. But then the Spanish sharpshooters lowered their sights and found their marks. One by one, Rough Riders crumbled in agony beneath the steady fusillade.

"I got it that time," one of the volunteers called out as he fell. Others began to curse.

"Don't swear—shoot!" Wood shouted.

"There was no more gossip in the ranks," Marshall reported. "The men sprang to their feet without waiting for an order. As they did so a volley which went over our heads came through the mysterious tangle on our right. A scattering fire was heard from the direction in which the scouts had gone. Then silence."

Although their shots were apparent, the Spanish soldiers were all but invisible, hidden in the high grass with their smokeless gunpowder that gave no hint of where they were. The denseness of the jungle added to the challenge of figuring out exactly where they were entrenched. Stephen Crane was particularly critical of Wood and Roosevelt's strategy. They entered the fray, he wrote, with "simply a gallant blunder. This silly brave force wandered placidly into trouble, but their conduct was magnificent."

The Spanish seemed to know beforehand precisely which path the Rough Riders would take, and they had positioned some sharpshooters on the heavily wooded slope near two blockhouses flanked by wood and stone entrenchments.

One of the first to be hit was the Native American scout Tom Isbell. Somehow he managed to survive the seven bullets that struck him in different parts of his body. Captain Capron and Sergeant Fish were not nearly as fortunate. Fish was the first to be mortally wounded, looking almost robust in death. He had been shot through the chest, and he sank to the ground with his back against a tree. Young Capron stood over him firing round after round, but he too was killed, just a few yards from Fish. The earth around him was covered with his empty shells. Capron's final words were "Don't mind me, boys. Go on with the fight!" Roosevelt nearly became a casualty himself when a Mauser bullet struck a palm tree and showered his face with splinters. He had been standing behind a large palm tree with his head sticking out to the side when the bullet struck, filling his left eye and ear with tiny shards of wood.

Ahead and to the right of the Rough Riders, Wheeler and Young advanced their black and white troops to within nine hundred yards of the Spanish lines. They had a better view of the enemy deployment, as the Spanish did of them, and both sides quickly took heavy losses. The casualties mounted during the first stages of the engagement. The Rough Riders tried to move forward through thick jungle growth, their ranks reduced now not just because of those who had dropped out along the trail but because many had fallen during the initial skirmish. Men had fallen wounded or dead in alarming numbers. Bogged down by the impossible terrain and caught off guard by increasingly accurate enemy gunfire, the Rough Riders had been unable to press their attack in an organized manner, and they suffered heavily for it.

13

Richard Harding Davis, who, like Hemingway, enjoyed adventure as much as he did writing about it, tried to point a path forward for the Rough Riders. "There they are, Colonel! Look over there! I can see their hats near that glade!" he shouted. The way forward looked like the walls of a maze to him. Each trooper had to remain aware of the men on both sides of him to keep his bearings in the thicket. At any moment, the entire field of fire could go from swarming with soldiers to empty of friendly troops, the only sign of them the racket of vines and tree limbs being pushed aside somewhere in the distance. Staying close, the men could hear the heavy breathing of their comrades with each step they took. Finally, they burst through into a clearing facing a curtain of dark vines, and the men fell to the ground and began to return the Spanish fusillade.

Roosevelt passed the dead and wounded, wincing at the sight of Fish as he lay with glazed eyes beside the tree on one side of the trail amid a tangle of jungle growth. Wood tried to maintain a semblance of control over the impossible situation, calling for the men to advance in an orderly fashion instead of rushing ahead on their own. But his commands fell on deaf ears. The soldiers' lack of combat experience prevented them from remaining calm and collected under the constant enemy bombardment.

Roosevelt admitted that they were moving ahead blindly. He couldn't see where most of his men were positioned at any given moment, and he had no idea where the Spanish soldiers were located. His basic instinct as a man of action was to simply charge forward toward the enemy gunfire. What was most infuriating of all was facing an enemy in battle whom he could not see. The jungle around them was dense, and as the men vanished into the vines, they seemed to be swallowed up. He began to worry that he would be court-martialed later if word got out that he had lost control of his men. It was the most confusing situation ever experienced by a leader who was normally on top of the events around him. After the battle was over, he learned that he was not the only officer who had trouble in the fight; the others he spoke to all admitted they had been as much in the dark as Roosevelt had been.

Through the jungle growth on the right, the firing continued nonstop as the white and black troops under Wheeler and Young engaged the Spanish at close range. The gunfire was amazingly heavy, according to eyewitnesses. The soldiers in the black Tenth tried to charge the enemy through "thick, prickly weed, through which paths had always to be cut with knives and sabers," reported Herschel Cashin. The Spaniards held their ground behind their barricades, firing in unison at the slowly advancing Tenth. A black soldier with the Tenth, with a ragged wound visible on his thigh, kept reloading and firing at the enemy from behind a rock. When another trooper told him he had been wounded badly, he laughed it off and replied, "Oh, that's all right. That's been there for some time."

American losses began to build heavily, and Wheeler grew concerned that his casualties would prove to be unacceptable in the event of a defeat—particularly since he had exceeded his authority in launching the assault, reason enough to get him court-martialed himself. He didn't want to admit it, but he needed Lawton to send him reinforcements as quickly as possible. Fortunately, Lawton had surmised as much, even before he got word from Wheeler; he had been listening to the deafening roar of guns and cannons with mounting alarm from his own base in Siboney. By the time Wheeler's messenger arrived from Las Guasimas, Lawton already had his own white infantry division plus the black Ninth, which had remained behind with him, ready to charge into battle.

The reinforcements, under the leadership of General Adna Chaffee, got there none too soon, although they were needed more by Wood, Roosevelt, and the Rough Riders than by Wheeler's forces, which were holding their own against the Spanish guns. Wood and Roosevelt, who knew nothing about Wheeler's plea for help from Lawton, were meanwhile struggling with the mule train, which was giving them more grief than it was worth. A soldier in charge of unloading the Colt rapid-fire guns from the mules accidentally let them slip and fall to the ground, damaging them beyond immediate repair. The Spanish Mauser bullets continued to rain down upon the men. Wood described the situation as desperate, with bullets cutting through the trees and dropping leaves like green snowflakes. Large branches crashed all around. The Rough Riders fired back blindly until one of Wood's men yelled out, "For God's sake, stop! You are killing your own men!"

The reporters with the Rough Riders were themselves in great danger, among them Edward Marshall, who fell to the ground when a bullet found its mark and smashed into his spine. He was standing close to Wood when he was hit, and the colonel later recalled that the reporter had shown his mettle by dictating a story to the *Journal* while he lay injured on the ground. Marshall let out not so much as a whimper while Stephen Crane took down the wounded man's dictation.

"In hard luck, old man?" Crane asked Marshall.

"Yes, I'm done for."

"Nonsense. You're all right. What can I do for you?"

"Well, you might file my dispatches. I don't mean file them ahead of your own—but just file them if you find it handy."

Crane agreed and eventually delivered Marshall's reports to the *Journal*, even though Crane himself was writing for the *World*—an act that was largely responsible for costing him his own job.

Crane helped a few others load Marshall onto a stretcher and carry him to a field hospital, where a doctor attended to his wound. After filing his dispatches, Crane saw to it that Marshall was transported to the *Olivette*, which had been turned into a hospital ship. He thought Marshall was a dead man as he waved him off. Crane was amazed that any man could remain so collected in such dire condition; Marshall had put his job as a reporter ahead of his personal agony, writing first-rate prose as he lay writhing on the ground. Crane was even more astounded that Marshall did not die from his injury.

Marshall not only survived the wound—although it cost him a leg—but he outlived Crane by more than three decades. He later wrote an article about his experiences in the war, and his account includes an interview with one soldier who recalled the horrors of battle in gruesome detail. He said his own breath left his body when he saw the man next to him hit by a bullet that blew the top of his head off, sending it flying into the air. The man collapsed to the ground, his body intact except for the shattered skull.

The black Ninth scrambled up the main path and joined the black Tenth and white troops on their right flank. General Chaffee directed the action on horseback. The Spanish defenders saw the reinforcements advancing rapidly to join the rest of Wheeler's troops and turned their machine guns in that direction. The Ninth fired back with enfilading fire—meaning it cut across the ranks and swept the entire Spanish line of defense, as distinct from defilading, or more targeted, fire. On the far left, the Rough Riders, under constant assault themselves, continued their own slow climb to join Wheeler's men where the two trails came together.

Part of the Tenth moved to the left, where they drew enemy fire without the ability to respond, since they were out of range with their carbines. They pushed ahead of Wood and the Rough Riders on the left, and came under heavy fire without letup for more than an hour. "Their coolness and fine discipline were superb," said a white officer with them. Another troop of the Tenth took command of the Hotchkiss mountain guns, which had a longer range, and zeroed in on the Spanish entrenchments—but sparingly, since their supply of ammunition was low. The rest of the Tenth was ordered to advance on the far right.

"I ordered the troops forward at once, telling them to take advantage of all cover available," said the lieutenant commanding the troop. The volleys from the Spanish were homing in heavily, striking the ground on all sides of the men. It was almost impossible for them to move forward from their cover with any confidence. The lieutenant ran back to where the black troops were positioned near a brick wall and ordered them to charge forward en masse. They dashed ahead in a single great outpouring of men, with three or four of them dropping as they were hit. The Spanish had erected a wire fence in the midst of thick brush, which stood on their right, making it difficult to push ahead. The black troops followed along the fence for a hundred yards or so, reaching a spot where most of them found an opening through which they could charge ahead toward the enemy.

The black Ninth and Tenth and white First pushed ahead into the relentless Spanish fire, advancing cautiously toward the crest up a sheer incline. Their movement was difficult because of the steep slope, the thick cactus, and the sharp-leaved grass, known as Spanish bayonet, that covered the hillside. The men sliced through it with their knives and sabers. The lieutenant who had ordered them forward recalled that it was impossible to see more than a few men at a time because of the thick foliage. But all of them made it to the crest at about the same time and, from there, began to advance steadily.

General Young had a similar view of the battle: "The ground over which the right column advanced was a mass of jungle growth, with wire fences, not to be seen until encountered, and precipitous heights as the ridge was approached." It was impossible for the troops to keep in touch with one another toward the front, he recalled, and they could only judge the enemy positions from the sound and direction of the gunfire. Their progress was remarkably difficult, yet they pulled together and moved ahead under continuous rifle fire, backed up by rapid-fire guns. Young noted that the troops under his command maintained perfect discipline in the face of the heavy onslaught. No one straggled or attempted to fall back as they kept up their steady advance toward enemy lines.

14

The battle raged on for more than two hours, with both sides suffering mounting casualties under the steady hail of bullets. The shrieks, groans, and deafening din of warfare shook the very air itself. The smoke from the American guns seared the men's eyes and choked them with every breath they took. As they slogged up the hill, branches crashed around them, inflicting even more injuries. Then, almost miraculously, the Spanish soldiers, despite their greater numbers, slowly began to pull back as the black Ninth and Tenth and the white First pushed past the crest and closed in on the enemy positions. Wheeler's voice rose above the roar as he uttered his famous cry, "We've got the damn Yankees on the run again!"

The Spanish were indeed pulling back as the American troops charged ahead in the face of blistering fire. Wood and Roosevelt could hear the rebel yells emitted by black and white troops alike as they forced the defenders back from their barricades to a new line of defense a few hundred yards to the north. When Roosevelt rode up to the junction of the two paths, he saw Wheeler's men whooping wildly near the brick walls of the abandoned sugarcane storage house. Nearby lay the bodies of two dead Spaniards, a pile of cartridge cases, and some canned beans, which the Americans immediately cooked over an open fire to assuage their hunger. The men were too exhausted to pursue the enemy to their new redoubt. They collapsed to the ground, shared their meal, and breathed a collective sigh of relief to be out of the hellish fire for a brief moment.

Herschel V. Cashin, the only reporter with Wheeler's and Young's forces, described the scene in his account of the war: "If it had not been for the Negro cavalry, the Rough Riders would have been exterminated. . . . The Negroes saved that fight and the day will come when General Shafter will give them credit for their bravery."

His message was prescient. When Shafter later learned of what took place during the first real battle of the war, he wrote to an aide, "The First and Tenth (colored) regiments of regular cavalry (dismounted) deployed and charged up the hill in front, driving the enemy from their position, but not until we had sustained a severe loss in both killed and wounded. . . . The conduct of the troops, both white and colored, regular and volunteer, was most gallant and soldierly."

Chaplain Steward penned his own version of what transpired at Las Guasimas, saying that "the colored regulars in three days practically revolutionized the sentiment of the country in regard to the colored soldier." The poem "The Negro Soldier" by L. B. Channing reflected Steward's view: "We used to think the Negro didn't count for very much, but we've got to reconstruct our views on color more or less / Now we know about the Tenth at Las Guasimas."

"I have it from men who were upon the field that had it not been for the boys in black, the recent victory at Las Guasimas would have been a second Custer massacre," wrote John E. Lewis with the Tenth. But he lamented that the Rough Riders and other white troops got all the glory and the promotions. The press failed to report how the black cavalry and infantry soldiers took the lead and urged the

Rough Riders on. After overrunning the Spanish positions, Lewis said, the black troops sent them scampering in retreat.

Colonel Wood, however, lost no time in constructing his own revisionist history of the battle. "I don't want to boast," he wrote in a letter to his wife, "but we had a brilliant fight. The Spaniards said they fought the entire American army for four hours. My men had the bulk of the enemy in front of them and the Regulars one-third."

Wood was privately seething over the attention most of the reporters were paying to Roosevelt when the battle was over. The press loved the colorful politician with his thick mustache, round eyeglasses, and jaunty campaign hat. He made good copy, and they reveled in following him around. And Roosevelt was an expert at cultivating writers whom he knew to be partial to him, and he was more than willing to report his own self-aggrandizing views of his personal history. The future president had handpicked the reporters who accompanied the Rough Riders at Las Guasimas.

His favorite was Richard Harding Davis, a writer whom he originally disdained as "unpatriotic" and "flamboyant." Roosevelt courted Davis without restraint, wined and dined him regally while feeding him stories not available to others, because he knew Davis's dispatches would land on the front pages of the *New York Herald*. John Dunning was useful because he wrote for the Associated Press, which had massive distribution, and Kennett Harris was totally loyal to Roosevelt and would report to the *Chicago Record* just about anything his larger-than-life source told him. Edward Marshall was a brilliant writer who could be counted on most of the time, and young Stephen Crane, only twenty-six at the time, was already too famous to be ignored, although Roosevelt had some reservations about his cranky temperament and independence. Casper Whitney of *Harper's* was a solid professional with a valuable reputation, and Frederic Remington, who had greater fame as an artist and sculptor than as a writer, was also in attendance, having been sent by William Randolph Hearst as an observer who could provide illustrations of the war for the *New York Journal*. Cashin was the only reporter who followed Young and Wheeler into action; other reporters and observers joined the troops after Las Guasimas.

So it was inevitable that the Rough Riders would receive most of the credit for the early victory at Las Guasimas—credit that Roosevelt was not about to disavow. And it was certain that Roosevelt would receive the lion's share of credit for the Rough Riders' success, rather than his autocratic superior, Colonel Wood, whom the press stuck with the moniker "Old Icebox."

What none of the soldiers at Las Guasimas knew, however— neither black nor white, volunteer nor regular—was that the bloodletting they were subjected to during the first battle in Cuba was merely a warm-up exercise for the hell that was soon to come.

It was all over by ten o'clock in the morning, roughly two and a half hours after Young's scouts had first spotted the enemy. General Chaffee looked around and observed the condition of the Rough Riders and knew they would have been decimated had his reinforcements not arrived on the scene when they did. The Cuban rebels, who were expected to be in the thick of the action, were the last troops to come sauntering up the slope, and Chaffee suspected that their leader, Castillo, had played a role in the ambush on the mountain trail. But he decided to keep his opinions to himself as he complimented Wood and Roosevelt for bearing up under the "disastrous attack" on their men.

The official count of dead and wounded Americans minimized the extent of the actual carnage. According to the tally released to the public, of the 534 men under Wood's command, 8 Rough Riders lost their lives and 34 were wounded. Wheeler and Young's contingent of 464 men saw 8 killed and 18 wounded. Roosevelt reported the same figures in his own book and claimed that only one of the dead was black. But other reports differed substantially, including an account written by Richard Harding Davis, who stated in *Notes of a War Correspondent* that "every third Rough Rider was killed or wounded at Las Guasimas." In other words, the true number was upwards of 150 dead or wounded on the Rough Riders' side alone. Assistant surgeon Bob Church, working under LaMotte, gave anecdotal evidence in support of Davis's figures, maintaining that he and his superior treated closer to 200 seriously wounded men at their makeshift battlefield hospital.

"Everybody was wounded. Everybody was dead," wrote Stephen Crane in his inimitable style. "First there was nobody. Gradually there was somebody. There was the wounded, the important wounded. And the dead."

The Spanish gave out their own version of events. One Spanish soldier had high praise for the black soldiers—"Smoked Yankees" the Spanish labeled them—who charged their barricades first. He reported to his officers that "when we fired a volley, instead of falling back they came forward. This is not the way to fight, to come closer at every volley. They tried to catch us with their hands."

The Spanish press, however, engaged in its own form of propaganda. The newspaper *Espagna*, published in Santiago de Cuba, reported that "the column of General Rubin [sic] was attacked . . . with vigor, and they fought without being under cover. They were repulsed with heavy losses." The official Spanish position was that 10,000 Americans attacked 4,000 Spanish soldiers on the hill, resulting in 265 casualties on the invaders' side. The actual numbers, broadly speaking, were closer to about 1,500 Spaniards defending their position against around 1,000 Americans. When General Shafter read the Spanish account afterward, he laughed. "Reports from Spanish sources from Santiago say we were beaten," he quipped, "but persisted in fighting, and they were obliged to fall back."

General Arsenio Linares, who commanded the Spanish forces in the area, actually had more than thirty-six thousand troops stationed throughout the province, ten thousand of them guarding Santiago and its harbor a few miles to the west. Had he deployed more of his men to Las Guasimas, there is little question that they could have withstood the American assault on the hill. Wood himself admitted that the odds were slim for a smaller group of attackers to overpower a larger defensive force uphill in well-entrenched positions. But Linares feared that the American presence in Siboney was just a feinting maneuver, and that the real target was Santiago, with its strategic harbor. His reluctance to defend Las Guasimas with strength turned out to be a tactical blunder of his own—even as the real fighting had scarcely begun.

15

One of the biggest problems facing the Spanish was their scarcity of provisions. The number of Spanish soldiers in Cuba was estimated to be close to two hundred thousand, but the great majority were located in and around Havana and were scattered in garrisons throughout the countryside, where they rode herd over their rebellious subjects. The troops near Santiago lacked decent uniforms and shoes and subsisted on small rations of rice, beans, and whatever game they could kill. Spain was having financial problems and had not paid its soldiers in Cuba in more than a year. Their ammunition supply was dwindling along with their morale.

Spain had also failed to understand the strategic difference between an occupying army and one that was geared for combat. The garrison troops whom Spain had stationed around the country were proficient at suppressing the locals—burning down their houses, setting fire to their crops, and keeping them under the boot—but what they had not been trained well for were the tactical skills required to defend a country against a determined invading army. The Americans had committed their own share of blunders during their first few days on Cuban soil, but they were experienced at charging enemy fortifications, and they had the resilience to alter their strategy when the situation called for it.

Wood, in an effort to share in the attention the press showered on Roosevelt, summed up the battle with garbled syntax that had none of Roosevelt's flair: "A superior force of the enemy was driven from a strong position of their own choosing and thrown into a disorderly fight in which he could readily have become destroyed," he said. Old Icebox seemed to be a nickname that suited him well.

Word of the American victory at Las Guasimas reached General Shafter, who was still nursing the gout aboard his ship. He was furious at first that Wheeler had disobeyed his orders and attacked without authorization, but he decided to let the matter pass in light of the favorable press his army was already commanding in the nation's newspapers. Besides, he had more immediate problems to deal with, as he observed the remaining troops and supplies being loaded onto the beach through his spyglass. He wondered out loud how long it would take all of them to get ashore.

After the battle was over, the Rough Riders made camp in the afternoon and took care of their wounded. Afterward, they chowed down on a cache of beans they had found on a Spanish mule that had been killed by an American bullet. Dr. Bob Church had ventured out onto the firing line himself and carried several men down the trail on his back or in his arms. Reporters on the scene noted his heroism in combat, and the great strength he exhibited in accomplishing what he did. Richard Harding Davis reported that he saw Church, a Princeton graduate, carrying a wounded man much heavier than himself across his shoulders, the man's blood saturating Church's breeches. He repeated the feat several more times that afternoon, carrying one wounded man after another a half mile or so down the trail from the firing line under relentless enemy fire to a makeshift hospital.

Those who could walk hobbled back to the field hospital on their own while Wood and Roosevelt wandered through the sea of carnage, searching for their dead and wounded comrades. Around the badly maimed, the two men observed the large, gruesome-looking land crabs gathered in an ominous circle, waiting for all signs of life to leave the bodies before they swarmed. The vultures had already discovered some of the dead before Wood and Roosevelt came upon them; the decision was to leave the soldiers where they died, with mangled bodies and eyeless faces.

"Well, some of the boys got it in the neck," one of the cowboys said to another.

"Many a good horse dies," the other replied.

The men improvised stretchers from their tents and carried the badly wounded back to Siboney that afternoon and the following morning. As the men treaded slowly down the trail, tales about how the black troops had saved the day reached Lawton's troops. There was much talk about how the Tenth Cavalry had encountered the enemy first and rescued the Rough Riders. The black regulars congratulated one another for their actions on the battlefield, remarking on how they had raised their standing in the eyes of the Spanish defenders. An illustration of the battle that was widely circulated afterward depicted the Tenth rescuing the Rough Riders and putting the Spaniards in flight down the other side of the hill.

Richard Harding Davis, loyal to Roosevelt in his public dispatches, wrote privately to his family that the Rough Riders were caught in a clear case of ambush. John Dunning was less reticent, reporting to the Associated Press that "as perfect an ambuscade as was ever formed in the brain of an Apache Indian was prepared, and Roosevelt and his men walked squarely into it."

All the dead Rough Riders except for Capron were buried on the battlefield in one long trench lined with palm leaves, each man wrapped in a blanket. Capron had wanted his remains interred at home, but when that proved unfeasible, they buried him on a hill behind the hospital, near the seashore. The rocks along the trail where the Rough Riders had walked were spattered with blood, the grass was matted with it, and abandoned blanket rolls, haversacks, carbines, and canteens lay strewn along the length of the trail.

While the men recuperated in Siboney, Shafter continued to oversee the unloading of the remaining men and equipment onto the beach, with the last of them putting in at Siboney, west of the original encampment at Daiquiri. From his perch aboard ship, Shafter devised a strategic plan for the next phase of the war. He dispatched orders to Wheeler to not take any direct action of his own—no more probes without consulting with him first—and he also sent along details about the next engagement. Shafter wanted to move first against the San Juan Heights, a few miles east of Santiago, before attacking the Spanish garrison there. Lawton's men would lead the charge, followed by Wheeler's forces, and then by the Rough Riders, all of them accompanied by a contingent of Cuban rebels, this time without the untrustworthy Castillo present. Fourteen thousand American soldiers were to participate in the major thrust toward Santiago.

William Randolph Hearst, who had been sounding the clarion cry for war from the beginning, interviewed Shafter aboard the *Seguranca* and found him to be "in bad humor because of losses in the skirmish," although later Shafter felt obliged to play down his anger to avoid having to court-martial Wheeler for insubordination.

The officers and men took advantage of the respite from the action, burying their dead, resting before their next encounter with the Spaniards, and restocking their larders with the new provisions being loaded onto shore. All the troops and supplies, including the black Twenty-Fourth under General Jacob Kent, were finally on land on the night of June 24, two full days after the first contingents hit the beach at Daiquiri.

North of Las Guasimas sat the town of Sevilla, flanked by the Agua-dores River, which flowed parallel to the main trail for a couple of miles, then zigzagged back and forth across it. Wheeler, once again interpreting Shafter's orders to suit his own ends, sent advance scouts ahead to Sevilla without consulting anyone else. He set up an American outpost there, where the river crossed the trail, and another outpost of Cubans about a mile and a half farther to the west, closer to Santiago. There the river made a sharp turn south toward a low hill called El Pozo—the Fountain, or the Well—where a hacienda sat on the eastern slope.

The trail continued for another mile or more westward beyond El Pozo, where it split, and crossed a valley toward the San Juan River. The trail picked up on the other side of the river and headed into the San Juan Heights, whose crown was San Juan Hill. A lower hill named Kettle Hill, which was topped by a sugar-refining kettle, sat a short distance to the right of San Juan Hill. Looking westward from El Pozo, the sea at Santiago Harbor was hidden from view by a high ridge, but the water and the city of Santiago could be seen through a dip in the ridge near San Juan Hill. North of the valley were the foothills of the Sierra Maestra range, where the village of El Caney lay nestled.

Wheeler's scouts could see the Spanish soldiers on San Juan Hill building a fortified line of trenches bound by barbed wire next to a blockhouse that adorned its crest. They appeared to be digging in for a strong defense of the area, and Wheeler knew that their positions would be impregnable once they completed their work. The Cuban scouts reported that General Linares was sending reinforcements toward San Juan Hill from Santiago. Once they arrived, any hope of a successful American assault on the position would greatly diminish. In Wheeler's view, a direct approach would be suicidal. His men would have to take El Caney first, then veer south through Kettle and San Juan Hills to achieve victory. Outside of El Caney, Wheeler thought he might be able to cut off the Spaniards' water supply, which flowed into the town from the mountains.

A long yellow pit was visible on the hillside leading up to San Juan, and the scouts could see the straw sombreros of the Spaniards bobbing up and down as the men in their blue uniforms built their fortifications close to the blockhouse. The higher-ranking among them rode around on white horses, overseeing the troops preparing their lines of defense. The soldiers worked like an army of ants, digging trenches on San Juan Hill and also to the north in the area around El Caney. The American scouts could see the enemy

San Juan Hill was the most famous of the hills taken by American troops during the long, brutal war against the Spanish in Cuba.

Library of Congress Prints and Photographs Division (LC-USZ62-58789)

marching through the streets of El Caney from their vantage point at El Pozo.

The Spanish had already built more than two miles of trenches throughout the San Juan Heights. They were rapidly constructing a greater line of defense snaking from the coast eight miles northeast to El Caney. Time was on their side, particularly if they could hold the Americans off a bit longer, which would allow for yellow fever and other tropical diseases brought on by infected mosquitos to kick in with a vengeance. The Spanish had been dealing with those ailments for decades, and although they themselves were far from immune, they believed the diseases would help weaken the attackers' morale and gut their ranks even before they climbed the hills.

The main areas of defense were the trenches around the block-house on San Juan Hill, but the Spanish had dug additional trenches and gun pits along the flanks of the hill to protect against an enveloping action by the invaders. A long line of barbed wire was strung in front of the trenches, mostly on Kettle Hill, to slow the enemy's advance. The Spanish miscalculated, however, in positioning their troops and fortifications on the top of San Juan Hill instead of along the lower promontory of Kettle Hill. The lower position would have afforded better command over the tree line less than five hundred yards below, where El Camino Real and another trail merged coming out of the forest.

The trenches sprawled for about two miles north of the block-house, where a stone bridge crossed the San Juan River onto the main road leading west to Santiago—the road that Spanish reinforcements were reported to be taking. El Caney sat two miles north of the bridge, about four miles north of El Pozo. El Caney was a small village with a big stone church, tin-roofed commercial buildings, and tiny houses with palm-thatched roofs. In and of itself it was hardly worth defending; its primary value was its strategic importance as a gateway of sorts to the Spanish bastion and harbor at Santiago. Hernando Cortés reportedly slept there the night before he sailed off to the Yucatán in February 1519 to conquer Mexico and expand Spain's empire in the New World.

Six hundred yards southeast of the village loomed a large fort named El Viso—the Lookout—providing defenders with a clear view of approaching armies from the south and east. The village itself hosted four blockhouses, which the Spaniards surrounded with trenches, gun pits, and barbed wire. They also posted troops on the west side of the village to protect it against an American advance from that direction. What the town lacked was a sufficient number of well-supplied soldiers to man the defenses, since Linares still believed the major American thrust would be a direct assault on Santiago. Linares deployed five hundred troops at El Caney and a similar number around San Juan Hill. The so-called reinforcements that the Cuban insurgents had warned the Americans about, along with much-needed food and equipment, remained only a rumor.

And so the stage was set for the next phase of the war, a battle that would surprise combatants on both sides of the conflict with its stunning ferocity.

16

The American troops used the time after Las Guasimas to nurse their wounds, rest up for the conflict ahead, and wait for additional supplies and troops to make it up the trail from the beach. It turned into an abysmal six-day hiatus in the fighting. With the rain pounding down every day, the trail became a mudslide with barely enough room for a wagon or mule train to climb in single file. The banks along the side of the trail were several feet high in many spots, channeling the trail with a mud-choked quagmire a foot deep. The new troops slogged on, slipping sideways and backward into one another as they approached the campsites of those who had left earlier. Soldiers lay where they could, wet and miserable in their dog tents, which were open to the elements in the front and back. The arrival of the new men and animals only added to the already unbearable congestion. The rains sometimes let up briefly, allowing the sunshine through for a while before the clouds closed in again and drenched the men and equipment with relentless fury.

As new troops arrived in established campsites, others moved farther up the trail to make space for them and find more breathing room of their own. The line of men, animals, and supplies stretched longer and longer. The Rough Riders joined Wheeler's men on the afternoon of June 25 and camped near them alongside a stream while they waited for new orders. General Jacob Kent, leading the black Twenty-Fourth, hastened up the trail as quickly as possible, with orders to join the others before the next assault. There was never enough food to go around, but the mules were loaded with new supplies of salt pork, hardtack, beans, and canned tomatoes, which they shared.

That afternoon, Kent reported to Wheeler with his Twenty-Fourth Infantry troops, and they bivouacked for the night near the landing. Two days later, on June 27, the entire division moved out on the road toward Santiago and encamped on the same ground that Lawton had occupied a few days earlier. Some of the men set up positions near Sevilla, while others, including the Twenty-Fourth Infantry, set up a new camp at Las Guasimas. The order they followed was now more or less what it had been at the beginning, in accordance with Shafter's original plan. Lawton was once again in the lead with the black Twenty-Fifth and other troops. Wheeler followed him with the black Ninth and Tenth Cavalry, and Kent took up the rear with the black Twenty-Fourth under his command.

The Rough Riders had already been instructed, on Sunday morning, June 26, to pitch a new camp three miles west toward Santiago, an assignment that did not sit well with Wood, Roosevelt, and some of their men. "Our camp ground was disappointing," one Rough Rider complained. "The brush made it quite a job to get to headquarters. The heat and wretched conditions have begun to tell on everyone." One of his sidekicks was more enthusiastic, however: "A finer country we never saw. There are mountains all around us covered with coconut and mango trees, with a few pineapples and limes." Wood and Roosevelt fumed that Shafter and the other regular army generals wanted the volunteers out of the way, shunted off to the side where they were unlikely to do any harm.

The American troops grew increasingly frustrated as they sat around idly waiting for orders. When their officers expressed concern about time lost while the enemy fortified its positions, the only response from Shafter was to do nothing until he had a chance to survey the scene himself and direct the next line of attack. In other words, stand by until you receive further orders. Wheeler, Young, Wood, Roosevelt, and others already deployed throughout the area could barely restrain themselves from commencing a new operation at once, and even Lawton had become restless in response to the general lack of direction that was affecting the men's morale.

Many of the soldiers had a clear view now of Santiago and the harbor from their new positions, and they were increasingly anxious to roll down over the enemy positions there. The trails around Sevilla were crowded with seven thousand American troops and nearly half as many Cuban rebels, and new soldiers recently landed at Siboney were trudging up the path, adding to the congestion. In Santiago, General Linares did his best to buoy his own troops' morale. "Soldiers, we left the coal regions because I did not wish to sacrifice your lives in unequal battle, under cover of armored ships," he explained to his men, referring to the American bombardment of the coast. "The encounter is at hand, and it will take place under equal conditions."

On June 27, General Shafter sent additional mule trains laden with ammunition, food, and medical supplies up the trail from the beach. The rotund old military man, however, had yet to set foot on Cuban soil himself, despite his desire to be among his men and get the lay of the land, as it were, from his own perspective. Until now, he had been forced to rely on reports from his officers in the field, some of whom had a tendency to disobey his orders and establish their own rules of engagement. He was determined not to let that happen again and have command of the battlefield taken from him by insubordinate underlings.

Shafter's process of supplying the troops fell far short of expectations, adding to his unpopularity among the officers and men. The food he sent was mostly the same putrid fare on which they had been subsisting for days on end—hardtack, salt pork, and rancid coffee—while fresh fruit and vegetables lay rotting on the transport ships, thanks to Shafter's inability to get them unloaded. The more innovative among the men supplemented their rations with produce they slashed out of the jungle and cooked according to their own improvised recipes. "We have become experienced cooks," one soldier wrote home. "Mangoes boiled in sugar is like applesauce; fried in sugar it is like sweet potatoes. We have hardtack fried in bacon grease which is as good as anything toasted. We also soak our hardtack in water until it is dough, add salt, then mix in some coffee, fry in bacon grease, put a little sugar on top and enjoy it."

Staying clean was another problem, since sentries prevented the men from jumping into the stream and contaminating the water supply, but the tropical downpours intensified, alleviating the sanitary conditions. Electrifying flashes lit up the sky, accompanied by booming claps of thunder and cataracts of water drenching everything in the field. The men stripped down, passed bars of soap around, and showered in the deluge to clean off the grime. They fought among themselves for higher ground, since every depression in the earth churned with whirlpools of muddy rainwater. It rained mercilessly every day, pounding rain that dumped three or four inches an hour onto the trails. When the rain stopped, they busied themselves shoveling the water off the rutted trails so they could progress farther along.

Finally, on June 28, General Shafter hobbled down the gang-plank of the *Seguranca*. His men hoisted him up onto his horse, and then he and his entourage slowly began to make their way up the path into the hills above the beach. Roosevelt couldn't resist chuckling that the absentee general probably outweighed the poor beast he rode on. The leader of the American forces arrived at El Pozo, where he saw with his own eyes the terrain that had been described in detail to him in dispatches from Wheeler and Lawton.

"I had never seen a good road in a Spanish country, and Santiago did not disappoint my expectations," Shafter announced from his horse as his eyes swept the landscape. The roads looked little better than bridle paths to him, except for the one running from El Caney and the San Juan River into Santiago. He had dispatched Lawton and Chaffee to make a more detailed reconnaissance in the area around El Caney, which Wheeler interpreted as an insult to him and a denigration of his earlier observations of the field. Lawton, too, took the opportunity to praise Chaffee at Wheeler's expense— settling the score that had been mounting since Wheeler counter-manded Lawton's, and Shafter's, authority a few days earlier.

"To General Adna R. Chaffee I am indebted for a thorough and intelligent reconnaissance of the town of El Caney and vicinity prior to the battle," Lawton reported, stating that Chaffee was one of the best soldiers in the army. Lawton pointedly recommended Chaffee for special distinction in proposing a battle plan that made sense to everyone and for conducting himself admirably in the battle that followed. About General Wheeler, Lawton said nothing.

Chaffee's battle plan was a long way from being adopted at this point, however. Shafter was still undecided about the best course of action to follow. At first he said he wanted to put a large force in El Caney and another farther to the west, near the pipeline running water to the city, making his main thrust of attack from the north-east and east. He wanted to "get the enemy in my front and the city at my back," he said. A few days later he altered his strategy, stating he wanted to position an entire brigade on the road between Santiago and El Caney to keep the Spaniards from retreating into Santiago. Then he changed direction again, saying he would attack the Spanish enclaves around Santiago directly. Even then, he was not decided. He went back and forth between concentrating his main line of attack on El Caney, then perhaps on San Juan Hill, or maybe it was best to make a direct run at Santiago and forget about the other positions.

When Chaffee told Shafter that they should be able to capture El Caney in about two hours of fighting, Shafter finally made up his mind and adopted Chaffee's strategy, agreeing to move his main forces against El Caney first, with Lawton directing the attack with the black Twenty-Fifth under his command. He would concentrate on the four wooden blockhouses on the west and north sides of the village, a stone church that had been converted into a fort with holes drilled for the Spanish to fire through, and El Viso about six hundred yards to the southeast. There were also the series of trenches around the village, barbed wire barricades, and rifle pits that had to be overcome.

And so the plan was set after several agonizing days of waiting while the Spanish built up their positions on the hills. Shafter came to the conclusion reached earlier by his subordinates that it was better to go straight at the Spanish on their northernmost encampments before attacking their main stronghold in Santiago. They all reasoned, erroneously as it turned out, that American losses would be kept at a minimum with that line of attack.

17

Examining the terrain more closely, the officers noted that the trail to El Pozo resembled the handle of a pitchfork, with two prongs fanning in roughly parallel directions from where they left the handle at El Pozo. The right tine reached out past El Caney, and the left tine descended into the valley and then climbed into the hills of San Juan Heights. For six long days following the victory at Las Guasimas, the men bivouacked in the area, crowded together along a three-mile stretch like ants on a hill, as the weather alternated rapidly from drenching downpours to blistering tropical sunshine laced with high humidity.

While they waited for final orders, General Shafter took his most decisive action of the campaign so far on the afternoon of June 30, sending one of his aides, forty-four-year-old Captain Albert L. Mills, up the trail to confer with Colonel Wood in his tent. Mills informed Wood that General Wheeler and General Young had both become ill and relinquished their command. As a result, Colonel Wood and General Samuel S. Sumner would replace them immediately, Wood taking command of the white First and black Tenth regulars, and Sumner overseeing the rest of their men, which put Roosevelt in sole command of the Rough Riders. Although both Wheeler and Young did appear to have come down with symptoms of a tropical fever, this rearrangement of power was the official reason for the change in command.

"Much to his chagrin, General Wheeler was confined to his Spartan hammock and stretched wagon sheet, with an attack of malarial fever," wrote Kennett Harris in the *Chicago Record*. "It was suicide, the division surgeon declared, for him to attempt to move." But it was inevitable, given Shafter's fury over Wheeler's insubordination in particular, that speculation about other reasons for the abrupt change on the battlefield made the rounds among the men.

At three o'clock in the afternoon, Mills directed Wood to break camp and move forward an hour later. This gave the men little time to strike their tents, roll up their haversacks and blankets, and load their weapons and ammunition onto their backs. "It was as though fifteen regiments were encamped along the sidewalks of Fifth Avenue and were all ordered at the same moment to move into it and march downtown," wrote Richard Harding Davis. "If Fifth Avenue were ten feet wide, one can imagine the confusion."

At that hour, Shafter ordered into operation one of the more ill-advised military strategies attempted since the age of artillery and the machine gun: he launched over the heads of the men, high among the treetops, an enormous observation balloon manned by live soldiers. There it rose, a giant floating bull's-eye, wafting above the jungle to get an aerial view of the Spanish emplacements—and, conversely, presenting a precise target and signal for the Spaniards to judge the paths taken by the attacking Americans. Shafter had imported the balloon from France, thinking it would make an ideal platform for aerial spying. The company's manufacturers had assured him that the floating surveillance sphere would be impervious to enemy gunfire, since both the gas-filled conveyance and the basket carrying the men were swaying targets and hard to hit with gunfire from the ground.

Nevertheless, the officers selected to ride above the treetops were not too keen on climbing aboard so close to the front lines.

To be fair, the idea did not originate with Shafter. The first hydrogen-inflated balloon was launched on June 5, 1783, in Lyon, France, by Joseph-Michel Montgolfier, who envisioned it as a way to capture Gibraltar. Benjamin Franklin became intrigued by the balloon's military possibilities for reconnaissance and airborne assaults. "Five thousand balloons capable of raising two men each could not cost more than five ships of the line," Franklin wrote. "Ten thousand men descending from the clouds might in many places do an infinite deal of mischief."

At a height of about seventeen hundred feet, men in a balloon were capable of distinguishing objects as far as eighteen miles away. They could then communicate with troops on the ground using flag signals, or by sliding down messages inside sandbags attached by rings to the cables that stabilized the aircraft. The French used the first "air force" to good effect against a coalition of British, Hanoverian, Dutch, and Austrian soldiers on June 26, 1794, during the Battle of Fleurus. In September 1861, the Union Army raised a balloon to fourteen hundred feet over Fort Corcoran, Virginia, south of Washington, DC, spotting two Confederate camps miles away at Falls Church. Shortly afterward, in the James River, another balloon rose two thousand feet from the deck of a Union ship, a converted coal barge named the *General Washington Parke Custis*, turning it into the first "aircraft carrier."

In at least two locations—Mechanicsville and Gaines' Farm—the use of balloons allowed the Union to achieve victories by directing their artillery fire on the Confederates during the Battle of Seven Pines. The so-called Balloon Corps served the Union Army until 1863, when it was disbanded following the resignation of Lincoln advisor Thaddeus Lowe. The British used balloons successfully at the Battle of Suakin, in 1888, and the Battle of Omdurman, in 1898.

But not all military leaders were convinced of the balloons' long-term efficacy. Napoleon scorned them, and other military strategists thought them unfair. The International Peace Conference at The Hague actually banned dropping munitions from them in 1899, a year after the war in Cuba. In any event, the development of more advanced machine guns and artillery rendered the balloons militarily obsolete—until they were developed into the types of rigid dirigibles used in the early 1900s.

The great, glistening hulk of the balloon rose high above the treetops as the men plodded below along their assigned routes, many of them staring upward with their mouths open wide. The officers aloft in the balloon descended before the great battle began and described the terrain they observed from their aerial perch. They could see in detail the Aguadores River approaching El Caney from the east, the streams and trails that snaked through the brush, the hills dotting the undulating countryside, the San Juan River flowing north to south. Both rivers joined south of the hills and ran together to the sea.

Fourteen thousand troops trudged slowly beneath the balloon, stepping on one another's heels as they slipped in three inches of muck, crammed together like sardines in a tin, inching ahead foot by foot until the sun sank below the trees and the moon ascended in the night sky to take its place beside the man-made sphere. It was an endless procession of men and beasts, mounted and dismounted soldiers, mules weighed down under their own loads, in what appeared at the moment to be a futile trek to nowhere. The procession moved forward at a snail's pace until after midnight, when the men were ready to drop.

General Sumner, now in command of part of Wheeler's and Young's troops, pitched his headquarters tent on the right side of El Pozo, with a view of the mist rising in the moonlight from the basin below. Sumner had served on the side of the Union during the Civil War and remained in the army afterward, fighting as a cavalryman on the frontier during the Indian Wars in the early 1890s. He had risen to the rank of brigadier general by the time war broke out in Cuba.

On the ground around Sumner, nearly seven thousand men attempted to get a little sleep before the next battle. Most stared up from their blanket rolls at the pitch-black, star-strewn sky, as the rains had mercifully departed for a while. Off to their right, General Chaffee, who had reinforced Wheeler's brigade with the black Ninth and some white divisions, camped among the bushes with his own men alongside the path to El Caney. The major surprise of the night occurred when Shafter's adjutant, Lieutenant Colonel Edward J. McClernand, looked in on his boss's tent at three o'clock in the morning and discovered him once again laid up with gout, complicated by fever and exhaustion from his struggle up the hill.

"He said he was very ill as a result of his exertions in the terrifically hot sun of the previous day," McClernand reported, "and feared he would not be able to participate as actively in the coming battle as he had intended." This meant that the bulk of battlefield generalship would fall primarily on Lawton, but also on Sumner, Kent, Wood, and Chaffee—a fragmented chain of command to say the least, since many of them had shown a tendency to go off in their own directions. When Roosevelt heard about it, he muttered, "The battle simply would fight itself."

18

eneral Lawton, Shafter's next-in-command, made immediate plans to oversee the American assault on the Spanish
positions—understanding that with so many idiosyncratic
personalities in the field, it would be like trying to herd cats. To
make matters worse, the morale of the American troops was
increasingly challenged by the steady downpours alternating with
blistering sunshine, unceasing harassment from assorted insects,
and scant and inadequate food supplies. Their drinking water was
contaminated, and with hardly enough time to boil it, the men
were coming down with dysentery and other intestinal maladies.

On the Spanish side, General Linares was contending with his
own array of problems. Cuban rebels were chewing up his reinforcements before they could reach the hills around Santiago to
bolster his defenses. His stores of food and ammunition were low,
and the soldiers under his command were dispirited and themselves prone to yellow fever, which was even more debilitating
than malaria, the other major mosquito-spread sickness. More
than one in ten had come down with the dreaded disease and were
unfit for duty.

Linares remained convinced that the Americans would concentrate their primary assault on the old forts guarding the entrance to the harbor at Santiago, and he located the bulk of his able-bodied forces there. As a result, other vulnerable areas were less protected. On the slopes around El Caney, Linares had stationed only 521 infantrymen supported by two Krupp light artillery pieces; on San Juan Hill, he had 137 men, which he later bolstered to 461; another 324 men were placed between San Juan and Santiago; and 1,500 soldiers spread across his main line of defense around Santiago.

So, both sides confronted mounting challenges as they dug in for the most decisive battle of the campaign—Spain's struggle to hang on to the vestiges of its crumbing empire, and America's effort to replace it as a major player on the global stage.

Before dawn on July 1, Lawton broke camp at El Pozo and marched with 6,650 men up the right prong of the pitchfork toward the village of Marianage, roughly halfway along the route to El Caney. The men were divided in two brigades, each supported by two light 3.2-inch field guns, with the artillery commanded by Captain Allyn Capron Sr., the father of the young Rough Rider who had been killed at Las Guasimas.

A British military observer from the Royal Engineers noted that an eerie quiet prevailed in the moments before the battle. "There was no sign of life beyond a few thin wisps of smoke that curled from the cottage chimneys," he reported. A few cattle grazed about in the valley, and on three sides around the men towered the peaks of the Sierra Maestra, glistening in the first rays of the rising sun.

Then, without warning, a great cacophony shattered the stillness. At around 7:30, the first shots of the battle boomed in the hills south of El Caney. Lawton had given Captain Capron permission to unleash his artillery at El Viso. The shells overshot their target, however, which turned out to be fortunate since, at that precise moment, a group of fifty Cuban horsemen was riding across the field of fire. The rebels had been scouting the area around El Caney to get a better fix on Spanish positions, but they sped away in fear of their lives when the shells from Capron's guns roared overhead.

The black Twenty-Fifth marched with Lawton to Marianage, where Lawton called for a halt from 6:30 to 7:30 while he sent search parties to scout the area. About a mile north of Marianage, there was a house where Lawton wanted all the troops to rendezvous after El Caney was taken. Lawton sent another reconnaissance team ahead to get a clearer picture of the precise Spanish positions on the left side of El Caney. He directed some of his troops to the left and others, including the black Twenty-Fifth, to the right. They were all to converge in the center when the charge was launched.

The men advanced slowly beyond Marianage to a low hill covered with bushes, about a mile south of El Viso, the large fort situated on the southeast slope of El Caney. General Chaffee deployed the men under his direct command onto higher ground to the right of the fort. Other troops under brigade commander General William Ludlow circled around to the left. At the same time, Shafter directed General Henry Duffield from his sickbed to engage in a feinting action by marching twenty-five hundred men along the coast toward Santiago, where Linares expected the Americans to attack, while Admiral Sampson bombarded the area from the sea to reinforce the deception.

General Kent headed directly along the trail toward the San Juan Heights with fifty-two hundred troops, including the Rough Riders and the black Twenty-Fourth, along with General Sumner and his twenty-seven-hundred-man contingent of black and white regulars. The Rough Riders climbed up the trail toward San Juan with them, Roosevelt, mounted on his horse, at the lead of his men and yelling that he was having a "bully time." He understood that Shafter intended for the main fighting to be done by Lawton and his soldiers, and that the Rough Riders were being used as a diversion. But in his own mind, Roosevelt had other ideas about what was likely to happen. In the heat of battle, who was to say which unit would swarm over the hill first?

The American lines of advance and chains of command were hardly models of organization. Anything could happen, and victory was the only thing that mattered. Roosevelt tied a blue bandanna with white polka dots around his neck in cowboy fashion and pushed his way ahead on the path he was assigned. He had been modest in accepting his new leadership role, saying that he wouldn't have wanted to undertake it until he was sure he had had enough experience. But after his first combat engagement at Las Guasimas, he believed he could handle the responsibility.

Overhead, the huge observation balloon, with a couple of officers riding in the basket, hovered about a hundred feet above the men on the ground. It might as well have had a bull's-eye painted on it, but even without one it made a perfect target for the Spanish defenders. "We did not like having that balloon over us, in range of the Spaniards' guns," wrote a colonel under Sumner's command.

"Is there a general officer below?" one of the men in the balloon yelled to the troops on the ground.

No one answered.

"Is there a field or staff officer down there?" was the next question.

Still, no one replied.

"Is there any officer?"

"Yes, quite a few," someone yelled back.

"I see two roads in front," one of the observers reported.

"Where do they lead to?"

"I can't tell."

That was the extent of the information provided.

A moment later, a cascade of Spanish bullets directed at the balloon fell down on the men, and they immediately dove for cover, wondering what to do next. "We are ordered to remain here in reserve," replied an officer, wishing he were somewhere else at that moment.

The storm of bullets missed the balloon, leaving it intact for a brief period, but its presence continued to take a horrifying toll on the men. From where the men at the front of the column lay on the ground and for a mile to their rear, hardly a yard of earth was outside the zone of Spanish fire. For a solid hour, the bullets poured in like cruel rain on the Americans, including the Rough Riders and the black Tenth, who were positioned near them. Dozens of troops were killed or injured, yet they were all under orders not to return fire until the command was given.

The ground, the grass, the trees around the men, and the men themselves were raked over and over with savage accuracy. Some tried to roll away or run for better cover, only to sink to the ground again, moaning as they clutched their shoulders, arms, or legs. Red Cross medics moved up the line and dragged the wounded back to the river, where they laid them near the muddy banks along the water's edge. The Spanish guns showed no mercy, riddling combatants and aides alike. Captain Mills, who had conveyed Shafter's orders to Wood and the other officers a day earlier, paid a heavy price when a Spanish bullet struck him between the eyes, blinding him temporarily. Incredibly enough, he survived the shot through the forehead, although he remained out of action until the war was over.

"When are we going to begin this thing?" Sumner asked McClernand.

"Our orders are not to do anything until Lawton gets through over there, but he seems to be pretty busy," McClernand answered.

Sumner was growing increasingly frustrated. McClernand noted his impatience, checked his watch, and finally said to Sumner, "Well, I guess you might as well begin."

With the sounds of war echoing from the north, twenty-four horses hauled four light Gatling field guns to the top of El Pozo, spurred on by whips and curses from artillerymen under the command of Captain George S. Grimes. Grimes positioned his guns facing a Spanish blockhouse on San Juan Hill, twenty-four hundred yards away. His field guns fired off about twenty rounds, but they caused more problems for the American forces than they did for the Spanish: the shells hit nothing of importance, but the smoke they emitted hung over El Pozo for a minute or more, giving the enemy a clear target toward which they could direct their return fire. A British war correspondent warned Wood that the artillery fire was likely to put his troops in greater danger.

"We have our orders and cannot move from here," Wood snapped at him.

The Spanish fired with deadly accuracy at a nearby barn, the only structure visible within a mile of El Pozo. Many of the Rough Riders were standing in the barnyard, while a group of foreign observers, newspaper correspondents, and other noncombatants huddled inside the structure. The Spanish shells flew in, killing and wounding some of the men. At the same time, the Spaniards' smokeless guns made it impossible for the Americans to see where the fusillade was coming from.

A Spanish rocket shell roared in, followed by another that soared above Grimes's battery of Gatlings, detonating in the air overhead and unleashing a shower of shrapnel on the men below. In the moments before it exploded, it had emitted an ominous hissing sound accompanied by a trail of white smoke. The shrapnel failed to find a human target, and the men breathed a sigh of relief. But the Spanish had found their range, and the next shell roared in like a railroad train, its timed fuse shattering the projectile into thousands of metal pieces that poured down on the troops. Some Rough Riders and Cuban rebels were killed or wounded, and Roosevelt felt the sting of enemy fire when a piece of shrapnel struck him on the back of his left wrist, raising a large welt. Wood's horse was shot through the lungs. Some of the Rough Riders were enraged at the sight of their stricken commander and started to charge forward, directly into the line of fire. Several were cut down, unable to fire back at the invisible enemy positions, and others ran off in different directions in a fog of confusion. Some tumbled down the western slope of El Pozo, others scampered to the right. Roosevelt wrapped a handkerchief around his wound and said, "Well, that's the first one. They'll have to do better next time."

Roosevelt got back on his horse and rounded up his men, castigating them for their lack of discipline in the face of hostile fire. He took roll call there on the hill while the medics moved up the line and hauled the dead and wounded back to the field hospital. The men stacked their blanket rolls, haversacks, and other equipment on the sides of the trail as they regrouped for the next stage of the battle.

Sumner was perplexed, trying to figure out the best way for his troops to respond. The trail they had taken was bound on both sides by a thick growth of trees and underbrush, but now they had reached a point where the trail opened onto a wide expanse, and Sumner could see the Spanish emplacements only a half mile ahead on the sloping hills at San Juan. The San Juan River ran across the trail where Sumner stood, and another stream intersected it about two hundred yards farther along. Sumner's men were stretched out along the trail with little protection except for the foliage, and the Spanish guns homed in on them with ferocious accuracy. His men were dropping all around him as they were struck by a pitiless swarm of Spanish bullets. Yet, Sumner and the men under his command were still unable to return fire effectively. He finally received his marching orders from Shafter shortly before 9:00 AM, when he was ordered to march his men forward from the peak of El Pozo toward the Spanish positions around the San Juan Heights.

19

The action heated up farther north near El Caney. The Spanish returned Capron's artillery fire with a relentless assault of their own directed at Chaffee's troops on the right of the hill. These included the black Twenty-Fifth and some Cuban rebels, both of whom suffered heavy losses in the early stages of combat. Ludlow and his troops veered farther to their left, within about one hundred yards of the west side of the village, where they supported Capron's artillery with a stream of rifle fire. His goal was to prevent the Spanish from circling around on that side of the hill in an attempt to envelope the American attackers. The Spanish defenders then began to sweep all the approaches into El Caney with a wide swath of devastating gunfire that hit the marks with growing accuracy. More of Lawton's forces moved ahead up the middle, past Capron's battery, with orders to approach El Viso and support Chaffee's troops, who remained under heavy fire.

Capron's artillery shells pounded the walls of El Viso but did little damage to the Spaniards, who were well protected behind them. For the next hour, Spanish gunfire inflicted heavy casualties on the American soldiers in a vicious, nonstop firefight. Ludlow's horse was shot from under him, sending the general sprawling onto the ground. His men dove for cover, with little to protect them against the steady downpour of Mauser bullets. "The buggers are hidden behind rocks, in weeds, in the underbrush," one of Ludlow's men complained. "We can't see them, and they are shooting us to pieces."

Ludlow decided that a change of plan was called for. He moved one of his regiments about three hundred yards farther to the southwest to serve as a blocking force against Spanish soldiers trying to encircle them from that direction. That regiment he replaced with two others armed with more modern Krag rifles. Capron's artillery continued to pound El Viso and the Spanish rifle pits and trenches on the southern side of the fort. Meanwhile, Chaffee inched his troops forward in the face of withering Spanish fire that kept them from making much progress. On the southeast slope of El Viso, they found a refuge of sorts in a ravine that provided some protection from direct enemy fire. The firefight continued for an hour longer, when both sides began to run low on ammunition. Lawton ordered his forces to rest while more ammunition was brought up from the rear, and the Spanish welcomed the opportunity to take a break from the action while they tended to their dead and wounded and restocked their own dwindling supplies.

The lull lasted for three hours while the sun climbed higher, pushing the humidity and temperature well into the nineties. While the troops were waiting for new supplies, Lawton ordered one of his colonels, Evan Miles, to move some of his troops farther to the right, between Ludlow's men and Chaffee's forces. Miles succeeded in positioning them there by noon, at which point the Spanish began firing again, pinning them down about eight hundred yards from El Viso. The losses mounted, and stretcher bearers started carrying the dead and wounded back down the trail. One of them yelled over to the men of the Twenty-Fifth on the right, "Give 'em hell, boys. They've been doing us dirt all morning."

But that was easier said than done. A battle that was supposed to last two hours according to earlier assessments was now dragging on for a good part of the day, with the Americans taking more losses than they were dishing out. Shafter, still laid up in his tent, was growing increasingly frustrated by reports about the lack of progress at the front. He sent a messenger ahead to tell Lawton, "I would not bother with little blockhouses. They can't harm us." Yet it was not the blockhouses that were harming his men, but rather the well-placed Spanish sharpshooters inside them. Wheeler, too, who had been replaced by Shafter, was beside himself with rage and struggled unsuccessfully to get up from his own sickbed and get back into the fight. Nothing seemed to be going right for the American forces at the moment. The Spanish were resisting every attempt to assault the hill to drive them out of their commanding positions.

Colonel Miles got word that the black Twenty-Fifth with Chaffee needed more support, so he dispatched forty Cuban rebels to circle around to their right to help them protect that flank southeast of El Viso. The Cubans pushed ahead the best they could, but the Spanish riflemen had them in range and cut them down, killing the lieutenant who led them. The Cubans and the Americans they came to support kept firing back, but the configuration of the terrain offered them little protection, restricting their ability to advance. The men inched forward "across a plowed field in front of the enemy's position," Miles reported, but "the latter's sharpshooters in the houses in Caney enfiladed the left of our line with a murderous fire." The attackers attempted to redirect their fire on the town of El Caney, but the Spaniards responded with a steady volley of their own that inflicted heavy losses on the Americans.

A new line of troops moved up to a position about sixteen hundred yards behind Miles, and from there they advanced through thick underbrush and three barbed wire fences to within a thousand yards behind the colonel and his men. And there they, too, got bogged down by heavy Spanish rifle fire that riddled the ground all around them.

The roar of battle near El Caney punctuated the thundering sound of guns pounding the American positions near the San Juan Heights. Shafter was growing more and more alarmed about the mounting losses of his men, and he sent word to Lawton to finish the job at El Caney as soon as possible and then head south to reinforce the troops attempting to assault San Juan. "You must proceed with the remainder of your force and join on immediately upon Sumner's right," read Shafter's frantic message to Lawton. "If you do not the battle is lost."

During the lull in fighting, however, Lawton realized that taking El Caney was going to be a bigger job than anyone realized. He couldn't spare a single soldier to send to anyone's assistance. He needed every man he had in his own brigades, and the forces at San Juan would have to fend the best they could on their own. Shafter later agreed that, given the pressure Lawton was under, he was right to continue the fight he already had at hand.

Shafter entrusted McClernand with the unenviable task of delivering his orders and finding some way for the men under Sumner, Kent, and Wood to overtake San Juan before they were all wiped out. "For a time it seemed as though every second man was either killed or wounded," reported Richard Harding Davis. White and black men, regulars and volunteers lay moaning on the ground, clutching at their arms, legs, and chests, braving it out by acknowledging their wounds with phrases like "I've got a punctured tire." A wounded black soldier with the Tenth said, "Oh, don't bother the surgeons about me. They must be very busy. I can wait." He had been shot through the intestines and was lying under a tree near the river, holding his stomach while three of his black brothers were sprawled around him. All of them had been hit in different parts of their bodies.

Every man had only a limited view of what was going on in the general battlefield, and most expressed fear that the enemy soldiers might come swarming in at any moment and finish them off while they were unable to fight back. As yet, despite their heroic efforts, the American forces had accomplished nothing of value. Making matters worse, the mammoth observation balloon rose about fifty feet directly overhead once again, an open invitation for the Spaniards to use it for target practice while foot soldiers marched helplessly beneath it. The enemy attackers sent a steady outpouring of bullets at the balloon, which was only six hundred yards away at this point, and much of their fire took a heavy toll on the men on the ground, members of the First and Tenth in particular.

Like so many fish at the bottom of a barrel, men continued to fall after being hit by bullets and shrapnel from timed charges. Their blood saturated the earth and their uniforms, which were already soaked with sweat and water from fording the streams. Many lay prostrate, suffocating in the blistering heat, their eyes rolling, their heads feeling as though they were on fire. The bullets showed no mercy as they came streaking in from the Spanish rifle pits, and the shrapnel screamed through the air for what seemed like an eternity. One of the officers yelled from the balloon, "I see men up there on those hills. They are firing at our troops!" The response from below went unrecorded and was probably unprintable.

Kent moved the black Twenty-Fourth farther up the trail to come to the aid of the white First and the black Ninth and Tenth, which were in the lead and taking the heaviest fire. General Hamilton Hawkins, a tall Civil War veteran with a snow-white mane, directed Kent's reinforcements along the crowded path as they worked their way toward the front. The route back down was completely blocked for two miles by Kent's forces as they inched their way forward. The entire route was packed with men—the living, dead, and wounded—with little room for anyone to maneuver. They were all entangled in a chute of death from which there was no visible means of escape.

Then, inexplicably, McClernand sent a courier with a message to Kent to move to the side and let the Rough Riders advance to the head of the line. McClernand seemed to have misinterpreted Shafter's orders in taking this action; Shafter had clearly wanted Roosevelt's volunteers to be held back in reserve, but the chain of command and disjointed string of orders got more and more garbled by the minute. Roosevelt, for his part, was only too happy to mount his horse and tell his men to follow him into battle. He rode up the trail, causing a considerable amount of resentment among the regular army vets who had thought from the beginning that the Rough Riders were receiving too much favorable press attention, at their own expense.

The air was still and hot as the men struggled ahead. The vegetation in the jungle around them stank, as though it was rotting from the overbearing humidity, and it was thick enough to block their view to the sides. The putrid stench emanating from the bodies of decomposing horses mingled with the general rot and brought some of the men to the point of nausea. Fortunately, the Spanish had failed to take advantage of the terrain by planning an ambush, and the troops were able to plod forward without resistance. The grumbling in the ranks of the regulars reached Sumner's ears, and he rode back down the trail to reassure his men that they would do most of the fighting, despite the role McClernand had assigned to the Rough Riders. Sumner intended to direct Roosevelt and his volunteers to the right, more in the direction of the lower-lying Kettle Hill, rather than toward their main objective on the peak of San Juan.

Although they were not yet under fire, the going was tough for the Rough Riders. In crossing several deep, fast-moving streams, some of the men were swept downriver, and many of the cowboys, unable to swim, choked on the rushing currents. Weighed down by the sweltering heat and their heavy, wet clothing, the volunteers discarded much of what remained of their personal equipment. The entire procession of men and animals came to a crawl, the slowest among them clogging the trail at various points like slugs in a drainpipe. There was scarcely an inch of extra space to move around. Kent grew incensed by Shafter's poor strategic planning, and he conferred with Sumner about what they should do next. None of the officers knew precisely where they were in relation to their objectives. Sumner commanded Kent and Wood to head straight ahead until they reached the Aguadores River and then halt there while they joined forces and reconnoitered.

20

At that moment, a wraith-like figure appeared in their midst in the form of General Wheeler. The feisty old veteran had forced himself off his sickbed, roused into a fury by the sound of guns booming in the hills. He somehow mounted his horse unseen by the medics or any of his aides and rode like a ghost on horseback toward the San Juan Heights. By the time he reached Sumner and the others, however, he was too weak to assume command and was forced to serve as a mere liaison between McClernand and the generals at the front. After another hour of slogging up the overgrown trail, they reached the spot where it intersected the Aguadores River. Roosevelt rode up to join them, leading the remnants of his troops strung out down the trail behind him.

"Colonel, better get down, or they'll pot you," one of the officers called out to Roosevelt.

"I'm not going to lie down for any confounded Spaniard!" Roosevelt answered.

From the banks of the river, they could see that the Spaniards had leveled most of the trees and heavy brush on the other side to create an open killing field for their riflemen. The observation balloon floated overhead, tethered in place by ropes held by troops on the ground. One of the officers in the balloon called down that there was a previously unseen footpath veering off to the left that provided another route to San Juan Hill. The observers couldn't see many enemy soldiers along the route, so they assumed that most of the defenders were hidden on the far side of the ridge. Sumner contemplated the situation, trying to figure out the next phase of the attack. Should he expose his men to the cleared banks on the other side of the river, taking a chance that the enemy was not waiting in ambush for them? Or should he play it safe and await further orders from Shafter, who was laid up with no firsthand knowledge of their predicament? Some of the men were already crossing the river on their own, with no orders from anyone, so Sumner felt he had little choice but to plunge across himself with the bulk of his forces.

Unfortunately, while the men holding the balloon were preoccupied, the giant aerial target drifted out over the water above the troops, showing the Spanish soldiers on the hill precisely where the Americans were crossing the river. The Spaniards launched a steady discharge of rifle fire that not only inflicted more death on the men below the balloon but also punctured it. The incoming fire was vicious and intense, shredding the balloon's skin and sending it into a freefall until it crashed ingloriously into the trees beside the trail. The men in the basket managed to get out with their lives, but many soldiers on the ground were not as fortunate. Spanish shells and bullets exacted a heavy toll, with the Rough Riders near the lead taking a good deal of the punishment. Many of them dashed off to the sides looking for whatever cover they could find. Sections of Kent's and Wood's regiments were trapped and unable to flee from the carnage. At least eighty men were killed, and many more were wounded.

Simultaneously, a thirty-eight-year-old captain rushed to the front of the pack, with the black Tenth charging behind him. The captain's name was John J. Pershing, the officer who would gain fame almost twenty years later as General "Black Jack" Pershing when he led the American Expeditionary Forces during World War I. Pershing had long been a champion of African Americans, having taught at the Negro School in Missouri, where he was born, before he entered West Point in 1882. He earned his nickname as a defender of black equality and a spokesman for their performance in battle when it was unfashionable to do so—the soubriquet first registering as "Nigger Lover," then "Nigger Jack," before it was sanitized as "Black Jack."

This was not the first time that Pershing had led black soldiers in combat. He had headed the Tenth and a white cavalry unit during the Indian Wars in the early part of the decade, praising their valor in combat. Pershing was an instructor of military tactics at West Point when the *Maine* exploded in February 1898, and he asked for permission to rejoin the Tenth when it was ordered to Cuba. He hooked up with the black troops in Chickamauga, Georgia, traveled with them to Florida, and sailed as the leader of the group from Tampa. Pershing complained bitterly about the conditions the men endured below deck on their way to Cuba, about the shabby treatment they received from their white compatriots, and even about the heavy, unsuitable uniforms the men were issued as they headed off to a tropical warzone. He marched with them every step of the way after they landed on Cuban soil, earning his men's respect and admiration. Now they followed him willingly into battle in the face of a murderous enemy onslaught.

Although Pershing thought that Shafter had botched the operation from the start, he came to the general's defense when a white officer complained about the "fat old slob" who was getting them all killed. "Why did you come to this war if you can't stand the gaff?" chastised Pershing, a military man through and through. "War has always been this way. The fat old man you talk about is going to win this campaign. When he does, these things will be forgotten. It's the objective that counts, not the incidents."

Pershing positioned himself waist-high in the middle of the fast-flowing river as he motioned the Tenth forward through exploding shells and heavy Mauser fire. He moved back and forth from the water to the shore, urging the men on. An enemy shell screeched in and landed between him and Wheeler, who was mounted on his horse. Pershing saluted Wheeler, who saluted him back and remarked, "The shelling seems quite lively." Then Wheeler rode off while Pershing continued to direct his men to the other side of the river. He stood exposed in the midst of the intense pounding as his men were hit and fell to the ground all around him. Every so often, he returned to land to find some of his men who were lost in the jungle and to direct them across the river. Pershing held steady amid the carnage, and when a man in his command was shot next to him, he calmly noted the way the soldier's arms flew up and his hands flapped downward at the wrists: "That's the way it is with all people when they are shot through the body," Pershing observed, "because they want to hold the torso steady, because if they don't it hurts." One of the black troops in his command, who had witnessed Pershing in action, commented later that through it all, "Pershing remained as cool as a bowl of cracked ice."

The American troops following the Tenth across the river started to refer to it as "Hell's Crossing," and they called the open field on the far side "the Bloody Angle." When Wood made it over, he looked back at the tattered balloon and said it was "one of the most ill-judged and idiotic acts I have ever witnessed." One of his officers agreed, saying, "What the balloon didn't get hit us."

Roosevelt followed in their wake and deployed the remnants of the Rough Riders to the right in the direction of Kettle Hill. Their numbers were significantly depleted, and more would lose their lives before the battle was over. Those who were left made it across with their leader. They passed the Tenth as they veered north, with orders to meet up with Lawton's men after the latter finished mopping up El Caney.

21

At about 1:00 in the afternoon, Ludlow's brigade commenced firing again at the Spanish emplacements from its position southwest of El Viso. Lawton ordered Miles and Chaffee to move forward with the white Fourth and black Twenty-Fifth to see if they could get any closer to the fort. A second line of black troops, led by Lieutenant James A. Moss, followed about two hundred yards behind them, firing over their heads in the direction of El Viso.

Moss was an 1894 graduate of West Point who had earned some earlier fame experimenting with the use of bicycles in war. In 1896, he formed the Twenty-Fifth Bicycle Corps, which covered forty miles a day over rugged mountain terrain, crossing streams, and even hauling their bikes over fences up to nine feet high. Each soldier carried a knapsack, blanket roll, and shelter-half strapped to his handlebars, plus a rifle containing fifty rounds of ammunition slung on his back. Moss designed the bikes himself and had them built by the sporting good company Spalding with steel rims, tandem spokes, extra-heavy side forks and crowns, gear cases, luggage carriers, frame cases, brakes, and special saddles. Fully packed, the bicycles weighed about sixty pounds.

Now Moss found himself leading black foot soldiers in battle. Two lines of trees that ran along a railroad track hid him and his second rank of attackers from the eyes of the Spaniards. Just north of the trees stood a line of barbed wire, beyond which lay an open field of pineapples. No sooner did Moss and his men in the rear cross over into the pineapple field than a hail of Spanish bullets and shells roared down on them, raking them as they crossed open ground with no protection. Moss was more concerned about the carnage inflicted on his men than he was for his own wellbeing. "It's raining lead!" he wrote later. "The line recoils like a mighty serpent, and then in confusion, advances again! The Spaniards now see us and pour a murderous fire into our ranks! Men are dropping everywhere . . . the bullets cut up the pineapple at our feet . . . the slaughter is awful. . . . Our men are being shot down at our very feet, and we, their officers, can do nothing for them!"

Chaffee, to the right, ordered his own men to move ahead, away from the deadly gunfire behind them and closer to El Viso. Slowly, his troops closed to within two hundred yards of the fort and could begin to make out the shapes of the Spanish riflemen inside the structure as well as in the rifle pits around it. He called for his best sharpshooters to come to the front of the line and take aim at the enemy. Close to forty of them inched forward, took their positions, and opened fire. This time, the American bullets found their marks. Spanish troops began to fall, shot where they lay in their rifle pits and winged in the head and shoulders by bullets that made it through the firing slots in the wall of the fort. The number of Spanish dead and wounded climbed rapidly.

"Thirty or forty of these dead shots are pouring lead into every rifle pit, door, window, and porthole in sight," read Chaffee's exuberant message from the front. "The earth, brick, and mortar are fairly flying! The Spanish are shaken and demoralized."

The black Twenty-Fifth surged forward, emboldened by the sudden turn of events—an almost instantaneous and unexpected reversal of fortune, it seemed. They got there first in the face of "a galling fire," about twenty minutes before the next wave of soldiers arrived at the fort, according to Lieutenant Colonel A. S. Daggett, a white officer with the group. When the Spaniards saw the Smoked Yankees—as they had referred to them earlier at Las Guasimas—charging forward, they retreated from the fort over the far side of the hill and ran toward the village of El Caney. One by one, those who were still able-bodied cut and ran off.

"Bareheaded and without rifles, they are frantically running from their rifle pits," Chaffee went on with undisguised elation. "Our men are shooting them down like dogs."

The Twenty-Fifth charged inside the fort, with their comrades closing in behind them. The Spanish dead and wounded lay everywhere, carpeting the dirt floor and soaking it with their blood. Bullet holes pockmarked every square inch of the stone walls. The trenches outside were layered with the dead and groaning enemy in contorted positions. Many had been shot through the forehead as they had peeked above their barricades. One officer noted that "their brains oozed out like white paint from a tube." Others had been maimed by shrapnel from Capron's artillery and writhed half-dead in the trenches. Men from the Twenty-Fifth seized the Spanish flag from the top of the fort and raised it overhead in victory.

From their vantage point at El Viso, the American troops could see some of the retreating Spaniards trying to circumvent El Caney and flee into the hills to the north. The route was blocked, however, by a band of Cuban rebels who were marching south in an attempt to attack the village from the other side. In effect, the roughly three hundred Spanish soldiers who were left to defend the village itself were trapped there by Cubans to the north and the Americans in command of El Viso, who now outnumbered the enemy twenty to one. Nonetheless, General Joaquín Vara del Rey y Rubio, who had been tasked by Linares with holding El Caney with so few men, decided to fight on. The battle may have been all but decided, but he knew the attackers would head south to reinforce the troops at San Juan at their first opportunity, and he figured he could at least deprive Shafter of about one-third of his army by bogging it down at El Caney.

The odds greatly favored the American forces, but the battle for El Caney was not yet over, not as long as General Rubio still had a breath of life in his fifty-eight-year-old body and a handful of soldiers under his command. The general regrouped some of his men in front of a blockhouse on the southeast corner of the village, and from there they launched a stream of bullets at the advancing American troops. A line of trenches ran from that blockhouse westward until it reached another blockhouse that anchored the southwest corner of El Caney. Spanish sharpshooters occupied a row of fortified houses extending northward along the west side of town, from which they fired down at Ludlow's men, who had circled to their left to cut off a Spanish retreat along the road toward Santiago. The Americans shot back, but their bullets had little effect on the well-entrenched enemy.

"As long as we remain in our present position," one of Ludlow's officers said, "we can accomplish but little, as the walls of the blockhouse are impervious to our bullets." The unfavorable situation prompted them to veer farther to their left, down the slope of the hill and then up to a ridge that overlooked the blockhouse and the houses on the west side of the town. The higher vantage point allowed them to fire down at the Spaniards in the blockhouse and in the row of houses from about two hundred yards away.

This line of attack proved more successful and caused many of the defenders to abandon the blockhouse and seek cover among the houses to their north. They tried to make a final stand there against the encircling Americans, who kept closing in on them like a noose drawing tighter every minute. The men of the Twenty-Fifth had continued on past the fort after seizing the Spanish flag and swarmed into the village from the east, shooting retreating enemy soldiers as they backed them into town. General Rubio rode through the village on horseback, exhorting his men to fight on against the Americans and deprive them of an early victory.

The conquest of El Caney took longer than anticipated, and much of the credit for the victory belonged to the black Twenty-Fifth, which launched the major assault on the village that led to its ultimate collapse.

Library of Congress Prints and Photographs Division (LC-USZ62-104748)

As the Americans moved closer from all sides, the Spanish kept up a steady attack from the center of the village, the heart of which was the old stone church that sat like a sentinel in the midst of the bloodshed. Despite their mounting losses, the Spaniards refused to submit to the overwhelming tide of American attackers. They held on for the next few hours, until reality overwhelmed them late in the afternoon.

"The action lasted nearly throughout the day, terminating about 4:30 p.m.," Chaffee wrote in his report. The sheer weight of the numbers against the Spaniards told the final story. Down to the last eighty-four soldiers of the more than five hundred they started with, the Spanish forces collapsed after ten brutal hours of combat.

One of the last to be killed was the general who had inspired his men to rise above their dire circumstances and accomplish the nearly impossible. Rubio was shot through the legs as he fired his gun in the square in front of the church. His men lifted him from his horse and were lowering him onto a stretcher when an American bullet crashed through his head and killed him where he lay. Two of his sons had been lost in action earlier that day. American soldiers buried the Spanish leader with full military honors, praising him as "an incomparable leader; a heroic soul," whose men had shown "magnificent courage" during the battle for El Caney. Later that year, Rubio's remains were repatriated to Spain, where he received his country's highest military decoration.

As Rubio's life fled from his body, so too did the will to continue flee from the bodies of his men. More than four hundred Spanish soldiers died or were wounded defending El Caney. The survivors escaped past Ludlow's troops and scampered down the road to Santiago. An equal number of Americans were killed or wounded taking the village—which the soldiers soon started calling "Hell Caney"—with the initial successful charge on El Viso spearheaded by the black Twenty-Fifth.

A British officer who witnessed the American assault on El Caney blamed their heavy losses—despite the overwhelming odds on their side—on poor generalship and disorganized planning overall, laying the blame squarely at Shafter's feet. "Is it customary with you to assault blockhouses and rifle pits before they have been searched by artillery?" the Brit asked an American officer.

"Not always," the officer answered, his embarrassment showing.

The British officer didn't need to point out that in this battle meant to be a speedy prelude to the main action farther south, nearly a tenth of the American troops were badly wounded, killed immediately, or else died later from untreated injuries because of poor medical attention. Adding to the poor showing was the absence of a major part of Shafter's army, who was not able to relieve their comrades at El Caney because they were trying to storm the San Juan Heights. Some of the blame fell on the cautious Lawton, the commanding general in the El Caney operation, but ultimately the buck stopped with the man presiding over the entire war, the bedridden Shafter, hampered by gout and other ailments.

22

With the battle for El Caney now ended, Lawton decided to rest his men for the night rather than risk more of their lives on a drive southwest toward San Juan over unfamiliar terrain. Instead, he marched them due south, back down the path taken that morning, past Marianage to El Pozo, where they bivouacked overnight. By the time they arrived that evening, Lawton's men were clearly spent, bruised and battered by the rigors of the daylong battle. And even had they headed directly toward San Juan to join the troops fighting there, according to the original plan, it was already too late for them to be of any help to the beleaguered American forces struggling to fight their way up a different set of treacherous hills.

Close to noon on July 1, before Lawton called an end to the ceasefire at El Caney, Roosevelt had deployed the Rough Riders to the right along the San Juan River toward Kettle Hill, hoping that Lawton's men would be heading southwest to their assistance. To his immediate left was Pershing at the head of the Tenth. Roosevelt led his men into a jungle on his right flank as Mauser bullets drove down on them in sheets through the trees, inflicting heavy casualties. Sumner sent a courier up to Roosevelt's position with instructions to send a search party to make sure the Spanish hadn't planned another ambush for his men. The best Roosevelt could do in the dense foliage was to lead a skirmish line farther into the jungle, taking the lead himself on foot.

His second order from Sumner was to refrain for the time being from firing at the enemy, since Pershing and the Tenth were in the process of advancing ahead of him through more open terrain and he didn't want the Rough Riders putting them in their line of fire. Roosevelt smoldered again at being relegated to reserve status, but he had no option except to follow orders as he waited for an opportunity to engage the Spaniards at closer range. He sent couriers of his own over to Wood, who was leading his own detachment in the direction of San Juan Hill. Roosevelt's men were tumbling around him, their losses growing by the minute, and he hoped that Wood would be more sympathetic to his plight. While Roosevelt inched his skirmish line through the jungle, he encountered six dark-skinned men wearing ragged uniforms he couldn't identify and that were all but slipping off their backs. They claimed to be Cuban rebels looking to return to their unit. Since they were unarmed and Roosevelt had no way of knowing for sure who they were, he let them disappear back into the jungle in the direction they had come from.

Wood could not spare any men to send to Roosevelt's assistance, and neither could Kent at the head of the Twenty-Fourth, or any of the other officers with orders to climb the Heights toward San Juan Hill. The Rough Riders were in no position to move forward as the rifle fire from the enemy's entrenchments blistered through the trees and savaged their ranks, reducing their numbers alarmingly from the more than five hundred they started with. All the men across the entire American front were pinned down by enemy fire, with the Spaniards mostly hidden from view through the heavy foliage. Roosevelt grew desperate to take more aggressive action before his troops were completely slaughtered as they groped through the brush blindly, unable to respond effectively. Neither Kettle Hill nor San Juan Hill could be clearly seen through the trees. Confusion reigned supreme as the casualties mounted, still with no definitive orders from Shafter on how to proceed.

Kent's men were in dire straits themselves, with Spanish bullets and shells ripping through their ranks. The white troops in front of them refused to push ahead, so Kent ordered them to step aside and let his men pass through. "For the love of country, liberty, honor, and dignity," Kent pleaded with tears running down his cheeks, "stand up like men and fight, go to the front!" Still, they would not move; some actually tried to head back the other way down the trail, out of the range of enemy fire.

So Kent rushed past them, leading his men in a mad fury in the direction of San Juan Hill. They stormed forward past "the prostrated bodies of the bewildered and stampeded Seventy-First," wrote Herschel V. Cashin. They rushed wildly across "an open field, attracting the attention of the entire Spanish line, and drawing their concentrated fire." Their own losses mounted heavily. Kent feared that they had entered a circle of fire, with Spanish guerrillas behind them as well as defenders bombarding them from the hills. But he was in no better position to observe the terrain behind his men than he was to see what faced them on the hill.

"At times I became melancholy and apprehensive as to my fate," J. W. Galaway, a soldier with the Twenty-Fourth, wrote later, "but it was not from fear, but suspense." The Twenty-Fourth continued along the route between the Aguadores and San Juan Rivers under heavy, unceasing fire, then Kent ordered some of his men to veer left onto the footpath that the observers in the balloon had spotted. The footpath had not been visible to the soldiers on the ground, but the Spanish were well aware of its existence and the alternative route it provided to their defenses on San Juan. They unleashed a torrent of fire along the trail, killing and wounding many of the men who had followed it, including four officers. Those who had not been hit by enemy bullets continued to inch ahead through the line of fire.

To their right, Pershing's Tenth faced a similar situation. Sergeant Horace Bivins, who was in charge of the Hotchkiss guns with the unit, said later that they had to stop innumerable times because of bloody mudholes caused mostly by the injured men, and because of other obstacles on the trail. Looking through his field glasses, he saw so much wild game fleeing in terror that he "did not know where to direct [his] first shot." When he finally did fire toward San Juan Hill, the puffs of black smoke from his guns attracted so much fire from Spanish marksmen that a few men went down around him immediately. Bivins was also hit by a Mauser bullet, which knocked him unconscious for a few minutes. He recovered quickly and got up to continue the assault.

The heat and humidity rapidly became another formidable obstacle bearing down on the American troops. Some stopped to slice their trousers off at the knees, exposing their legs to a wide assortment of biting insects and thorny underbrush. The heavy uniforms chafed their skin, raising red rashes from prickly heat, prompting the men to discard more clothing on the sides of the trails. As they plodded through the chaparral, they reached a point where the San Juan River continued north and the Aguadores River forked to the east and flowed north of El Pozo. Roosevelt abandoned all hope of getting help from Wood or Kent and of hooking up with Lawton heading down the trail from El Caney, so he drove his men forward toward Kettle Hill as best he could in the face of the heavy enemy gunfire.

The Rough Riders came to a halt in the jungle as they waited for further orders from Sumner, Wood, or Shafter. Enemy fire roared in on them from three locations—San Juan Hill, the Heights, and Kettle Hill—yet they were still under orders from Sumner to hold their fire until Pershing and the Tenth had taken their own advanced positions to their left. The Americans now formed two broken lines as they inched ahead toward the Spanish emplacements. The first, composed mostly of black troops, had approached a meadow on the west side of the San Juan River. Wood's men were behind them spread across both banks of the river, and the Rough Riders were farther to the north facing Kettle Hill. Pershing's Tenth was also ordered to hold its fire once they were in place until new orders were received from Shafter's camp. All of them were more than ready to continue the assault, but still no orders arrived.

Roosevelt decided to pull his men back to the river where they could find some protection behind the western bank. Besides the lethal fire from the hills, Spanish snipers were hidden in the trees shooting the hell out of his men. His blood was boiling, driving him into a rage.

"Boys, this is the day we have trained for!" he yelled to his troops. "You know you are being watched by the regulars. Don't forget you are a Rough Rider!"

Roosevelt was down to about fifty troops now, a tenth of what he had at the onset of hostilities. He panicked that his Rough Riders would be totally wiped out unless he took some drastic action to alleviate the situation. The clatter and din of war rattled the men's eardrums as Spanish shells roared in and Mauser bullets zipped through the grass and leaves.

Indeed, enemy fire put not just men but their animals in danger as well. Horses made tempting targets for Spanish sharpshooters, as many of them reared up on their hind legs in fear, presenting themselves as larger and more visible targets than the men did. Some threw off their riders, and other cavalrymen dismounted, preferring to take their chances on foot. Roosevelt's horse, Texas, was tethered to a tree nearby, and the future president feared he would be hit by incoming fire, yet his mount stood there neighing nervously and was unharmed through the carnage.

Stephen Crane reported later that the entire battlefield was roaring like a brushfire on the prairie, having observed the action himself through field glasses as he stood in the open. Richard Harding Davis told him impatiently to stop showboating and tempting fate and to look for some protection behind a tree.

Beyond the jungle growth, the chaparral, and the denser foliage lay an open meadow with grass and plants that ran up to the foothills of San Juan and Kettle Hills. The Americans halted at the edge of it, waiting for an opportunity to storm up the slopes. To Roosevelt's left, Pershing's Tenth opened up a round of fire in the direction of San Juan Hill, although their view of the Spanish emplacements was still obstructed. Roosevelt wanted to support them with his own men, but as he turned to one of his aides, Lieutenant Ernest Haskell, on leave from West Point, the lieutenant's body stiffened as he froze in place without crying out. The leader of the Rough Riders could see that Haskell had been shot in the stomach by a Mauser bullet.

"Oh, don't bother about me," Haskell said when Roosevelt reached out to him. "I'm going to get well." The twenty-two-year old officer survived the serious wound and lived for another thirty-two years.

Two of Roosevelt's other top aides went down by his side, one overcome by heat and exhaustion and the other wounded by a bullet that slammed into his neck. A third keeled over dead when a bullet ripped through his brain. Then Roosevelt suffered one of the greatest losses of the battle so far when his favorite sidekick, Captain Buckey O'Neill, the man who dove into the water in an attempt to save two black troops from drowning at the landing, was shot in the mouth.

23

William Owen O'Neill was born on February 2, 1860, either in Ireland, St. Louis, Missouri, or Washington, DC. His precise origin remained as much a mystery as the man himself, partly because he was a larger-than-life adventurer and entrepreneur, fond of spinning tall tales, some of them about himself. The claim that he was born in Ireland is most likely an invention of his; although his father served in the so-called Irish Brigade during the Civil War and was wounded at the Battle of Fredericksburg, his parents had been in the United States since the 1850s.

Buckey—a nickname he earned because he liked to "buck," or gamble, against the odds in poker and other card games—migrated from the east to Prescott, Arizona, in the spring of 1882 making brief stops along the way. The first was in Tombstone in 1880, where he reported on the war between the Earp brothers and the Clanton-McLaury gang of murders and cattle rustlers, which culminated in the Gunfight at the O.K. Corral on October 26, 1881. Next he dallied in Phoenix, a town he didn't like all that much. Prescott suited him better, and it was there he made his home.

Buckey was first and foremost a man of action, but he was also a literary man—traits he shared with the leader of the Rough Riders and which endeared him to Roosevelt. He started his career as a court reporter, then moved up the ladder and became editor of the *Prescott Journal Miner*, after which he founded, wrote, edited, and published the *Hoof and Horn*, a livestock periodical. The action side of his nature took over when he ran for various offices and was elected sheriff of Yavapai County and later mayor of Prescott. Twice he ran for Congress as a territorial representative for the Populists, but he lost those races, in 1894 and 1896, to major-party candidates.

O'Neill made his real money developing onyx and copper mines and building a railroad line to the South Rim of the Grand Canyon. He exhibited an interest in archaeology when he led a Smithsonian expedition to explore the Sinagua Indian ruins known today as Montezuma Castle in Arizona's Verde Valley. Buckey indulged a taste for military adventure at the same time, joining a local militia and helping organize the Arizona National Guard. Like an earlier Hemingway, the man of action turned his hand to fiction, publishing stories in the *San Francisco Examiner* and *Argosy*.

His path met up with Roosevelt's in 1898 when Buckey helped found the First United States Volunteer Cavalry, the unit headed by Colonel Wood that was destined to become the heartbeat of the assemblage Roosevelt put together for the war in Cuba. Roosevelt and Buckey O'Neill hit it off from the start. Buckey was the prototypical cowboy Roosevelt had become intrigued with during his many trips out west, a man who could ride, shoot, and fight with the best of them. He was one of the first who volunteered to join Roosevelt in Cuba, telling him, "I am ready to take all the chances." He shared Roosevelt's philosophy that the war would not be over until every officer in the unit was killed, wounded, or promoted.

On that fatal day, July 1, with the Rough Riders pinned down at the bank of the river, Roosevelt ordered Buckey O'Neill to lead an advance team to get a better view of the Spanish positions on top of the incline. Buckey motioned his men forward toward a field of waist-high grass near the edge of a clearing on the other side of the river. The men dove to the ground in the grass and lay flat, still obeying orders not to fire back until they were commanded to do so. Buckey stood upright at the head of his detail, about twenty yards from the riverbank, smoking one of his hand-rolled cigarettes. Roosevelt thought he was taking unnecessary risk, but the captain didn't believe an officer should dive for cover when the men he led were in danger.

"Captain, a bullet is sure to hit you," a sergeant said to Buckey, all but begging him to lie down.

Buckey blew out a cloud of smoke, laughed, and replied according to witnesses, "Sergeant, the Spanish bullet isn't made that will kill me."

Moments later, he turned on his heel to face the Spanish guns, and a Mauser bullet flew into his mouth and exited through the back of his head. Buckey O'Neill was dead before his body hit the ground. The manner of his death and the life that preceded it grew into a legend, and the man was even lionized in a 1997 TV miniseries, in which he was portrayed by actor Sam Elliott. A bronze statue of Buckey erected in 1907 has become a Prescott landmark and occupies a prominent spot in front of the Yavapai County Courthouse.

Roosevelt was beside himself with anguish, grief, despair, and mounting anger. He clearly had to do something. He couldn't wait forever while the best of his men were falling dead around him with orders to hold their fire. He sent another message to Sumner and Wood, pleading for permission to shoot back and advance. Wood's and Sumner's impatience and frustration were also boiling over, as they themselves had no clear orders from Shafter on how to proceed. Sumner, whose troops included the black Ninth, later said that it had become "necessary either to advance or else retreat under fire." Roosevelt was at the point of taking it upon himself to move toward the hill when the long-awaited message arrived a little after 1:00 PM from Sumner's camp, with Shafter's approval, to "move forward and support the regulars on the assault on the hills in front."

It was the summons Roosevelt had been hoping for, and he sprang to action without delay. He mounted Texas, pointed his men in the direction of Kettle Hill, past the body of Buckey O'Neill, and led the charge in the midst of a blizzard of enemy gunfire.

As Roosevelt rode up from the riverbank, he saw one of his men lying in a bush off to the side. Roosevelt ordered him to get up and join the charge. The trooper staggered to his feet and tried to move forward, and it was then Roosevelt noticed that he had already been raked across the length of his body by Spanish gunfire. The man fell over dead. Roosevelt blanched when he realized that the bullets may have been intended for himself, an easier target mounted on his horse, but had claimed the life of one of his volunteers instead. That he was putting himself at greater risk by charging ahead of his men on horseback had not occurred to Roosevelt before then. But it was not his nature to shy away from danger; the incident rattled him temporarily, but he shrugged it off and rode on.

Ahead and to the left of Roosevelt, Pershing told his men to charge. He positioned himself at the head of the black Tenth as he observed the entire field of combat. They were all engaged now, as Pershing reported on the action afterward: "Each officer or soldier next in rank took charge of the line or group immediately in his front or rear and halting to fire at each good opportunity, taking reasonable advantage of cover, the entire command moved forward as coolly as though the buzzing of bullets was the humming of bees. White regiments, black regiments, regulars, and Rough Riders . . .

unmindful of race or color, unmindful of whether commanded by ex-Confederate or not, and mindful of only their common duty as Americans."

Pershing's Tenth Cavalry and Sumner's Ninth Cavalry rushed directly ahead toward San Juan Hill. Farther south, Kent also advanced with the black Twenty-Fourth and other men under his command toward San Juan, with some of the troops approaching along the smaller footpath seen from the balloon. The Rough Riders pushed on toward Kettle Hill north of them, and Wood's brigades formed another line of attack across the entire range of battle. When Pershing saw most of the attackers heading up the incline through the brush to San Juan, he veered the Tenth off to the right to reinforce Roosevelt's left flank and support the Rough Riders' steep climb to Kettle Hill.

The first ranks of attackers had now moved within about five hundred yards of Kettle Hill and could see the sugar refinery and some of the enemy emplacements through the constant cloud of Mauser bullets that continued to inflict heavy casualties on the Americans. The enemy was almost in sight, but what the attackers didn't know yet and would soon discover was the hills were protected by barbed wire fences that were all but invisible as they snaked through the thick brush around the Spanish entrenchments.

24

The advance was made under heavy infantry fire, through open flat ground, cut up by heavy wire fences," Sumner recalled later. Beyond the barbed wire, the jungle growth ended and the incline became steeper. To his right, Pershing's Tenth joined up with Roosevelt and the Rough Riders as they continued to push slowly up the hill. Roosevelt wanted his men to get to the top before the others, and he urged them on while still mounted on Texas, shouting at the soldiers to not fall behind. Some of the Rough Riders ran a few steps before the hill became more demanding, and then they found themselves panting for breath and falling to the ground, trying to crawl up the incline when their legs gave out. Pershing's Tenth was beside the Rough Riders on the left, with Sumner's Ninth to the left of them, most of the black troops in better physical condition due to long years of battlefield experience. Together, they slogged their way closer to the enemy lines.

The Mauser bullets steadily took a toll, finding their marks from the riflemen on the hill and from snipers hidden in the trees to the right. The American lines of attack devolved into a welter of confusion, with troops strewn out along the slopes from Kettle Hill over the Heights to San Juan, and down along the trails behind them with the rear guards still moving up from El Pozo. Medical corpsmen scampered up and down, pinning white tags on the slightly wounded, blue-and-white tags on those more seriously injured, and red tags on the more critical cases. They carted away the wounded as quickly as they could and left the dead where they had fallen, to be buried later. "We thought we had a soft snap," a medic recalled later, referring to the outnumbered enemy, "but we got a tough proposition here."

The front ranks of American attackers encountered the first strands of the Spaniards' barbed wire defenses. The enemy had strung the fences between palmetto poles sunk into the ground in a zigzag pattern about twenty-five yards apart. The Tenth reached the first jagged line of wire before the others and started to tear at it with their bare hands. Roosevelt tried to move ahead on horseback, but Texas began to stumble and rear up in fear as the hill grew more challenging. The horse almost became ensnared in the wire, temporarily bringing horse and rider to a halt. But Roosevelt was able to guide Texas across the fence when the troops pulled the poles out of the ground and flattened it.

At that moment, a sniper's bullet from the rear—or, possibly, an errant shot from one of his Rough Riders—grazed Roosevelt's cheek and ripped his eyeglasses from his nose. His nearsightedness was severe enough that he could barely see without them. Fearing such an event, he always kept a few pairs in reserve, one of which he put on. His luck was still holding out; three times so far bullets had nicked him or hit a nearby tree, and three times he came through with no serious injuries. His men scrambled with him over the downed fence and continued up the slope. One of them said later, "If Teddy was not on that horse, the bullets would not be coming so close."

The men continued to receive head and chest wounds as they carried the yellow Rough Rider banner up the hill, which had now steepened to about a forty-five-degree angle. One of the troops had his hat shot off, the bullet just missing his head as it ripped through the crown. "I'll have to patch that up with a bit of sticking plaster, or I'll get my hair sunburned," the redhead joked, drawing laughter from his comrades. Buffalo Soldiers from the Ninth and Tenth moved slightly ahead of them to their left as they drew closer to enemy lines. A British correspondent reported that the troops advanced slowly but steadily, likening their climb to his own country's Charge of the Light Brigade against the Russians during the 1854 Crimean War. Many of the American soldiers fell out with wounds or from exhaustion, but the majority didn't falter as they pushed on in the face of deadly fire.

They were progressing slowly through the shrubbery and stands of small trees when Roosevelt experienced his fourth close encounter. A bullet from the hill clipped his elbow, drawing a copious flow of blood, and a couple of bullets grazed Texas without doing serious damage. Roosevelt patched up his wound with his neckerchief and soldiered on.

The troops climbed slowly, struggling, some dropping to their stomachs to fire a few rounds of their own now and then. Some of the men criticized the Spaniards for hiding behind barricades while the Americans were easy targets, with nowhere to find good cover.

The uphill assault toward Kettle Hill dragged on for twenty more minutes before the Tenth discovered another strand of wire strewn through the brush. This time they could not pull it down quickly enough to help the men behind them, and Texas stumbled right into it, cutting a deep gash across his chest and forelegs, drawing him up short. The horse was badly wounded and could go no farther. Roosevelt dismounted, checked out the injury, and handed the reins to one of his men. From that point on, he had to proceed on foot like the others.

They were now within three hundred yards of the crest and could make out the Spanish flag at the top for the first time. The sight of the ensign seemed to invigorate the troops and propel them upward at a faster pace. To everyone's surprise, they found there was a lower ridge protruding from the hill about one hundred yards below the peak of Kettle Hill, a feature that had previously gone unnoticed. This, according to military strategists, would have been the so-called military crest, the ridgeline that should have been the Spaniards' first line of defense. Compared to the geographical crest, it would have provided them with an even better vantage point over the American attackers and the entire field of combat. General Linares, however, had determined earlier that his heavily outnumbered forces stood little chance of ultimate victory against such overwhelming odds, and, realist that he was, had positioned his troops for retreat. Having expected the main line of assault to be at Santiago, he had ordered his five hundred or so defenders to the top of the hill, to be better prepared for an eventual withdrawal when the Americans finally, inevitably, overran his positions.

Buffalo Soldiers with Sumner's Ninth and Pershing's Tenth rushed ahead first, one of the men in the Tenth carrying his unit's guidon as they ascended to within fifty yards of the peak. They were whooping and yelling, the taste of victory in their mouths as they closed in on the enemy entrenchments. "By God, there go our boys up the hill! Yes, up the hill!" one of the troops yelled out, astonished. A moment earlier, it had appeared that they would all be cut down.

The cries of impending victory grew louder as they charged ahead, with most of Roosevelt's remaining Rough Riders now beside the Buffalo Soldiers. Roosevelt was startled when a disoriented Spanish bugler, attempting to run away, ran into his arms instead and was taken prisoner. The yelling intensified when the first rank of Americans saw the Spaniards leaving their trenches and streaming southwest toward San Juan Hill, some returning fire as they ran, but most intent on avoiding the newly energized American army. The soldiers of the Tenth planted their guidon on the hill as the troops swarmed across the crest, with a clear view of the retreating defenders heading down the back slope in the direction of San Juan Hill. Roosevelt later claimed that the Rough Riders had planted their standard first, but one of his Rough Riders, Nova Johnson from New Mexico, said later, "You should have seen the amazement Colonel Teddy's face took on when he reached the top of that first ridge, only to find that the colored troopers had beat us up there."

"That day we fought pretty hard and my gun became so hot I could hardly hold it," wrote C. D. Kirby with the Ninth in a letter to his mother. "The soldiers were falling all around me and I thought every minute would be my time." Kirby shot and killed two Spanish snipers hidden in their perches on nearby trees.

"We had a hard fight," wrote Sergeant Bivins of the Tenth. "Our loss is very heavy. . . . I got hit myself and was stunned for five minutes. . . . Bravery was displayed by all of the colored regiments. The officers and reporters of other powers said they had heard of the colored man's fighting qualities, but did not think that they could do such work as they had witnessed."

One of the Rough Riders, Frank Knox, who would go on to become secretary of the navy during World War II, wrote afterward, "I joined a troop of the Tenth Cavalry, and for a time fought with them shoulder to shoulder[,] and in justice to the colored race I must say that I never saw braver men anywhere. Some of those who rushed up the hill will live in my memory forever."

A reporter with the *New York Mail and Express* headlined his article ALL HONOR TO THE GALLANT TROOPERS OF THE BLACK TENTH. He reported that they fired "as they marched, their aim was splendid, their coolness was superb, and their courage aroused the admiration of their comrades. Their advance was greeted by wild cheers

The black Ninth Cavalry was particularly effective during the battle for Kettle Hill, earning the accolades of American commanders and war correspondents, who said they had never seen men fight more bravely.

Library of Congress Prints and Photographs Division (LC-DIG-ppmsca-11342)

from the white regiments, and with answering shouts they pressed onward over the trenches they had taken close in pursuit of the retreating enemy. The war has not shown greater heroism."

Another account of the battle, which appeared in the *New York Sun*, bestowed similar accolades on Sumner's Ninth. "The Spaniards, pouring shot into them at a lively rate, could no more stop the advance than they could have stopped an avalanche. . . . The enthusiasm of the Ninth Cavalry was at its highest pitch and so it was with the other troops. Only annihilation could drive them back; the Spaniards could not."

With the Buffalo Soldiers' guidon waving prominently on top of the hill, the Americans paused a moment and looked to the south. They were too exhausted after the arduous climb to pursue the retreating Spaniards, but from their vantage point on the peak, they had a clear view of the action that was still going on in the Heights. As bloody as the battle for Kettle Hill had been, the war was not yet over. Other violent encounters still lay ahead—the campaign to overtake San Juan Hill and, finally, the conquest of the primary Spanish defense around the city of Santiago de Cuba.

25

o the south, Kent led the march on San Juan Hill with three brigades, a little more than five thousand men in all. Three officers marched with Kent, each in command of one of the brigades: General Hamilton Hawkins with roughly two thousand men in the First Brigade; Colonel E. P. Pearson commanding about fifteen hundred troops in the Second Brigade; and Colonel Charles A. Wikoff leading another fifteen hundred in the Third Brigade, including 534 with the black Twenty-Fourth Infantry. The Spanish had strung three lines of barbed wire along the foothills leading up to San Juan, beyond which lay three hundred yards of open meadowland that offered no protection as the men tried to cross it.

A Spanish blockhouse dominated the peak of San Juan, which was the highest hill in the region. Wikoff's Twenty-Fourth moved ahead on the path to the left and took the lead as the Spanish defenders poured a heavy fusillade down along the trails leading to their positions. The Twenty-Fourth pushed slowly through the ranks of the other troops on the trail. The Ninth, the Tenth, and the Rough Riders to the north tried to descend the slope of Kettle Hill and join them, but they found themselves in range of the Spanish guns on

San Juan, which forced them to take cover where they could find it. The Spaniards were far fewer in number, but they still controlled the approaches to their trenches and barricades from the top of San Juan. A battery of two mountain guns, plus troops from the First Provisional Battalion of Puerto Rico, the First Talavera Peninsula Battalion, and a unit of sailors from the harbor, were sent up from Santiago to reinforce their defenses. General Linares also arrived on the scene and joined his men near the blockhouse.

Shells from the mountain guns now began to soar down on the American attackers trying to climb the hill. Linares had also sent up additional ammunition for the riflemen, who kept up a steady rain of fire from the blockhouse, trenches, and rifle pits. Below the crest of San Juan, the barbed wire fences zigzagged across the trails and through the brush on the slope of the hill. The east side of San Juan Hill was particularly steep, presenting more difficult terrain for Kent's men to traverse with their ranks strewn out for a mile or more to the rear. The cries of victory emanating from Kettle Hill suddenly seemed premature to the three brigades struggling in their own theater of the battle.

The three hundred yards of open space beyond the wire fences appeared more and more like an invitation into a slaughterhouse. It was a veritable killing field, with anyone entering it offering himself as an easy target for the Spanish marksmen. The Buffalo Soldiers of the Twenty-Fourth sliced through the barbed wire fences with their bayonets and rushed into the meadow first from the left, with shells and Mauser bullets falling all around them. The number of American casualties grew rapidly, among them Colonel Wikoff, who fell as he led the Twenty-Fourth and the rest of the Third Brigade into the open.

His death was witnessed by First Lieutenant Wendell Simpson, who stood beside him when it happened. "The first line upon reaching a slight ridge in the field, one hundred yards from the creek bank, took position lying down and was rapidly joined by other lines in succession," Simpson reported. "The second battalion pushed promptly forward, prolonging the line to the left. A terrific fire was continually poured from the entire line upon the works on top of the hill in front—Fort San Juan. It was just at this stage of the action that Colonel Wikoff received a bullet wound through the chest from side to side, which caused his death."

The fifty-one-year-old Wikoff was the most senior-ranking American officer to die in action against the Spanish. He lingered about fifteen minutes before succumbing to the wound. Two regimental commanders behind him were also shot dead. Kent sent messengers back to Shafter for detailed instructions on what course of action to take from that point on. Precious minutes passed by with no word from the general's camp.

The commanders in the field decided it was time to take matters into their own hands. Kent met with Sumner and Wood, and together they decided that "the Heights must be taken at all costs." There could be no turning back. They dispatched couriers to the regimental commanders with the message that a full-blown assault on San Juan Hill was the only option left for them—either that or an unthinkable retreat back down the various trails leading to the coast. Onward and upward was the only acceptable decision for them.

At around the same time, the troops in the rear had managed to push the four Gatling guns farther along the trail and maneuvered them to within seven hundred yards of San Juan Hill. As soon as they were in position, the men fired the guns, which boomed like thunder and echoed across the hills. The American troops in the lead were startled at first, believing they had come under a new line

of fire from Spanish artillery behind them. Once they saw the deto-
nations on the peak of San Juan, however, they shouted jubilantly,
"It's the Gatlings, it's the Gatlings!" They rose to their feet to get a
clearer view and could see that the American shells were hitting the
enemy fortifications with great accuracy.

To the north on Kettle Hill, the Ninth, the Tenth, and the
Rough Riders were also thrilled by the turn of events. The American big guns were taking a toll on the blockhouse and gun pits. The
Spaniards lifted their heads above their barricades to get off some
rounds, presenting easier targets for the Buffalo Soldiers and others
on Kettle Hill, who fired at will as the enemy's attack began to sub-
side. The Gatlings fired round after round for almost ten minutes
straight, sweeping the peak of San Juan and the trenches around it
with a ceaseless outpouring of devastating firepower. The Twenty-
Fourth moved forward across the meadow, which gave way to a
sharp incline three hundred yards away, where the base of the hill
rose out of the valley floor. Lieutenant Jules G. Ord with Kent's First
Brigade screamed out, "Come on! We can't stop here! I will not ask
for volunteers, I will not give permission, and I will not refuse it!
God Bless you and good luck!"

As on Kettle Hill, the Spanish had chosen to defend the geographical peak of San Juan instead of the military crest below it.
The strategic miscalculation created for the Americans a protected
zone of sorts beneath the military crest. Once the Americans had
crossed over the meadow, the slope of the hill rose sharply to the
lip of the lower ridge, which offered them cover from the defenders'
line of fire. There was no choice but to get through the killing field
to reach it, but the American guns hammered the Spanish positions more and more effectively, encouraging the troops to step up
their advance. They continued to climb even as the firing from the
Gatlings and the danger from Kettle Hill decreased.

General Linares knew the moment was at hand when he saw his soldiers falling in growing numbers all around him, shot dead or wounded by American gunfire. It was now about 1:30 in the afternoon of July 1, and the sheer force of the invaders' manpower advantage had proved to be overwhelming as they swarmed over the peak and took possession of the blockhouse. The Buffalo Soldiers of the Twenty-Fourth and the other first-line attackers howled as the Spaniards abandoned the blockhouse and their trenches and began the retreat down the far side of the hill toward Santiago. The Americans fired at them as they ran down the hill, and for the moment they ignored the wounded soldiers left behind, who groaned where they lay writhing on the ground. One of the last Americans to be killed in the battle was Lieutenant Ord, who had sparked the American assault when he urged the men to charge. One of the British officers who had earlier been critical of the Americans' performance was moved to cry out, "It's a great day for us Anglo-Saxons!"

Roosevelt and his men were still on the peak of Kettle Hill as the Spanish fled down the far sides of both Kettle and San Juan. At about 1:35, he asked Sumner and Wood for permission to follow the Spaniards as they scrambled over to San Juan and down to the harbor. His objective was to take the northern spur of San Juan Hill with his men. Both officers agreed, and Roosevelt began to descend in their wake. At the same time, the Ninth and Tenth had charged down the back slope of Kettle Hill, screaming as they started to run toward the northern slope of San Juan Hill as fast as the terrain and the condition of their legs allowed. The smell, the very feel and taste of victory spurred them on.

When Roosevelt saw that only five of his Rough Riders were following him—the others claimed to have not heard his command— he returned and berated the rest of the group for not charging with him. The Rough Riders and some other regiments then joined him, about eight hundred in all. But before they took off, a Spanish shell smashed into the sugar-refining kettle, killing two of the men with flying shrapnel and wounding a third. The men moved on and sliced through one of the barbed wire fences protecting the northern slope of San Juan Hill. The remaining troops on top of Kettle Hill fired at the Spaniards in support. The Rough Riders, the Buffalo Soldiers of the Ninth and Tenth, and other troops ran ahead together. They detoured around a small lake that sat in a cradle of land in the Heights. The charge across the narrow, marshy valley straddling the two hills was exhausting, but they rushed on in the face of enemy fire from the northern slope.

They made it to the top a little after 2:00 PM, when Roosevelt (who had again been nicked, this time in his left hand by a spent bullet) was surprised by two Spaniards who leapt out of the trenches and fired at him from ten yards away. Miraculously, their bullets missed the leader of the Rough Riders. Roosevelt fired his own gun twice, missing one of the defenders, who ran off, and killing the other. Rough Rider Cliff Scott witnessed the encounter and reported, "The colonel jerked his gun and made a hip shot that was good." Roosevelt's kill was especially rewarding, since he had made it with a gun that had been removed from the *Maine*, whose sinking triggered the war in the first place. The Rough Riders ran to the peak of San Juan Hill, where they joined the Twenty-Fourth and other regiments that had already taken the blockhouse and overrun the Spanish trenches.

Sumner and Wood rode up on horseback moments later with the rest of their brigades, and Sumner strung them out across the hill in a long defensive perimeter in anticipation of a Spanish counterattack. They were prepared for any surprises the Spanish might have planned for them, as they now commanded the topmost peak between the Heights and Santiago de Cuba, the latter of which they could see from the ridge about three hundred yards west of the blockhouse. But the Spanish had little if anything left and launched no counterattack.

The Americans were half-starved after their momentous victory and were unexpectedly rewarded when they found a huge pot of Castilian stew cooking over a slow fire burning in the officers' mess tent atop the hill. Besides the stew, there was bread, smaller pots of rice and peas, salted fish, and most satisfying of all, bottles of wine and a demijohn of good Cuban rum. The men began to attack the provisions without waiting for an invitation to assuage their hunger and thirst. The Spanish defenders, however, had fewer mouths to feed than the Americans did, so the officers made the men line up in an orderly fashion in an effort to stretch the food as far as it would go.

26

From the western ridge of San Juan Hill, the American troops had a clear view of the harbor and the city, its streets empty except for the commotion of Spanish troops wandering shell-shocked in every direction. A number of Buffalo Soldiers from the Tenth and some white regulars started to run down the hill toward Santiago without authorization, but an officer called them back and told them to remain on the ridge until they received orders to proceed. Stephen Crane had joined them at the overlook and described the men as "dusty" and "disheveled," their shirts glued to their backs with sweat as they gazed down the hill, weary from all the "marches and the fights." And still, they had been ready to continue the battle without anyone ordering them to fight on.

The Spanish, for their part, were not yet ready to concede defeat. They reformed into three lines of defensive positions, forming a triple perimeter to protect the city, and then commenced firing artillery shots up at the hill to keep the Americans from charging down on them. The Americans remained on the peak of San Juan, digging trenches of their own with anything that came to hand— their own shovels and abandoned Spanish equipment, including cooking utensils, dishes, cups, cans, machetes, and the sharp edges of their mess kits. Around 2:30 in the afternoon, the generals sent word down to Shafter that the Heights had been taken. Shafter struggled from his cot, mounted his horse, and attempted to assess the situation from El Pozo. His aides told him that Lawton was apparently still bogged down at El Caney and had yet to march from there to support the troops on Kettle and San Juan Hills. Shafter was concerned that the spread of land between Kettle and El Caney remained unoccupied by American forces.

Shafter's repeated orders to Lawton to abandon El Caney and head southwest to reinforce the troops in the Heights fell on deaf ears throughout the afternoon. The battle had dragged on far longer than anyone had anticipated, but Lawton considered El Caney to be strategically important and was determined to take it before moving on. In Lawton's report after the siege on El Caney ended, Lawton didn't acknowledge receiving any orders from Shafter. Lawton would not make it over to San Juan until the following day, July 2, after he rested his battered brigades overnight. The troops on top of San Juan exchanged fire with the Spaniards throughout most of the afternoon, and it wasn't until around 4:00 PM that the Spanish attempted their first offensive operation in the campaign. Linares sent a contingent of four hundred men up the Heights in an effort to encircle the Americans from their right flank. The effort failed, however, when the Gatlings opened up on them, sending them retreating back over the ridge toward Santiago.

There was little left to do now but hold the positions on the Heights and wait for further orders. The officers took stock of the situation and used the opportunity to count their losses. They knew their casualties were heavy, but the final toll of those killed or seriously wounded in the brutal conflict would not be known for a while to come. Adding up the final numbers after any war has

always been a dicey business, complicated both by imprecise report-
age in the field and by the information's potential use as political
propaganda. But there was little doubt that both sides had suffered
badly. Lawton's cost in dead and wounded at El Caney numbered
450 men—7 percent of his forces. The outnumbered Spanish suffered 300 casualties, almost 60 percent of the defenders in the village. Lawton's men took 127 Spanish soldiers prisoner, and another
100 escaped down the trail to Santiago.

Over on San Juan Hill, the American dead and seriously injured
came to more than 10 percent of the troops engaged there, a total of
almost 1,500 men when added to the losses at El Caney. About 200
Spaniards were mortally wounded and another 300 were captured.
Linares himself was wounded as he stood near the blockhouse, but
he lived on to return to Spain, where he died sixteen years after
the war at age sixty-six. Among the Rough Riders, about half of the
500 Roosevelt started with were rendered unfit for duty because
of illness suffered during the various campaigns, 86 were killed
or wounded, and others went missing. Fifty of his men were with
him as they dug into their positions on San Juan Hill. The Buffalo
Soldiers suffered the heaviest losses in percentage terms: about 17
percent of the 1,685 that they started with.

The commanding generals on both sides, Shafter and Linares, were
heavily criticized for their strategic decisions during the campaign.
"Shafter's conduct of the campaign was incompetent and culpable,"
read a report disseminated by British military strategists, "and his
ultimate success was undeserved good fortune. No precautions
were taken against reverses. The daring of American troops was
exceeded only by their extreme rashness." The Brits called Roosevelt
and the Rough Riders examples of audacity laced with imprudence.

Linares was excoriated for holding back ten thousand of his men in Santiago and sending so few to defend the Heights and El Caney. The Spanish general, however, shifted the blame to Cuban rebels, whom he claimed diverted his forces, and to the "inappropriate" and "unorthodox" fighting style of the American invaders.

The American forces remained vigilant in their positions on San Juan Hill through the long night of July 1 and the early hours of the next day. They were determined to not give up any ground, but they were aware of the number of Spanish troops guarding the city and the harbor in Santiago. They expected a counterattack at any time in a last-ditch effort by the Spanish to reverse the fortunes of the war.

But it never came. The small hours of the morning of July 2 remained still and silent. When Lawton arrived later in the morning with his own forces, which he had rested overnight at El Pozo, the men on the hill knew that the battle for San Juan Hill was truly over. Lawton brought up his big guns, which opened a constant bombardment on the troops forming the perimeter around the city. The Spanish squadron guarding the harbor was also in range of the American artillery. American ships now began to move in toward Santiago from the open water, closing in on the Spanish flotilla. The Spaniards felt the noose tightening. Their options were limited. Should they attempt to withdraw the Spanish fleet from the harbor or risk being ensnared by an American blockade—or worse, watch their ships being sunk by the advancing American armada?

The Spanish naval defenses fell under the command of Admiral Pascual Cervera, whose fleet consisted of several cruisers and destroyers, none of which were in particularly good condition. The cruiser *Cristóbal Colón* lacked much of its armature, and another, the *Vizcaya*, was hampered by a porous bottom. Also at Cervera's disposal were his flagship, the *Infanta Maria Teresa*, the cruiser *Oquendo*, and the destroyers *Pluton* and *Furor*. An attempt to run the American blockade with its superior ships and firepower would be tantamount to suicide. Cervera's best hope, short of surrender, was to try to ram the fastest American cruiser, the USS *Brooklyn*, with the *Infanta Maria Teresa*.

On land, Shafter tried to assume command of his operation on July 2 and the morning of July 3, moving his troops down the slope of San Juan Hill, closer to the eastern side of Santiago, already under cover of his heavy guns. He positioned the men in a semicircle about a mile east of the city, where they faced the triple perimeter of the Spanish land defenses, who met the Americans' advance with artillery of their own. Faced with the prospect of suffering even more casualties than he had taken already, Shafter cabled Secretary of War Russell Alger—a distant relative of rags-to-riches storyteller Horatio Alger—with a request to withdraw his men to a point at which they would be out of range of the Spanish guns. Alger had already been attacked for appointing Shafter to head the Cuban expedition in the first place, and for inadequately preparing the army for the war. Alger's response to Shafter was immediate and emphatic: *Hold your ground!* The press was at that moment trumpeting the news of the great American victory in Cuba, under Alger's watch, and there was no way he wanted Shafter to let the victory be clouded by even the appearance of defeat.

Alger also cabled Admiral Sampson to close in on the harbor as quickly as possible, to relieve Shafter's troops who were still facing strong enemy resistance. Sampson turned his command over to Commodore Winfield S. Schley and boarded his cruiser *New York* with orders to sail to Siboney to confer with Shafter, whom Alger ordered to meet there with Sampson. At dawn on the morning of July 3, the Spanish held a mass to pray for victory, and at 8:00 AM they weighed anchor. Fifteen minutes later, Cervera flashed the signals to his naval commanders. "Sortie in the prescribed order! ¡Viva España!" An aide to Cervera was moved to remark, *"Pobre España"*— poor Spain—as the Spanish ships pushed away from their moorings into the face of almost certain suicide. Schley had anchored the American fleet four miles offshore to avoid the heavily mined harbor. At 9:30 he was stunned to see the first of the Spanish ships moving slowly away from land, in his direction. He knew he had them outgunned with his seven-ship fleet, the well-conditioned battleships *Iowa, Indiana, Oregon,* and *Texas,* and his cruisers and armed yachts *Brooklyn, Gloucester,* and *Vixen.*

Schley kept his spyglass trained on the Spanish fleet as it sailed slowly toward the mouth of the harbor. Cervera's ships started to head west along the coast in an attempt to outrun the Americans and escape toward Cienfuegos. The *Infanta Maria Teresa* was in the lead, followed at six- to ten-minute intervals by the other cruisers and destroyers. Sampson had sunk an American collier in the harbor channel earlier to block a Spanish escape, and the enemy ships had to move gingerly around it. Once past it, they would no doubt build up a head of steam as they sailed into open water. Schley gave the order to close in and cut them off. "Go right for them!" he sounded the alarms. The *Iowa* opened fire first, ripping shells into the *Infanta Maria Teresa* with devastating firepower. The American sailors could see the dead and wounded enemy crewmen flying in all directions across the deck. Cervera seized upon his only opportunity for victory. He directed his flagship directly at the *Brooklyn.* If he could ram it and knock it out of action, he might have a chance to punch through the blockade and make it to Cienfuegos.

Cervera's desperate plan failed as quickly as it was hatched. Every ship in the American flotilla turned toward the Spanish flagship and pounded it to pieces, silencing most of its guns. Explosions rocked the ship, and flames broke out from stem to stern. By 10:15, the Spanish flagship ran for the beach and its commander hauled down its colors. Schley turned the American guns next on the *Oquendo* with similar results, and the ship ran aground and raised a white flag. But Cervera was not yet defeated. With Sampson reversing course and sailing back on the *New York* to join the engagement, the *Cristóbal Colón* fired on the *Iowa*, hitting her twice and forcing the American vessel to reduce speed. Both sides set off their guns from a distance of twenty-five hundred yards. The *Furor* and *Pluton* were struck next, with the first hit by the *Gloucester* and running aground in a fiery explosion, and the second sinking shortly after 11:00 AM, when it was pounded nearly in half by shells from the *Iowa*.

The fastest of the Spanish fleet, the *Cristóbal Colón*, escaped the blockade and dashed westerly along the coast. The *Brooklyn*, *Texas*, and *Oregon* chased after the fleeing vessel for the next two hours. The Spanish cruiser raced through open water five miles ahead of the pursuing Americans, until the *Oregon* opened up on it with its biggest guns, thirteen-inch behemoths that fired shells weighing eleven hundred pounds each. The first five missed their target, but the sixth flew through the distance and landed just in front of the prow of the *Cristóbal Colón*, sending a powerful cascade across its deck. At that moment, the ship's commander realized the American guns had his range; the next shells would be lethal. He raised his white flag and headed for land.

At 1:00 PM, the naval battle for Santiago was over. When the American sailors on the *Texas* filled the air with cheers, the captain said, "Don't cheer, boys! Those poor devils are dying."

The Spanish sailors under Cervera had fought bravely, giving back as much as they could with their inferior ships and firepower. The crew of the *Iowa* rescued the Spanish admiral and gave him a standing ovation when they took him on board. Of the 2,200 men in the Spanish fleet, 328 had been killed and 151 were wounded. The rest were rescued that afternoon by American sailors who pulled them out of the water, away from the sharks and the Cuban rebels, who surely would have treated them cruelly had they captured them on land. Indeed, the rebels had already shot several of them as they tried to swim ashore. Unlike the land battles for the hills north of Santiago, the American casualties in the naval engagement were minimal: one man dead, and one badly wounded.

As was the case after many hard-fought encounters, the Spanish and American sailors recognized the humanity in their enemy combatants and began to fraternize when all the fighting at sea was over, the Spaniards trading swords, wine, cigarettes, and jewelry for American hardtack and bacon. The men (and now women) who fight in wars often find common ground in the same manner that two street fighters will shake hands and drink together after they've battered each other without mercy.

Although the naval situation had been settled, Shafter was still not finished with his battle to occupy the city of Santiago de Cuba. Linares having been relieved of command after he was wounded in battle, his replacement, General José Toral, had agreed to an exchange of prisoners with Shafter but not to a surrender of the strategically located city. Toral was stubborn, even in the face of logistical problems arising from the vast number of men under his command. He still had 10,000 troops in the area, another 20,000 scattered around the province, and a total of 140,000 Spanish soldiers remaining in the numerous encampments located throughout the island—all of them with mouths to feed. The Americans had cut off his water supply, and his positions were being pummeled by ongoing attacks from American naval guns now in control of the harbor even as the sailors broke bread with one another. His soldiers were suffering, but he was under orders from his government not to capitulate as long as it was possible to resist. Shafter, on his part, was impatient to negotiate a peace agreement immediately. His own men were exhausted, and more and more of them were coming down with malaria, yellow fever, and other tropical ailments. And he had never stopped worrying about a counterattack on his rear by Spanish reinforcements.

The matter remained at a stalemate for the next few days, until Toral proposed Shafter a deal on July 8, offering to abandon Santiago if the American general allowed his men to march off unharmed to a different location. Shafter was tempted to accept, but Alger and others in Washington were adamant that he refuse any peace offers by the Spanish until he received further instructions. The American ships continued to bombard the city from the harbor, the troops east of Santiago rained shells down from the hills, and a few days later General Nelson Miles arrived in Cuba with three thousand more soldiers to bolster the American offense. With Miles now on the scene in virtual command, he ordered Shafter to make a peace proposal of his own on July 11. The United States would agree to ship the Spanish defenders back to Spain if they laid down their arms and ceased hostilities.

Toral needed to confer with his government before making a decision. He advised his country about the hopelessness of the Spanish situation in Santiago and, indeed, throughout the entire Cuban countryside. Morale was low, ammunition was running out, and yellow fever was taking a toll on his men. On July 13, the generals of both armies met under a large tree equidistant from their opposing lines and worked out a settlement that was acceptable to each warring party.

The precise language of the agreement was paramount. The Spanish insisted on avoiding the word *surrender* to save face. The war in Cuba was unpopular at home, and the appearance of leaving the island in disgrace could stir a civil uprising, and possibly a revolution against the government. Instead, the Spanish agreed to *capitulate* to the reality of their plight and head for home. A flurry of cables flew back and forth across the Atlantic for the next few days, and finally the United States and Spain forged a ten-point agreement that amounted to surrender without actually using the offending word.

The two countries signed the document on July 16. At 9:00 the next morning, Shafter and Toral met in a field just outside Santiago with their chief advisers and units of cavalry officers. Included on Shafter's team was General "Fighting Joe" Wheeler, who reported afterward that "the Spanish troops presented arms, and the Spanish flag which for 382 years had floated over the city was pulled down and furled forever." Later that day, July 17, the entire contingent of Spanish troops in Santiago de Cuba marched unarmed out of the city they had fought so diligently to defend. They stepped into captivity aboard American ships that would guarantee their safe passage home—to a country riven by unending strife that would lead to a brutal civil war less than forty years later.

Many of the American troops would also be leaving the island of Cuba, but not necessarily sailing back to their homeland. There were other Spanish territories remaining to be conquered, several more battles on the horizon to topple what was left of the crumbling Spanish empire. And not all of the American troops who had fought in Cuba left after the battle was concluded. Some were ordered to stay behind to occupy and secure the city, and to stand guard over the prisoners until they were shipped home later.

Most of the American fighting men who remained to garrison Santiago and keep it safe from any further hostilities were Buffalo Soldiers—the all-black units that were deemed more suitable for war in tropical climates because their government considered them to be less susceptible to malaria and yellow fever than white soldiers were.

PART THREE

The Collapse

27

The colored troops did as well as any soldiers could possibly do," Roosevelt said when the battle was over. "I wish no better men beside me in battle than these colored troops showed themselves to be." The black soldiers are "an excellent breed of Yankees," he added. Later, he softened his praise, saying, "Between these two cavalry regiments and ours" there was a tie, "which we hope will never be broken." Still later, Roosevelt claimed that the Buffalo Soldiers performed their duties well, but only because they were "peculiarly dependent on their white officers." His assessment soured further when he said he had to pull his gun to restrain some leaderless black troops who were trying to retreat in the face of enemy fire. "Negro troops were shirkers in their duties and would only go so far as they were led by white officers," he wrote.

Black and white soldiers alike attacked Roosevelt's shifting views on the performance of the black troops in Cuba. Presley Holliday, a member of the Tenth, explained that Roosevelt was well aware that a few black troops had headed to the rear only to replenish their ammunition. "Everyone who saw the incident knew the Colonel was mistaken about our men trying to shirk their duty," he wrote in a letter to the *New York Age*. As far as white leadership was concerned, Holliday said that many black noncommissioned officers filled in for the whites when they were killed or wounded in combat. Roosevelt's statement was "uncalled for and uncharitable," Holliday wrote. "Considering the moral and physical effect the advance of the Tenth Cavalry had in weakening the forces opposed to the Colonel's regiment, both at Las Guasimas and San Juan Hill," Roosevelt's assessment did the black troops a great deal of harm, according to Holliday. He also added that not all the black troops who charged the hills were urged on by white officers.

Pershing thought the Buffalo Soldiers were the finest troops he had ever fought with. "We officers of the Tenth Cavalry could have taken our black heroes in our arms," he wrote. A white journalist with the *Baltimore Morning Herald* reported that "the colored citizen makes an admirable soldier in many respects," and *Leslie's Weekly*, a national magazine, stated that black soldiers were "heroes, as good as any in the land." George Kennan, another correspondent, wrote that "they fought with the utmost courage, coolness, and determination." The *Republican* of Springfield, Illinois, carried an article stating that "at San Juan Hill three companies of the Twenty-Fourth Infantry (colored) lost every one of their officers before the fighting was over. . . . It is said that the Twenty-Fourth bore the brunt of the battles around Santiago, the Spaniards directing their main attack upon the theory that the Negroes would not stand the punishment. Yet whole companies remained steady without a single officer."

Many communities throughout the North and South honored the Buffalo Soldiers with parades, receptions, luncheons, gifts, and other accolades when they returned to American soil. Philadelphia invited all the black units that had fought in Cuba to a "Peace Jubilee," during which the city showered them with cheers that were "almost deafening, and lasted until the last of the soldiers disappeared," according to the *Army and Navy Journal*. New York City's black West Fifties neighborhood, then called the "Tenderloin" district, was renamed San Juan Hill in their honor. Compliments about the performance of the black troops in combat even came in from the enemy camp. "If you will be as brave in the future to your country as you have proven yourselves today," said General Toral when he addressed them after the battle, "it will not be very long before you will have generals in the army of the United States."

The real reason for Roosevelt's betrayal of the Buffalo Soldiers in his evolving public comments appeared to have been the competition they presented to the Rough Riders as the true heroes of the war in Cuba. In the immediate wake of combat, Richard Harding Davis and many of the other correspondents reported on Roosevelt's exploits in hagiographic language, creating the myth that he had charged at the head of his men up San Juan Hill and taken it by storm, almost singlehandedly. The lopsided coverage created a rift between the volunteers, especially the Rough Riders, and the regular army troops who did much of the fighting. Some of the regulars retaliated by saying that they had never actually seen Roosevelt on top of San Juan.

General of the army Nelson A. Miles said during a speech he gave in Washington that Roosevelt "was not at San Juan Hill at all," based on reports he received from officers in the field. Captain John Bigelow, a white officer with the Tenth, maintained that he never saw Roosevelt on San Juan, although he fought with him on Kettle Hill. Roosevelt almost certainly did make it up to San Juan Hill after the main battle was over, but comments to the contrary probably were made to restore some balance to the publicity bestowed on the Rough Riders. Regarding the Buffalo Soldiers, Bigelow wrote, "Their conduct made me prouder than ever of being an officer in the American Army, and of wearing the insignia of the Tenth United States Cavalry." Wheeler remarked sarcastically in a letter to the *New York Herald*, "It is touching to see the regulars get American newspapers, read how redoubt after redoubt was taken by the volunteers, with scarcely any mention of the regular army. How disappointed and disgusted they are!"

One black private speculated in a letter, "I thought we would be the whole thing on account of having taken the hill[,] but the adjutant says the Rough Riders will get all the credit because they have their press agents along. And what do you think, they were not even in the fight. They say our charge will make Roosevelt President someday. Well, I suppose I shouldn't kick, as I am looking for a laurel wreath myself." Another wrote that he knew from the beginning that the Rough Riders would "steal their thunder."

The war to kick the Spanish out of Cuba had ended, but the public-relations war would continue for another fifteen years and longer. In a sense, Roosevelt got in the last word when his own book on the war, published the next year, outsold and outlasted all others on the subject. His bully pulpit as president also enabled him to drown out the other voices. Years later, he finally grew tired of all the carping after someone claimed that "his one military deed was firing his pistol at some poor devil who was running away." He retaliated by replying, "He wasn't shot in the back, but in the left breast as he turned."

Yellow fever, dysentery, and typhoid fever struck with a vengeance in the days after the warring parties signed their peace agreement. "The starving time was nothing to the fever time, where scores died per day," wrote a black trooper in a letter to Chaplain Theophilus Steward of the Twenty-Fifth. "We were not permitted to starve; but had fever, and had it bad; semi-decayed beef, both from refrigerators and from cans. We had plenty of fever, but no clothing until very late; no medicine save a little quinine which was forced into you all the time, intermittent only with bad meat."

The ailments had already stricken many men in the days leading up to the battle at San Juan Hill, but by mid-July the American army officially announced that they had become epidemic. Doctors ordered the men to boil the water before drinking it, but in the intense heat their thirst was unquenchable, and many of the soldiers drank water wherever and whenever they could find it. Sergeant Horace Bivins, who had been in charge of the Hotchkiss guns with the Tenth, found fresh, uncontaminated water flowing from two springs near a mango grove. He placed a detachment of troops there to guard it, while hundreds of men lined up to take their turns filling their canteens. Bivins succumbed to illness himself on July 26, and he was carried back on a stretcher to the camp hospital in Siboney, where he lay for twelve days "at the point of death."

The Buffalo Soldiers were assigned to an all-black hospital. It was no more than an open tent in which they had to lie on the ground, getting soaked by torrential downpours that blew in on them from both ends with the shifting winds. Major A. C. Markley of the black Twenty-Fourth referred to it as "a charnel house of the wrecked army." Men were dying every hour, and even the doctors, nurses, and medics were laid low by the diseases. The chaplain of the Tenth, William T. Anderson, had a degree in medicine as well as divinity, and he complained in no uncertain terms about the conditions the black troops were forced to endure, until they were finally moved to an enclosed tent near Wheeler's headquarters. There they could rest in bunks while they waited to receive better medical attention. "It seems he was just in time to save us," Bivins wrote.

The call went out for soldiers to volunteer as nurses when the medical professionals became ill, and the entire Twenty-Fourth stepped forward after most of the whites refused. Sixty of them were initially selected, and within days forty-two of the men had contracted fevers. Again, the need for more help arose, and the rest of the unit volunteered to the last man. They pitched in where necessary, unloading supplies, putting up and striking tents, carrying the sick from place to place, digging graves, and mopping up the mess resulting from widespread dysentery. They kept at it until all the "deaths warned us to stop," wrote Markley. Out of a total of 456 members of the Twenty-Fourth, 432 lost their lives to the rampaging disease.

By August, conditions in Cuba had become intolerable, and the troops left behind in Cuba were ordered home to convalesce in Camp Wikoff, named in honor of the colonel killed in Cuba who had headed the Twenty-Fourth. The government chose the camp—in Montauk, New York, near the tip of the South Fork of Long Island and east of the Hamptons—since the remote site had a deep-water port where the big ships could dock, and it also provided a quarantine zone of sorts a safe distance from heavily populated areas. In Cuba, bands played and ships flew the colors as the Twenty-Fourth marched to the vessel that would take them back to America. But only 198 men and 9 officers could make it aboard under their own power; the rest of the Twenty-Fourth were carried onto the ship on stretchers. Another thirty of them died from tropical illness after their arrival at Montauk. The official report stated that the transport ship entered the waters of Montauk on September 2 with 385 troops on board, many of them sick, but there were no deaths during the voyage.

Other troops, including the Rough Riders, had already departed on different vessels to make the journey from Cuba to Fort Pond Bay in Montauk. Once back on US soil, they were directed to find accommodations among ten thousand tents stretched in rows across the rolling hills. Most of the men were emaciated and incapacitated. More than thirty-two hundred men were so ill they had to be carried down the gangway on stretchers. Eighty-seven died during the voyage. Wheeler admitted in his report on the campaign that "the great bulk of the troops that were at Santiago were by no means well." Compared with the men of the Twenty-Fourth, those of the Ninth, Tenth, and Twenty-Fifth fared reasonably well and recuperated rapidly.

One of the healthiest men to land at Montauk was the hometown favorite from Long Island, the leader of the Rough Riders. As his ship the *Miami* pulled into port in mid-August, Roosevelt waved from the railing at the crowd assembled on the dock to greet him. He was distinctive in his Rough Riders hat, bushy mustache, and thick spectacles. "I'm in a disgracefully healthy condition!" he

Roosevelt returned to a hero's welcome after the war in Cuba. Always a favorite with the press, he received most of the credit for the victory on San Juan Hill, which he was happy to accept.

Library of Congress Prints and Photographs Division (LC-DIG-stereo-1s01903)

shouted. "I've had a bully time and a bully fight! I feel as strong as a bull moose!"

Most of the others were not as fortunate. Chaplain Steward thought a radical improvement in the men's diet would be the best medicine they could get, and he sent a note to the *Daily Evening News* in southern New Jersey asking local farmers to ship fresh fruit and vegetables to Montauk to help the returning veterans—whites as well as blacks—if they were so inclined. The community complied, and when word of its generosity made the rounds, new shipments of melons, peaches, homemade pies, and vegetables started to pour in from the locals of Long Island, Brooklyn, Philadelphia, and other areas. The fresh food produced the desired effect; the men responded almost immediately, and their health was slowly restored.

The logistics of caring for ten thousand sick men in a remote camp hours removed from a major city were almost insurmountable, but more help began to come in from diverse locations throughout the country. The Merchants' Relief Association sent supplies worth thousands of dollars, then distributed them equitably among the recuperating troops. Other charitable organizations followed suit. The Women's Patriotic Relief, the Women's War Relief, the International Brotherhood League, and the Red Cross shipped food, medical supplies, and other goods to Montauk to assuage the suffering. The *Brooklyn Daily Eagle* set up a tent to organize the relief effort and provide a refuge for wounded warriors unable to return home. For a while, the racial barriers evaporated as blacks, whites, and some American Indians fraternized with one another, joined by necessity in their common plight. For the moment, it was comforting to believe that racial antagonism was now a plague of the past.

"This short war has done so much for America at home and abroad," wrote Reverend Sylvester Malone in a letter he sent to Camp Wikoff, "that we must take every soldier to our warmest affection and send him back to peaceful pursuits. . . . This past war must kindle in our souls a love of all the brethren, black as well as white, Catholic as well as Protestant, having but one language, one nationality, and it is to be hoped, yet one religion."

The healing time continued over the next few weeks. By the time President McKinley arrived in a flag-bedecked train on September 1, the camp community had already grown to a sprawling

President William McKinley traveled to Montauk at the eastern tip of Long Island to bask in the afterglow of the victory in Cuba and to welcome back returning heroes of the campaign, including Theodore Roosevelt and the Rough Riders.

Library of Congress Prints and Photographs Division (LC-DIG-ds-04492)

complex of tents, wooden buildings, two hastily built hospitals, and a power plant that stretched from an eighteenth-century building on the western edge to another old structure on the eastern rim, which was torn down and replaced by Montauk County Park. He shook hands with his leading officers, including Roosevelt, gave a speech, and checked out camp conditions. Roosevelt departed with the Rough Riders to great fanfare and cheers from the throngs gathered to see them off on September 13. But the sickest among the troops, including most of the men of the Twenty-Fourth, had to remain for another month before they fully recuperated.

When they left, however, they would not be going off to "peaceful pursuits," as Reverend Malone had envisioned. The campaign in Cuba was over, but the war against Spain still raged on in other remote regions of the globe. The service of the Buffalo Soldiers was required to finish off what remained of the crumbling Spanish empire.

28

The war guns boomed, beckoning the Buffalo Soldiers to battle once again. Five men of the Tenth were awarded Medals of Honor, and twenty-five other black troops received Certificate of Merit Medals for their actions in Cuba. Now it was time to prove that they were patriotic and fit enough for duty on different islands to complete the final collapse of the Spanish empire. Puerto Rico was next, but it was only a warm-up exercise for the vigorous fights they would face in more far-flung battlefields, including the Philippines. The battle for Spain's stronghold in Puerto Rico had actually begun in May 1898, around the time the American troops were gathering in Tampa to await orders to sail for Cuba.

It started with a naval engagement on May 12, as American gunboats pounded the island's capital city of San Juan and established a blockade around the harbor. The Spaniards tried to break it without success during three separate battles, during which the US Navy inflicted considerable damage on the Spanish fleet defending the city. The naval war continued through much of the summer, until Secretary of War Alger ordered a land offensive in July that would include some of the Buffalo Soldiers who were able to leave

Montauk earlier than their brothers. He ordered General Nelson A. Miles to land his men on the northeast section of the island, where a lighthouse lit the waters off the coast with sweeping beams of light. The town that Miles's military strategists selected was Fajardo, about five miles inland from the coast and, under normal conditions, an easy thirty-mile march from the strategically located capital of San Juan. But conditions were anything but normal, as the Spanish had troops stationed in the area, and their resistance might mean a potentially long and costly engagement with no guarantee of victory. When Miles reappraised the situation, he revised his plan of attack.

Instead of striking at the northeastern quadrant of Puerto Rico, the American troops would land at a place the Spaniards least expected them to attack, in a dismal little barrio named Guánica, situated on a bay along the southern coastline. Guánica had less than one thousand inhabitants scattered among sixty houses and a variety of shacks, but its bay was one of the best on the island, with a solid wharf and steep banks on the eastern side. A sole, poorly manned blockhouse on the hill overlooking the harbor was its primary fortification. The Spanish defenses there consisted of a handful of soldiers belonging to a Puerto Rican militia unit, commanded by Lieutenant Enrique Méndez López. Miles arrived on July 25 at 5:45 AM with a convoy of transport ships carrying 3,314 troops, escorted by a small battleship, the USS *Massachusetts*. As the American fleet approached from the south, lighthouse keeper Robustiano Rivera was shocked to spot the flotilla out at sea and sounded the alarms. As it turned out, most Puerto Ricans were as eager as the Cubans to be free of Spanish domination, and they ran off rather than engage in combat against men they regarded as liberators.

In addition to the *Massachusetts*, the American armada consisted of the *Gloucester*, the *Yale*, the *Windom*, the *Columbia*, the *Dixie*, the *Wasp*, the *Lampasas*, the *Unionist*, the *Stillwater*, and the *Specialist*, plus two captured Spanish ships, the *Rita* and the *Nueces*. The black troops who were healthy enough to make the journey to Puerto Rico had been reorganized as Company L and incorporated into the Sixth Massachusetts Regimental National Guard. Miles sailed aboard the *Yale*. The *Gloucester*, a former yacht named the *Corsair* that had belonged to J. P. Morgan and was donated to the government, was the fastest in the fleet and the first to establish a beachhead. Twenty-eight sailors and marines lowered rafts into the water at 8:45 AM, set up a machine-gun nest when they hit the sand, and surrounded it with a ring of barbed wire.

López and his remaining militia opened fire on the machine-gun nest from three hundred yards away. The Americans responded in kind, supported by heavy shells directed at the blockhouse by the *Gloucester*. The land battle for Puerto Rico had now begun. One by one, the rest of the US fleet anchored in the harbor and began to lower rafts into the water for the troops to ride to the beach. The Sixth Massachusetts with its unit of Buffalo Soldiers hit the shore right behind the first wave of sailors and marines. The landing of troops onto the beach was concluded by 11:00 AM, and the initial skirmish was brief and conclusive. Six Spaniards lay dead with gunshot wounds, and López and three others suffered serious injuries. The rest of the militia, including lighthouse keeper Rivera, ran toward Yauco, a town located six miles to the north where a larger defense force was entrenched.

Yauco's main industry was coffee, although tobacco, sugarcane, and fruit also grew throughout the area. The town, home to about twenty-two thousand inhabitants, was situated in a coastal plain, but the slopes of Puerto Rico's central mountain range and a heavily forested region bordered it on the north. At the time of the invasion, 11 masonry houses, 166 wooden houses, 77 huts, a church, and the municipal building fleshed out the main part of the town. On the outskirts were several manufacturing plants producing furniture, crackers, pasta, chocolate, and other goods. The villagers had rebelled against the Spanish several times, most recently on March 24, 1897, when sixty armed insurrectionists commanded by Fidel Velez tried to topple the colonial regime. Most of the men who survived were taken prisoner.

In Guánica, the American troops lowered the Spanish flag, raised their own, and proceeded to build a landing dock to complete their debarkation. Seven companies of the Sixth Massachusetts, including the Buffalo Soldiers in Company L, and one from the Sixth Illinois left shortly after midnight in pursuit of the fleeing defenders. There were no American casualties during the brief encounter.

Alger was enraged when he first learned about the American landing at Guánica in an Associated Press report the next day. Miles had disobeyed his order to attack the area around San Juan, and had changed his battle plan without consulting with Alger beforehand. It was only when Miles cabled Alger three days later, after Miles was able to set up a telegraph connection to Washington, DC, that Alger realized the operation had gone smoothly. At that point, he decided to let the issue rest. "Spanish troops are retreating from southern part of Puerto Rico," Miles reported. "The army will soon be in mountain region. Weather delightful; troops in best of health and spirit. Anticipate no insurmountable obstacles in future results. Results thus far have been accomplished without loss of a single life." Had Miles botched the skirmish, there is little question that Alger would have slammed Miles with disciplinary action.

Walter J. Stevens, a corporal with Company L who claimed kinship with Crispus Attucks, the first man killed in the Boston Massacre in 1770, wrote later that while the American invasion force suffered no casualties at Guánica, the battle took its toll in other ways. Puerto Rico was teeming with typhoid, malaria, and yellow fever at the time. "Our boys also endured many other diseases and one of the things they suffered a great deal was diarrhea. Some died of this dreadful ailment and many of the men, including myself, contracted it and were eventually brought home to good old Boston on the hospital ship." Of the battle itself, Stevens attributed the quick American victory to poor enemy marksmanship. They shot "haphazardly from the hip," and most of their bullets flew over the heads of Company L as it lay in a wheat field.

Rivera and the retreating militia informed the authorities in Yauco that the Americans had landed and taken control of the harbor in Guánica. Captain Salvador Meca ordered the Third Company of his Twenty-Fifth Patria Battalion to march south and intercept the Americans before they could reach his garrison in Yauco. Meanwhile, along their way north, the pursuing Americans ran into some Puerto Rican units that jumped out of their hiding places with their hands raised and pledged their loyalty to the invaders. The Americans welcomed the locals and asked them to join forces against the Spaniards.

But not all of the islanders were hostile toward their Spanish overlords; many were loyalists who hated the Americans more than they did the Spaniards, with whom they at least shared a common language. This contingent of volunteers was known as the Puerto Rican Civil Guards, mounted guerrillas from Yauco and nearby villages. About three miles south of Yauco, Meca's men were also reinforced by two companies of the Cazador Patria Battalion, commanded by Lieutenant Colonel Francisco Puig. And so the stage was set for a clash not only between Spaniards and Americans but also between Puerto Rican collaborators and Puerto Rican rebels.

The Americans' main objective was to capture the terminus of the rail line that ran between Yauco and Ponce, the largest city on the south side of the island, in an effort to cut off supplies and lines of communication. The main track, which extended across the island, cut east about six miles from Yauco to Ponce, which boasted a deeper harbor than the one at Guánica. If Miles could shut down that city, the conquest of the southern part of Puerto Rico would be all but assured. The combined forces of the Spanish and Puerto Rican defenses under Puig's command positioned themselves on both sides of the main road leading from Guánica to Yauco, around a coffee plantation known as the Hacienda Desideria. The Puerto Ricans who had hooked up with the Americans knew precisely where the main lines of defense would be and warned the invaders beforehand, as they approached the area around 2:00 AM under the cover of night.

General George A. Garretson, who commanded the troops heading north, ordered three companies, including the Buffalo Soldiers of Company L, to branch off to the right and occupy the Seboruco Hills overlooking the hacienda. The sky was clear and glinting with stars, and despite the late hour, there was enough light to illuminate the movement of the oncoming Americans and alert the defenders. The Spaniards fired first, pouring in a fusillade of bullets from their smokeless repeating Mausers. Most of the shots missed their marks, and the Americans responded with a deadlier stream of firepower from their smoky Springfield rifles.

Garretson decided to seize the moment as soon as the first rays of sun painted a pink glow across the eastern horizon. Dawn had revealed the first enemy position on a slope just south of the hacienda, and he gave the order to charge. The companies of the Sixth Massachusetts sprang forward, spearheaded by Company L, and ran toward the gun emplacements in front of the building. The Spaniards fell back almost immediately, seeking cover behind the walls of the hacienda. Some of Puig's men had deserted their positions during the night, and the remaining men began to panic when the reinforcements they expected from Yauco didn't materialize. Rather than retreat in the face of the enemy attack, Puig tried a flanking movement around the charging Massachusetts and Illinois companies, temporarily taking the Americans by surprise. The Buffalo Soldiers and their white compatriots held their ground, however, and pressed forward, forcing the defenders to pull back farther along the road leading to Yauco.

By the time dawn had fully blossomed on the horizon, Meca's and Puig's soldiers were in full retreat. Sixteen had been killed or wounded, while the Americans suffered no deaths and only four minor injuries. All were racing north toward Yauco, with Puig accepting most of the blame for his failed defense, since his men had been the first to face the enemy and the first to give up critical ground. In their panic, the Spaniards continued to retreat through Yauco, with Garretson's troops closing in from behind.

Puig realized that his predicament had become hopeless; the Americans were rapidly narrowing the distance between them, leaving him with little or no opportunity to blow up the all-important rail line linking the village to the city of Ponce. In doing so he would have been fulfilling the Americans' goal to do just that, but with the invaders poised to occupy both cities, Puig would be denying them the link that previously had benefited the Spanish. Company L and the other troops entered Yauco, surprised to hear the cheers from some locals who welcomed the American forces on their land. Garretson ordered the Buffalo Soldiers to secure and garrison the town. The Spaniards' only option was to continue toward the next barrios up the line—Maricao, Lares, Adjuntas—abandoning their artillery and heavy equipment along the way.

The race continued through the afternoon and evening of July 26, throughout the night, and into the morning of the next day, with little time for sleep or rest. With Company L policing Yauco, the rest of Garretson's troops pursued the Spaniards across the thirty-five-mile breadth of the island for the next two days until the remaining defenders—those who had not dropped out into hiding places in the fields, woods, and other remote areas—made it into Arecibo, on Puerto Rico's northern coast, on July 29. The US troops, who had thoroughly routed Puig and his men, now controlled most of the southern part of the island. Four days later, Puig took the only course he deemed honorable for a military leader in his position: he raised his pistol to his head, pulled the trigger, and sent a bullet flying through his brain.

The battle for total control over the island of Puerto Rico was almost over, only a few days after it began.

29

Puig's suicide, as honorable as it seemed to him, turned out to have been a desperate act of misdirected idealism. No sooner had the Americans come storming through Yauco, the town Puig was entrusted with defending, than Yauco's mayor, Francisco Mejia, switched sides and embraced the invaders as saviors. Their arrival was "an act of the God of the just," he said.

"Today the citizens of Puerto Rico assist in one of her most beautiful festivals," he pronounced in an address to the local populace. "The sun of America shines upon our mountains and valleys this day of July, 1898. It is a day of glorious remembrance for each son of this beloved isle, because for the first time there waves over it the flag of the Stars, planted in the name of the United States of America by the Major-General of the American army, General Miles."

Around the same time that Mejia was extolling the virtues of the victors, new American ships carrying more troops arrived in the bay at Guánica with orders to proceed east toward Ponce with its deeper harbor. A column of troops marched in the same direction, tracking the progress of the reinforcements. The Spanish soldiers defending Ponce absconded to the north, while the Puerto Ricans formed a delegation to greet the Americans as soon as they entered the city. The troops aboard the newly arriving ships could see the US flag flying in Ponce's harbor, as well as the flags of other nations except for Spain. Even before the American vessels had anchored offshore, the townspeople had gathered to celebrate their liberation from the Spanish stranglehold. Miles lost no time issuing guidelines for his men's behavior on land, to ensure they did not jeopardize the trust of the locals. He then set up his headquarters, using the existing network of underwater cable lines to communicate directly with Washington, DC, which included a message to Alger informing him of his prior change in battle plans.

On July 30, the French ambassador to the United States, Jules Cambon, sent a message to President McKinley on Spain's behalf to discuss peace terms. But McKinley was not yet ready to negotiate for peace. With the Buffalo Soldiers securing Yauco and the rest of Miles's troops commanding most of the land in the south, a larger invasion force was closing in on Puerto Rico from the north. McKinley would not settle for anything less than unconditional surrender. Again, Fajardo was the target, with the conquest of San Juan as the ultimate goal.

The Spanish did not go down without a heroic struggle, even with most of the population turning against them and cheering on the Americans. Three US ships—the *Amphitrite*, *Leyden*, and *Hannibal*—passed along the coast near Fajardo on August 2 and could see the Stars and Stripes already flying from the lighthouse, raised high by the local citizenry. A reconnaissance party of American sailors and marines, plus Puerto Rican volunteers, quickly swarmed onto shore and moved within a half mile of the town center, located five miles from the coast.

There were only twenty-five Spanish soldiers on hand to defend the town, which they abandoned shortly after the invaders landed. A local civic leader, Dr. Santiago Veve Calzada, sent message after message to San Juan pleading for help to fend off the American attack. When it became clear that no assistance would be forthcoming, Calzada went to the American encampment by himself and asked for mercy for the townspeople, which the Americans were happy to provide. The Spanish subsequently made several attempts to recapture lost ground, suffering heavy losses for almost two more weeks, with town after town falling in the face of the American onslaught. Finally, on August 13, it was officially over when the warring parties signed the Treaty of Paris, which was ratified by the US Senate and signed into law by McKinley on February 6, 1899, and approved by Spain on March 19.

According to the terms of the agreement, Spain ceded Puerto Rico, its last colony in the Western Hemisphere, which was annexed by the United States. The war in Puerto Rico was costly to Spain in lives, prestige, and standing as a major global empire. The Spanish forces on the island totaled 18,000 men, and of that many, combined with their Puerto Rican allies, there were 105 casualties, including 17 dead and 88 wounded, with an additional 324 taken prisoners of war. The American losses were light by comparison, with 40 wounded and only 3 men killed of the 15,400 troop landed over the course of the campaign.

As a result of the victory in Puerto Rico, Nelson A. Miles became the Douglas MacArthur, so to speak, of an earlier generation. Just as MacArthur became ruler of Japan following its surrender in 1945, so did Miles serve as the first US military governor of Puerto Rico when the war ended in 1898. His change in military strategy was totally vindicated by his success, and it put to rest any question of disciplinary action by Alger, who basked in the reflected glory of Miles's conquest of the island.

For the Buffalo Soldiers, the battle in Puerto Rico was a brief prelude to the struggle that was about to erupt on more distant soil.
The Philippines, another region of the globe infested with a toxic
variety of tropical diseases, was exploding. And, notwithstanding
the ailments the black troops succumbed to in Cuba, the government of the United States still believed they could more readily
withstand those diseases than their white counterparts.

This time around, the Buffalo Soldiers would be fighting
not Spaniards but Filipino *insurrectos*, led by a fiery revolutionary named Emilio Aguinaldo, known among his men as Aquino.
Aquino established his own ad hoc government in the northern
region of Luzon and drew up plans to attack the American occupiers in and around Manila to the south. Admiral George Dewey had
defeated the Spanish fleet protecting the Philippine Islands, but the
United States failed to put enough boots on the ground to secure
order throughout the Spanish colony.

Julius Caesar had articulated a formula two millennia earlier:
if you want to totally shut down a country, you need to send in an
occupying army equal to 2 percent of the population. The population of the Philippines in 1899 was about 7 million, which, by
Caesar's calculations, called for an American occupation force of
140,000 men, more than ten times the number the US government
put in place.

Aquino and his followers didn't care for American domination
any more than they liked being trampled under the boot of Spain,
and he raised an army of forty thousand men to clear their homeland of the twelve thousand US troops stationed there. Independence from foreign rule was what the insurrectos wanted, and they
didn't much care if the colonialists called themselves Spaniards or
Americans. The Americans would soon learn that they were con-
fronting a far more dangerous enemy in the Filipinos than they had
against the Spaniards, especially as the locals' tactics transformed

from traditional military maneuvers to guerrilla-style fighting. American forces realized it would be a different experience to combat dedicated rebels rising up for liberty on their own turf—much as American revolutionaries did against the British—rather than to battle an occupying force of underequipped colonial soldiers.

Orders went out for the four contingents of Buffalo Soldiers that had fought in Cuba, plus two newly authorized volunteer black units—the Forty-Eighth and Forty-Ninth Infantries—to report to the Presidio in San Francisco, from which they would embark for the Philippines. The Twenty-Fourth and Twenty-Fifth were the first to arrive in San Francisco at the beginning of 1899, and they landed in the Philippines over the course of two days, July 30 and 31. The Ninth and Tenth were sent on the long journey across the Pacific Ocean as reinforcements, arriving in September, while the Forty-Eighth and Forty-Ninth completed the Buffalo Soldiers' presence on the islands during a three-week stretch between February 2 and 25. Altogether, seven thousand Buffalo Soldiers would see combat in this remote corner of the globe.

The hostilities erupted when Aquino launched an attack against the American troops on the island on February 2, 1899, and declared war against the United States two days later. But before the Buffalo Soldiers left the Presidio, black resentment of yet another colonial war against dark-skinned people had already begun to mount. Ida Wells-Barnett, an African American journalist who had long been advocating equal treatment for black citizens in her articles and speeches, told the Afro-American Council in the nation's capital on January 7, 1899, that "Negroes should oppose expansion [abroad] until the government was able to protect the Negro at home." Mob violence and anarchy brutalized blacks in the North and South, she said.

She was not alone in her opposition to American imperialism, particularly as it involved risking the lives and limbs of black soldiers to feed the country's growing appetite for a global empire. While the United States is embarking on a "hare-brained attempt to go into the colonizing business against its own Declaration of Independence," stated an editorial in the *Washington Bee* on June 24, 1899, "and while she is making such frantic clamor of some kind of independence which she has up her sleeve for Cuba and the Filipinos, would it be extremely wise for the American Negro to show to the entire civilized world the class of liberty they enjoy here?"

"The colored American is for 'expansion,' but he wants expansion on lines consistent with the human principles, for which he has given his labor and shed his blood in four wars," read an article in the *Colored American* on December 2, 1899. A prominent African American bishop, Henry M. Turner, called the crusade in the Philippines "an unholy war of conquest." Some black voices defended the war. "It is now said that colored troops are to be sent to the Philippines. The sooner the better," editorialized the *Indianapolis Freeman*, a black publication, on July 1, 1899. "The enemy of the country is a common enemy and the color of the face has nothing to do with it." Again, on October 7, the same newspaper declared, "It is quite time for the Negroes to quit claiming kindred with every black face from Hannibal down. Hannibal was no Negro, nor was Aguinaldo. We are to share in the glories or defeats of our country's wars; that is patriotism pure and simple."

There was little question, though, that the vast majority of opinions among black Americans tilted against what was increasingly viewed as an imperialistic adventure. Many Buffalo Soldiers heading off to do battle again for white America openly expressed their views. Private William Fulbright adamantly stated that the war was "a gigantic scheme of robbery and oppression." Robert L. Campbell, another black trooper, told the press that "these people are right

and we are wrong, terribly wrong." No man "who has any humanity about him at all would desire to fight against such a cause as
this," he added. Booker T. Washington said, "Until our nation has
settled the Indian and Negro problems, I do not think we have a
right to assume more social problems." E. E. Cooper, another leading black intellectual of the period, warned that it was "impossible
to Christianize and civilize people at gunpoint." And the black dis-
senters were not alone; many influential whites, including Mark
Twain, were increasingly alarmed by McKinley's imperialistic foreign policy. "We can have our usual flag," the great satirist wrote,
"with the white stripes painted black and the stars replaced by the
skull and crossbones."

30

The Buffalo Soldiers who set foot on the soil of the Philippines were greeted by posters and leaflets addressed to "The Colored American Soldier" and describing the lynching, discrimination, and abuse black people had suffered in the United States. The rebels asked them if they really wanted to be the instruments of white imperialist ambitions to oppress other people of color. If they were willing to switch sides, not only would Aquino and his followers welcome them with open arms, they would reward the black Americans with positions of responsibility and power.

For the most part, the Buffalo Soldiers resisted the attempt to sap their fighting spirit and turn against their compatriots, even as they understood the logic behind Aquino's message. On October 7, 1899, the men of the Twenty-Fourth exhibited great valor as they waded through waist-deep mud in an attempt to assault rebel outposts in San Agustin, north of Manila, on the periphery of Aquino's base of operations. The thrust was successful. Both sides exchanged a few rounds of gunfire, and the insurrectos fell back to the north, where they had more support from their fellow revolutionaries.

The Twenty-Fourth moved northward in pursuit of the rebels and engaged them a few days later in the mountain village of Arayat, where they overran enemy trenches and sent them fleeing, with the Twenty-Fourth suffering only a single casualty in the operation. The troops were rolling ahead in harsh terrain, so far encountering only minor opposition as the other black units circled in on the mountainous region toward the heart of Aquino's stronghold. Under the command of Captain Joseph B. Batchelor, a force of 350 Buffalo Soldiers entered an area of the islands where few non-Filipinos had ever ventured. They continued to close in on the enemy through the final weeks of October and into November and December. The early victories came easy, with the insurrectos pulling back and regrouping on more familiar turf as the Americans attempted to close in on Aquino and his followers. Then, suddenly, the momentum of the war suffered an unexpected reversal, and the road to American victory seemed loaded with pitfalls.

The insurrectos changed tactics and adopted a guerrilla style of fighting more suitable to their mountain redoubt. It was an unconventional kind of warfare, one that Americans had not faced before, and it proved highly effective for the inhabitants of the mountains, who were familiar with every square inch of their land. In addition, Aquino's message exhorting the Americans to join his fight for independence instead of advancing the cause of US imperialism began to take root in the minds of both some white troops as well as a handful of Buffalo Soldiers. During the course of the war, sixteen Americans would defect to Aquino, six of them Buffalo Soldiers. The most famous among them, and the one most valuable to the cause of Filipino independence, was Corporal David Fagen of the Twenty-Fourth, who switched sides on November 17, just as his brothers were scoring their early victories in San Agustin and Arayat.

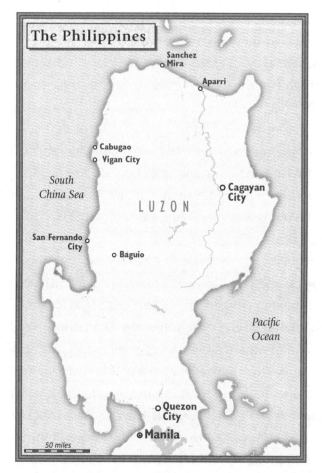

Ground hostilities in the Philippines commenced when a band of *insurrectos* led by Emilio Aguinaldo attacked US troops stationed on the island in February 1899.

Based on a map produced by www.Google.com/maps/place/Philippines.

While most of the Buffalo Soldiers remained loyal, Fagen had his sympathizers among the ranks. "We're only regulars and black ones at that," one soldier wrote home. "I expect that when the Philippine question is settled they'll detail us to garrison the islands. Most of us will find our graves there." Sergeant Major John W. Galloway of the Twenty-Fourth was even more adamant about the bind that ensnared the black troops. "The whites have begun to establish their diabolical race hatred in all its home rancor in Manila," he wrote in a letter. He maintained that white Americans were determined to intimidate both Spaniards and Filipinos right from the start in order to impose white supremacy in the colony after the war was over.

Fagen had enlisted in the army in Tampa in June 1898 and was honorably discharged the following January. He was considered a model infantryman by his white officers, who had high praise for his combat performance in Cuba. They rewarded his efforts by promoting him to corporal in short order. Fagen reenlisted in June 1899 and sailed with the Twenty-Fourth from San Francisco to the Philippines. He fought against the Filipinos mostly around Arayat, until he decided he was on the wrong side of the conflict. Swayed by Aquino's appeals to black Americans to join his revolution, Fagen arranged to be conducted over to the insurgents' side on horseback by one of Aquino's men, who slipped away with him into the jungle. Fagen rose through the ranks of the rebel army during the next year and a half, being promoted first to lieutenant, then to captain, and finally leading a band of rebels who called him General Fagen.

His exploits in Luzon earned him a front-page story in the *New York Times*, which reported that he was a "cunning and highly skilled guerrilla officer who harassed and evaded large conventional American units." The article maintained that Fagen had been particularly brutal toward his former comrades, routinely murdering those who were taken prisoner. But two members of the Twenty-Fourth—black trooper George Jackson and white lieutenant Frederick Alstaetter—said that Fagen treated both of them humanely after he captured them, although Alstaetter claimed that Fagen did steal his West Point ring. Other soldiers with the Twenty-Fourth insisted that Fagen had only reluctantly switched sides after having endured several racially motivated altercations with some white officers.

His legend in the region as a formidable supporter of Aquino grew to the point where a US commander, General Frederick Funston, placed a $600 bounty on his head, stating that Fagen was "entitled to the same treatment as a mad dog." A Tagalog hunter named Anastacio Bartolome delivered a decomposed head and a West Point ring to Funston on December 5, 1901, saying that he and other hunters had killed Fagen while he was bathing in a river. But the rebels insisted that Fagen was still alive and well, living in the mountains; the hunter had brought in someone else's head, they said, to collect the bounty money. The rest of Fagen's body couldn't be found where Bartolome said he had buried it alongside the river, so the evidence was deemed inconclusive, with a head and a ring on one side of the argument and a missing body supporting the other. In any event, the Americans were content to put an end to the mythology surrounding Fagen's exploits in the mountains of Luzon.

"Fagen was a traitor and died a traitor's death," read an editorial in the black *Indianapolis Freeman* the same month the hunter delivered the unrecognizable, decomposed head, "but he was a man no doubt prompted by honest motives to help a weaker side, and one with which he felt allied by ties that bind."

Notwithstanding Fagen's betrayal and the ambivalence many Buffalo Soldiers experienced as they climbed over the mountains and slogged through the jungles of Luzon, the great majority of them fought loyally with their white compatriots as the war to suppress the insurrectos wore on longer than anyone anticipated. On November 23, 1899, less than a week after Fagen's defection, the Twenty-Fourth marched forty-five miles from Cabanatuan City north of Manila to Tayug and reported to General Kent, who had led the unit in Cuba. The plan called for the men to cross over the mountain range to the east, down into the valley floor marked by the Cagayan River, to head off Aquino's men before they could reach the strategically important area. It was a treacherous stretch of real estate over poorly mapped mountains that required several days of hazardous trekking, with every available horse roped into service for a pack train.

The troops ground their way over steep cliffs, "hardly any of them surmountable except by zigzag paths cut on shelves from a foot to eighteen inches wide," Lawton wrote in his report of the campaign. Private Bruce Williams with the Twenty-Fourth said that the men ate "so much rice that we are ashamed to look at it. I, for one, am sick of it." For a while, their diet consisted of nothing but rice and bitter green coffee, with little or no potable water to drink. They also ate sweet potatoes given to them by friendly natives, Williams added, although they tasted as though they were "cooked by barbarians."

As they wound their way down into the valley, they learned that Aquino was approaching with a force of his own from the north. Lawton directed Captain Batchelor to take the 350 black troops in his command and block Aquino's path by following the river all the way to the coast on the northern rim of Luzon. By commanding the valley floor from south to north across the region, Lawton and Batchelor would protect their men from being enveloped by the insurrectos. They skirmished with the enemy along the way, but most of the encounters were brief hit-and-run attacks, with little damage inflicted on either side as Aquino's guerrillas disappeared back into the dense jungle. The biggest hurdle for the Twenty-Fourth was the high, sharp-bladed grass that sliced through their trousers like bayonets and cut their legs, ankles, and hands when the men tried to brush it away.

Batchelor pushed his men onward toward the coast. They marched along the banks of the river toward Naguilian, where the Cagayan intersected a smaller stream called the Magat River. When they approached the confluence of the two waterways, the Buffalo Soldiers could see a band of several hundred rebels staring down at them from a cliff overlooking the far bank. They exchanged fire with the insurrectos, with neither side prevailing because of the distance. The Americans had little choice but to ford the stream to reach the other side, but the water ran deep and the current was swift. The men searched the area and were unable to find any suitable materials to build a viable raft, so they tore down a hut at the edge of the jungle and began to cobble together a workable model.

As they were laboring away on it, four Buffalo Soldiers and one of their officers attempted to swim across the river, but one of the enlisted men, Corporal John H. Johnson, drowned in the effort. The four survivors made it across and found enough wood along the shore to construct a raft of their own. Amazingly, they pulled off the feat without being riddled by insurrecto bullets. They completed the job and floated back over to get their guns and help the other men complete the raft they were building. Finally, nine of them set off across the Magat on their makeshift rafts of wooden planks and bamboo poles tethered together with vines, canteen straps, and shelter-halves torn into strips. To the surprise of their comrades who stood on the shore cheering them on, the troops made it safely across and drove the insurrectos off into the brush. No one was more astonished by their success than their commander, Captain Batchelor.

"To see nine men," he later reported to Lawton, "the officers in their drawers and the privates naked, cross such a stream by such means, and drive an entrenched force not less than ten times their number, in broad daylight where their number must soon become known, is something not soon to be forgotten."

It was a victory badly needed by the American forces, who had been getting cut up by the insurrectos' guerrilla tactics in other regions and had little to show for it. On December 7, 1899, they scored another telling victory when the commander of the one thousand insurrectos in the area, General Daniel Tirona, surrendered to Batchelor. The Buffalo Soldiers took them prisoner and confiscated their canoes and other supplies before continuing on. Batchelor advanced his 350-man contingent farther along the Cagayan River, reaching Tuguegarao, the capital of the province of Cagayan, on December 12. From there it was on to Solana and Amulung as they headed for the coast, encountering little opposition in this theater of operation. They made it to Aparri, their destination on the northern coast, on December 17, where they set up camp to rest and wait for badly needed supplies, including food and fresh clothing.

The swiftness of Batchelor and the Buffalo Soldiers' accomplishments was all the more astonishing considering that they had traversed three hundred miles of rugged, unknown territory inhabited by hostile forces; crisscrossed unfamiliar trails in variable weather conditions; forded back and forth over rushing streams and rivers more than one hundred times; and suffered for more than three weeks with limited food supplies and filthy and ripped uniforms. One of Batchelor's superiors, General Elwell Otis, commented afterward that the march was "memorable on account of the celerity of its execution, the difficulties encountered, and the discomforts suffered by the troops."

For the men of the Twenty-Fourth, it was a victory worth savoring. But it was only one of many battles in a long and drawn-out campaign. The war to bring on the total collapse of the Spanish empire had barely begun.

31

Just before the year ended, on December 19, 1899, Lawton succumbed to enemy fire, taking a bullet in the chest and becoming the first American general killed outside of North America and the highest-ranking officer killed in the Philippines. In his characteristic style, he was striding over the ground at the head of his troops at 9:15 AM within three hundred yards of an insurrecto trench near San Mateo. At six-foot-three, wearing a large white pith helmet and a yellow raincoat, he presented an easy target for enemy sharpshooters under the command of General Licerio Gerónimo. Lawton's men implored him to take cover, but shrinking in combat and leading from the rear had never been his style. The insurrectos fired a round of bullets, most of which clipped the grass around the general's feet. But one found its mark, drilling him through the chest. "I am shot!" were his last words as he fell dead into the arms of one of his staff officers. Not only was Lawton the highest-ranking officer killed in the Philippines, he was the only American fatality during this war.

The business of governing and maintaining order in the land now occupied would prove to be costly and hazardous. Early the following year, the Buffalo Soldiers of the Twenty-Fifth were sent in to garrison other cities and villages, including Santa Cruz, Iba, and Subic Bay, on the western coast of Luzon. Part of their job was to erect and maintain the telegraph lines that provided links to other parts of the island and to the outside world. But no sooner did they put them up than the insurrectos tore them down. The Americans simply did not have enough manpower to guard the entire network, and the rebels moved in from their hiding places in the brush and wreaked havoc on their work as soon as the Americans left an area. Even worse, the rebels, who were familiar with the terrain, observed the Americans' every move as they themselves remained hidden, and the Buffalo Soldiers were in constant danger of having their men picked off one by one before the enemy scampered back into the jungle.

With their limited numbers, the occupiers resorted to stationing small units in each village, scarcely enough personnel to maintain law and order. They became, in fact, the only working govern-ment along the coastal towns, performing routine civil functions including serving as policemen, firemen, and even tax collectors to pay for ongoing expenses—the last of which hardly endeared them to the local populace. Keeping up morale in a war that many of the troops considered less than just, and in which they found themselves oppressing natives who had fought to free themselves from one group of colonialists only to find themselves attacked by others—others who they felt should have been sympathetic to their cause—was challenging in the extreme. Yet, the great majority of the Buffalo Soldiers loyally performed the tasks assigned to them by their white officers, even while they questioned the morality of what they had been sent to accomplish, a sentiment reinforced by constant criticism from home.

"I boil over with disgust when I remember that colored men from this country are fighting to subjugate a people of their own color," wrote Bishop Henry McNeal Turner, a leading voice in the

African Methodist Episcopal Church. "I can scarcely keep from saying that I hope the Filipinos will wipe such soldiers from the face of
the earth." Maintaining their loyalty in the face of such harsh, vit-
riolic rancor from their own religious leaders was simultaneously
heroic and conflicting. "If it were not for the sake of the 10,000,000
black people in the United States," wrote a Buffalo Soldier in a letter
to the *Wisconsin Weekly Advocate*, "God alone knows on which side
of the subject I would be."

The longer the war dragged on, the more elusive the insurrectos
became. One day early in the year, the Twenty-Fifth located a band
of them in a swath of jungle near the western coast. The Buffalo
Soldiers split up into two units, breaking camp at 4:00 AM, one
group moving along the coast and the other proceeding through
rice fields toward the insurrectos' rear. When they had them enveloped, the two units moved in from both sides believing they had
the guerrillas trapped between them—only to discover that their
prey had vanished into the mist, as it were. They had simply disappeared into their environment. The Twenty-Fifth, Twenty-Fourth,
and other black contingents attempted similar operations several
times, with the same results. The enemy became invisible when the
Americans thought they had trapped them, and sometimes managed to kill a few of the invaders before they vanished from sight.

Aquino and his men outnumbered the twelve thousand Americans
committed to combat in the Philippines by more than three to one
during the course of the war. After a string of frustrating encounters, the Twenty-Fifth turned the corner in late January 1900 when
they "scaled heights of great difficulty" and crawled through dense
brush in the region around Mount Arayat, an extinct volcano,
to capture the rebels' barracks and free five American prisoners.

Around the same time, they seized the village of O'Donnell, taking 128 guerrilla fighters prisoner and confiscating more than two hundred of their rifles, plus ammunition and food. Suddenly coming across these extra supplies was especially fortunate, as the Americans—unlike the insurrectos, who enjoyed the support of the locals and were used to living off the land, hunting, fishing, and gathering food and other materials as needed—were otherwise dependent on supplies that had to be shipped across long stretches of ocean and then over arduous terrain to their scattered outposts.

Their victories in these skirmishes turned the men of the Twenty-Fifth into heroes in the eyes of their white comrades—at least temporarily—and earned them immortality, of sorts. One white writer who championed them was the novelist John Dos Passos in his bestselling trilogy of novels, *U.S.A.*, with the opening lines of a verse poem: "It was that emancipated race / That was chargin' up the hill / Up to where them insurrectoes / Was afightin' fit to kill."

The battles raged on throughout the year, with the casualties mounting on each side of the conflict. On January 14 and 15, 1900, the warring parties fought the only artillery duel of the war on the summit of a mountain that climbed a little higher than three thousand feet above the Cabugao River along the northwest coast of Luzon. The American forces scored a decisive victory thanks to their greater firepower, but the elusive Aquino, who they thought was trapped in the area, managed to slip away across the mountain passes with a large band of his followers. Once again, he had pulled off the vanishing act for which he had become notorious, and which frustrated his American pursuers. The American troops who searched the battlefield after the last shot was fired discovered the bodies of twenty-eight rebels, but the commanders of the outpost had escaped with Aquino.

Later the same month, with the area north of Manila largely abandoned by the enemy, the Americans diverted some of their forces, including the Buffalo Soldiers of the Forty-Eighth and Forty-Ninth, to new hot spots erupting in the southeastern corner of the island around Bicol. Deep-water ports dotted the bays in the area, which made them ideal for freighters transporting hemp and other products to far-off countries. On the afternoon of January 18, Brigadier General William A. Kobbé sailed south with five ships with orders to take possession of Sorsogon Bay, which he captured with little opposition. He seized the town and posted a garrison of Buffalo Soldiers to maintain order while he continued on to the ports at Bulan and Donsol, then through the San Bernardino Strait to confront the rebels in Albay Province. They encountered heavy resistance from a determined band of insurrectos but forced the enemy to retreat on January 23. The skirmish cost the American forces seven wounded, and they killed or wounded fifty Filipinos.

Through the spring, the Americans recorded a series of small victories, taking villages including Albay, Nueva Cáceres, and Camarines. They once again had Aquino in their sights, with the insurrectos becoming increasingly desperate, forced to melt church bells and whatever metal objects they had in hand to make bullets. Aquino and his men appeared to be on the verge of collapse as the Americans moved in. Then, surprisingly, the insurrectos mounted a counterattack, impelling the invading troops to abandon a captured town, Catubig, on April 15 after a four-day siege. Aquino slipped the American stranglehold, vanishing from sight and falling back to Manila on May 19, where he dug in and regrouped his rebels. He launched what would later come to be known as Phase Two of the Filipino revolution against the Spanish empire—and the burgeoning American empire that was determined to replace it.

Through the summer and fall of 1900, the war for control of the Philippines continued—memorable battles included Macahambus, Pulang Lupa, Mabitac, and scores of others—while at home McKinley was reelected after a hotly contested campaign against William Jennings Bryan, whose party received Aquino's endorsement. As the Filipino resistance grew more intractable, the US commanders in the field adopted what amounted to a scorched-earth policy, burning down homes and villages and resorting to torture, including using a method that precursed the water-boarding technique used more than a century later in Iraq. Twenty towns in Bohol alone were razed to the ground, their most prominent citizens were tortured, and their cattle were killed and destroyed to deprive the insurrectos of food.

It was a dark hour for US military might in more ways than one. Victories were sporadic at best and hard to achieve. The Filipinos were fighting on familiar turf in their homeland and outnumbered this latest group of imperialists who were determined to deprive them of self-rule. And their hit-and-run, guerrilla style of fighting was both effective and frustrating. When their bullets ran out, they dashed out from the bushes and attacked the American troops with machetes, bolos, and other primitive weapons, inflicting telling casualties before they disappeared back into the jungle.

Even before the war ended, elements of the US government began to look into allegations of war crimes committed by troops in the field. Forty-four separate trials were launched before March 1901, many culminating in convictions for the murder of civilians, rape, the razing of villages, and other crimes—although many of the more severe sentences were later reduced or commuted to fines by Roosevelt after he became president.

"I deprecate this war, this slaughter of our own boys and of the Filipinos," General Felix A. Reeve was moved to write, "because it seems to me that we are doing something that is contrary to our principles."

But the trials and entreaties fell on the deaf ears of some of the commanders in the field, who grew increasingly incensed by the heavy losses inflicted by the insurrectos. After a devastating defeat on Samar, an island south of Luzon, Brigadier General Jacob H. Smith roared to one of his majors, Littleton W. T. Waller, "I want no prisoners! I wish you to kill and burn! The more you kill and burn the better you will please me!" He added that he wanted to turn Samar into a "howling wilderness" following the deaths of fifty-nine American soldiers and twenty-three others wounded by insurrectos disguised as women. Smith left no doubts about his orders, saying he demanded the execution of all Filipinos more than ten years of age. The major carried out his orders and earned the sobriquet "the Butcher of Samar" for his efforts. After the court-martial that followed, Smith was "admonished" for his action, and Waller was acquitted of all charges.

During the 1902 Senate hearings in the wake of the war, Senator Joseph Rawlins asked General Robert P. Hughes, who commanded many of the campaigns, about the morality of burning villages and killing women and children. "The women and children are part of the family," the general responded, "and where you wish to inflict punishment you can punish the man probably worse in that way than in any other. These people are not civilized." Hughes added that the Buffalo Soldiers were somewhat to blame for the developments of the campaign in the Philippines: "The darky troops . . . sent to Samar mixed with the natives at once. Wherever they came together they became great friends. When I withdrew the darky company from Santa Rita I was told that the natives even shed tears for their going away."

So, the Buffalo Soldiers were damned if they did and damned if they didn't. After fighting valiantly in the Philippines against the backdrop of widespread criticism from the black community at large, they were then used as scapegoats by the very commanders who ordered them to violate the tenets of "civilized warfare."

32

No war lasts forever, and the war in the Philippines was no exception. One by one, the insurrecto leaders surrendered to US troops. The capture of Aquino on March 23, 1901, at his house in Palanan, on the coast northeast of Manila, marked the beginning of the end of the insurgency. Twenty of his followers stood guard outside at about 3:00 PM, when Aquino heard shooting in his courtyard. "Not suspecting any plan against myself," Aquino wrote in a memoir, "I thought it was a salute with blank cartridges."

He ran to a window and told his men to cease firing, but when he saw that an attacking party was aiming bullets in his direction, he ran to an inner room and grabbed his revolver. He was about to race back and defend himself against the Americans, but he was restrained by subordinates who told him not to sacrifice himself because "the country needs your life." Four hundred US troops surrounded the house, killing and capturing Aquino's men. Five high-ranking officers entered his home. "Which one of you is Aguinaldo?" one of them asked. Aquino was then put under arrest by the five American officers leading the invasion force.

After a long, bruising campaign that tested American military strength to the limits, the war in the Philippines effectively drew to an end with the capture of the insurgents' leader in March 1901.

Commons.Wikimedia.Org

With Aquino's capture and the adoption of what amounted to war crimes tactics by military commanders in the field, the only unanswered question regarding the final fall of the Spanish empire was when it would happen. The hostilities continued for the rest of the year, but by 1902 the war essentially ended with the adoption of the Philippine Organic Act, passed by the US Congress on July 1. The law called for the establishment of an interim government along with the cessation of the insurrection, the completion of a census throughout the islands, and official recognition of the authority of the US government over the Philippines.

For many of the Buffalo Soldiers, however, the war would drag on long after most of the troops had returned home. Hot spots erupted in different regions throughout the islands, and the US government assigned the men of the Twenty-Fourth the task of putting down the mini-rebellions where they occurred, mostly in the Muslim districts in the south. For the next four years, the Buffalo Soldiers and members of a new Philippine constabulary killed more than fifty insurgents who refused to submit to US rule. The Filipinos were now "our little brown brothers," a term coined by William Howard Taft, the first American governor-general of the Philippines, who was elected the twenty-seventh president of the United States in 1908. But the white officers overseeing the mopping-up operations made no distinction between the Filipinos and the Buffalo Soldiers who remained abroad. They were all "niggers" as far as the officers were concerned. A popular song of the period captured their attitude clearly: "You are told he is your little brown brother, / and the equal of thee and thine. / Well, he may be a brother of yours, Bill Taft, / but he is no relation of mine."

The Buffalo Soldiers who did return to their homeland after the conclusion of the major campaigns passed through the San Francisco Presidio in 1902 before departing for other assignments. Four men of the Ninth remained there until 1904, becoming the first black troops ever garrisoned at the Presidio on regular duty. In May 1903, Captain Charles Young, the third African American graduate of West Point and the only black officer authorized to lead men in combat, left with a contingent of troops from the Ninth and Tenth. His mission was to patrol the national parks at Yosemite, Sequoia, King's Canyon, and other locations, and "to establish a camp with the purpose of protecting the park from injury and depravations." Young was a prominent hero of the action in the Philippines, spearheading attacks against the insurrectos in Samar, Blanca Aurora, Durago, Tobaco, and Rosano for a year and a half with the simple command, "Follow me!"

When an assassin's bullet claimed McKinley's life on September 14, 1901, Roosevelt succeeded him as president. The leader of the

Rough Riders toured California from May 12 through 14, 1903, and Young and his men flanked both sides of his carriage as the president rode down Market Street in San Francisco. It was a reunion of sorts between Roosevelt and the Buffalo Soldiers, who had last seen one another during combat on the hills in Cuba. Roosevelt's selection of them as his "Guard of Honor" was viewed by some as an apology for his disparaging remarks after the historic war.

Roosevelt followed this event with an invitation in 1904 to have black educator Booker T. Washington dine with him at the White House—the first time an African American appeared there as a guest of honor. But he undid the goodwill he earned with the black community two years later when he summarily dismissed 167 Buffalo Soldiers following a shooting spree in Brownsville, Texas, that ended with the death of a white bartender and the wounding of a police officer. The War Department had actually precipitated the problem several months earlier, in May 1906, when it sent two battalions of the Twenty-Fifth to military bases in Texas—Fort McIntosh and Fort Brown. The army criticized the order, knowing that the locals in Brownsville were particularly bigoted against black people.

"Citizens of Brownsville entertain race hatred to an extreme degree," the white commander of the Texas National Guard had warned. Black chaplain Theophilus Steward had accurately predicted that "Texas, I fear, means a quasi-battle ground for the Twenty-Fifth Infantry." Upon their arrival, the Buffalo Soldiers were greeted by signs banning African Americans from stores, restaurants, bars, parks, and other public facilities.

By the end of July, the tension in town was reaching the breaking point. Not allowed to drink in Brownsville's white-only bars, the Buffalo Soldiers set up a tavern of their own, which promptly became a favorite hangout for the men. Fights broke out between whites and blacks on several occasions, and it all came to a boil on the night of August 13. Around midnight, a group of about twenty men gathered on Cowen Alley and started to shoot into buildings on both sides of the narrow passageway. Near the intersection of the alley and Thirteenth Street, a gunshot wounded a police officer, and then a half block farther along, bullets fired into a saloon killed the bartender inside.

The white officers at Fort Brown insisted that the black troops were in their barracks at the time of the incident, which came to be known as both the Brownsville Affair and the Brownsville Raid. The mayor and some prominent white locals, however, maintained that they had seen black soldiers firing guns indiscriminately at the time, and the army and the president were quick to use the Buffalo Soldiers as scapegoats. None of those dishonorably discharged, which included many longtime regulars with distinguished careers—six of them Medal of Honor recipients—were tried and found guilty of the crime, yet their dismissal from the military cost them their pensions and other benefits.

In the aftermath of the shooting, investigators discovered spent cartridges and clips strewn throughout the street. Roosevelt referred to the men of the Twenty-Fifth as "bloody butchers" who "ought to be hung," even though none of the bullets recovered were fired from the rifles of the black troops, according to white senator Joseph P. Foraker, who believed that local townspeople committed the crimes during a night of revelry.

The man who came to dinner two years earlier, Booker T. Washington, intervened on behalf of the black soldiers and pleaded with Roosevelt to reverse himself on the grounds that the evidence was inconclusive. The president denied his request, and a 1908 US Senate Military Affairs Committee hearing endorsed Roosevelt's decision. The Buffalo Soldiers of the Twenty-Fifth would have to wait another sixty-four years for vindication, when the army reopened the case and found the men innocent in 1972. The soldiers who were deceased received honorable discharges posthumously without back pay for their families. One of two survivors, and the last man standing, Private Dorsie Willis, eventually got a check for $25,000 and was honored at ceremonies in the nation's capital and Los Angeles in 1973. "It was a frame-up straight through," Willis said. "They checked our rifles and they hadn't been fired." He died in 1977 at ninety-one years of age, outliving everyone who had rigged the case against him and his fellow soldiers.

In 1907, Congress moved to discharge all black troops from military service, but the effort went down in defeat. Instead, the army attempted to make amends for the framing of black soldiers in Brownsville by allowing more African Americans to enter West Point for cavalry training and instructions in mounted combat. As it turned out, the army—and, increasingly, the navy—needed black warriors for ongoing eruptions in the Philippines, where they dispatched the Twenty-Fifth again to put down uprisings by Moro tribesmen in 1907 and 1908.

On the home front, with forest fires raging throughout the West, the government depended on greater numbers of men with the courage and training to put their lives on the line in an effort to tamp them out. There simply weren't enough white firefighters and military personnel available to get the job done, so the government once again called on the Buffalo Soldiers to fill the breach wherever more manpower was required. And then, as in the past, it was just a question of time before a new war broke out and black men were asked to do their part in expanding the growing American empire.

PART FOUR

The Aftermath

33

The enemy was closer to home this time around, but they were brown-skinned once again: Mexican revolutionaries under the leadership of José Doroteo Arango Arámbula—more famously known as Pancho Villa—and a few of his rivals. Mexico had freed itself of Spanish rule in 1821, following eleven years of revolution launched by a Catholic priest, Father Miguel Hidalgo y Costilla, on September 16, 1810. Spain had ruled New Spain, as it called Mexico before the revolution, for three bloody centuries. *"¡Mexicanos, viva Mexico!"* was Father Hidalgo's call to arms for the oppressed lower classes to reclaim the land stolen from them by their Spanish overlords. Sadly, as was the case with most revolutions, the following years were chaotic, with the presidency changing hands seventy-five times during the next fifty-five years. The United States and Mexico went to war in the middle of the nineteenth century, and attempts at liberal reform within Mexico were largely unsuccessful. A series of dictators ruled the land until the early part of the next century.

The troubles along the southwestern border of the United States had begun to erupt in 1912, when different bands of rebels attacked

Mexican government installations during the reign of Victoriano Huerta. The hostilities spilled across the border from time to time, fueling skirmishes with American troops patrolling the area from the mouth of the Rio Grande River in Texas all the way west to the Pacific Ocean in San Diego, California. It was a long stretch of border to protect, seventeen hundred miles of arid, treeless desert

Mexican revolutionary José Doroteo Arango Arámbula, better known as Pancho Villa, eluded capture by American troops for almost a year before President Woodrow Wilson ended the action and shipped the soldiers to Europe during World War I.

Library of Congress Prints and Photographs Division (LC-DIG-npcc-19554)

with scarcely a square inch to find cover from the sun or protection against armed, hostile forces.

The US government retaliated by beefing up American military presence along the border, shipping the Buffalo Soldiers of the Ninth to Douglas, Arizona, in 1912, and the Tenth to Fort Huachuca, Arizona, in 1914. Their ranks were thin as they patrolled the long stretch of sand and scrub, sporadically getting shot at by raiding parties of Yaqui Indians and Mexican rebels. The incidents were few and far between, but every now and then a man was killed or wounded on either side of the conflict before the rebels scrambled back to safer ground a few miles from the border. Despite the outbreaks of violence on US territory, the American government was not inclined to launch an all-out war against the insurgents. Rather, the War Department issued an order to the troops to make sure the gunfights did not "complicate the present situation."

The so-called situation was a conflagration in the making, however; violence inevitably begets more violence, and it was all but inevitable that the rebellion would totter onto more volatile terrain. The US government, which had attempted to remain neutral in the beginning, decided to send arms across the border to support one of the rebel leaders, Venustiano Carranza, in his struggle to overthrow the Huerta regime. The tactic worked, briefly, when Carranza and his men forced Huerta to resign on July 15, 1914, forcing the former dictator into exile. Carranza then took over the government, with the endorsement of President Woodrow Wilson. But the United States had backed the wrong horse, as it were, since another rebel leader who had originally allied himself with Carranza decided that he should be the leader of the new Mexican government. His name was Pancho Villa.

In 1894, Villa returned home from the fields where he worked as a sharecropper and caught the owner of the estate in the act of trying to rape Villa's twelve-year-old sister. The sixteen-year-old boy grabbed a pistol, shot and killed the child molester, and then took off into the mountains. From that point on, Villa lived the life of a bandit and rebel, establishing a name for himself as a Mexican Robin Hood of sorts, championing the rights of the disenfranchised peasants against the wealthy landowners and upper-class gentry. He attracted a loyal band of followers who helped him establish a base of operations in the mountain town of Chihuahua, in northern Mexico, just south of the US border.

During the next decade, Villa's fame grew. The revolutionary leader now commanded the Division del Norte and its crackerjack cavalry, Los Dorados. Following his defeat at a Carranza stronghold near Vera Cruz in 1915, Villa retreated again to his bastion in Chihuahua, where he contemplated his next move. Villa and his "Villistas" blamed the Yankees for engineering his defeat by Carranza and his followers, and they were regrouping their strength closer to US territory than the US government cared to see. In effect, the American government had unleashed a raging pit bull on the patio outside the hacienda door.

While the United States officially recognized the new Carranza regime, Villa had other ideas. War was what he wanted—not war between his band and the Americans, but between the Americans and the Carranza government, an action that would, he thought, ultimately create a void he intended to fill. In January 1916, Villa and his men raided a train that was crossing through Santa Ysabel in northern Mexico, removed sixteen American miners, and shot them to death. He followed up that attack when he crossed the border into the town of Columbus, New Mexico, early on the morning of March 9. As a local newspaper reported the day before, "Villa had been sighted 15 miles west of Palomas Monday night and was camped there all day Tuesday. . . . He is reported to have between 300 and 400 men with him. They are all well mounted and since arriving near Palomas have been slaughtering large numbers of cattle."

Palomas sat just across the border from Columbus, a small frontier town with about three hundred residents and a cluster of adobe houses and wooden retail buildings. When he crossed the border on March 9, setting fire to parts of the town and looting horses, mules, ammunition, and other military supplies, the pit bull had crossed over the threshold onto US territory. Not surprisingly, the task of subduing Villa before he rampaged at will throughout the house would fall to a great extent on the shoulders of the Buffalo Soldiers.

The US Thirteenth Army Cavalry stationed at Camp Furlong outside of Columbus killed eighty of Villa's men and lost eighteen of their own before driving Villa's band back across the border, where Villa regrouped his forces. President Woodrow Wilson had little choice but to retaliate for the incursion, so on March 19 he ordered John Pershing, now a general, to assemble a "punitive expedition" to track down Villa and destroy his rebel army. Black Jack included the Buffalo Soldiers of the Tenth in his expedition, commanded by Colonel William Brown, whose chief adviser was newly promoted Major Charles Young, the black officer whose fame had grown since his heroic leadership during the Philippines campaign.

Pershing divided his troops into two "flying columns," as he called them because of the speed they would move. They would head south across the border from different locations. The first comprised various white regiments, including the Thirteenth Cavalry, the Eleventh Cavalry, an artillery unit, the First Aero Squadron, and a company of engineers that left from Columbus. The faster column was made up of the black Tenth Cavalry, the white Seventh Cavalry, and another field artillery unit, all of which departed from Hachita, a few miles west of town. Their goal was to destroy Villa and his men, but without inciting the wrath of the Carranza government—a virtually impossible mission to accomplish, since it involved invading Mexican territory with US military units without authorization from the Mexican government.

As Pershing had anticipated, Carranza refused to grant him permission to use the Mexico North Western Railway to supply his men, so Pershing had to improvise a "train" system of his own. He put together a truck convoy to carry food and ammunition, and he established a wireless telegraph network to communicate with his officers in the field. On March 19, 1916, Pershing sent a Curtiss JN-3 aircraft of the First Aero Squadron into Mexican airspace to conduct an aerial reconnaissance of the terrain. When everything was ready to go, he set his plan in motion, crossing the border in force into Mexico. The two columns headed southward and hooked up at Colonia Dublán on March 20.

At that point, Pershing decided it would be more effective to split his troops into three columns instead of two, with two of the columns containing squadrons of Buffalo Soldiers from the Tenth, an indication of the high regard Pershing had for the black troops in his command. Once inside Mexico, he commandeered the train located there without Carranza's permission. As it turned out, the Mexican train cars near the border were an unholy collection of twenty-eight dilapidated boxcars in various stages of decay. The Buffalo Soldiers went to work immediately, taking on the jobs of patching up holes in the floors, cutting windows and doors in the sides to allow entry by the troops and their horses, and placing bales of hay on the roofs so the men who couldn't fit inside had places to ride more or less comfortably on top. The black troops then hopped aboard and commenced a search for Villa and his men that would send them riding in pursuit for more than a week before they exchanged gunfire for the first time with the Mexican rebels.

The troops headed south in the patched-up railroad cars with no real logistical support from their government, which was growing more and more focused on events in Europe. Their food supplies and ammunition were limited to what they had been able to load onto the train. Along the way, they abandoned the train and continued their journey on foot and horseback, purchasing additional supplies from locals who were willing to sell them anything with whatever money they could scrounge together. During the next few days, they encountered no signs of Villa and his followers, and the peasants they questioned were not inclined to provide them with any information they might have had.

Then, on March 27, Colonel Brown got word that a group of Villa's men were entrenched on a ranch about eight miles away. After a long march through the mountainous region, Brown gave the order to attack the ranch at dawn the following day. The Tenth's official diarist cabled the information to Pershing: "Arrived as per plan and surprised the inhabitants some sixty-five in number and undoubtedly Villistas but proof of same lacking."

During the five-hour battle, the Buffalo Soldiers killed or wounded most of the men and forced Villa to escape into the mountains. Only five Americans were wounded in the first skirmish of the expedition. The men marched or rode in the saddle for as much as seventeen hours a day as they pursued Villa farther into the mountains, an area that was unfamiliar to them but home territory for Villa. The frustrations built as the rebel leader eluded them each time they thought he was trapped. Not only was the terrain as familiar to Villa as his own backyard—which to a great extent it was—but he enjoyed the loyalty of the local peasantry, who supplied him and his band with food and ammunition. As the Buffalo Soldiers drew closer to Aguascalientes on April 1, Major Young ordered his men to charge about 150 rebels dug in at the Villa stronghold, only to find that the rebels had retreated once again into the surrounding mountains.

34

The men of the Tenth chased after the Mexican rebels for seven miles through rugged territory, but they finally had to give up pursuit when the light started to fade and most of their horses ran out of steam. Again, the Villistas seemed to vanish into the mist, similar to the way Aquino had pulled his disappearing act time after time in the Philippine jungles. When the Tenth did encounter the enemy, however, Villa and his men proved to be some of the most formidable guerrilla fighters the Americans had ever fought.

The next testing ground was in the town of El Mesteno, where a continuing stream of rifle fire from Young's troops failed to dislodge the rebels from their positions. Colonel Brown ordered Young to mount his men and attack the Villistas' right flank, while he attempted to envelop them from the left with units of white soldiers. Young readied his cavalry and galloped on horseback with them, their rifles and pistols drawn. They roared toward their prey yelling and screaming in the same way they had charged up the hills in Cuba, but they failed to get a single shot off when the Villistas refused to meet their charge and instead scampered again back to their mountain retreats. Again, their efforts to engage the enemy ended in frustration as Villa's guerrillas eluded what appeared to be certain defeat.

The pursuit continued deeper into Mexican territory without incident through early April 1916. But on April 12, Villa finally achieved the goal he was after. The US expedition onto Mexican soil infuriated Carranza to such a point that he dispatched regular army units north from Mexico City to halt the American advance. War—or at least what looked like the start of one—between Carranza's government and the United States appeared likely, and Villa was content to remain in hiding with his men while the two sides fought it out. At 6:30 on the evening of April 12, three troopers of the Thirteenth burst into Young's camp in Sapien. They informed the major that Carranza's contingent of more than five hundred regular troops had attacked the one hundred men of the Thirteenth in the nearby village of Parral. The white Thirteenth was on the verge of being wiped out. Those who could escape were retreating north toward Santa Cruz de Villegas.

The Buffalo Soldiers mounted up and charged toward Santa Cruz de Villegas. It took them less than an hour to reach the town, where they found the remaining soldiers of the Thirteenth ensconced behind barricades in the street and on rooftops, waiting for Carranza's men to attack again. The Tenth arrived just in time to prevent a complete disaster for the white troops, sending Carranza's men fleeing in the face of American reinforcements. Pershing was reported to be "mad as hell" when he saw what had happened. US troops had been on the march for weeks on end and had penetrated more than five hundred miles into Mexican territory by the time they reached Parral, with scant results to show for the effort. A total of ten thousand American troops would eventually be deployed into Mexico, and still they were unable to destroy

Villa and his band. And now Pershing had Carranza to deal with. He wired Washington, asking for permission to redirect his forces north from Santa Cruz de Villegas and capture Chihuahua, Villa's base of operations. But President Wilson refused to expand the expedition as Europe occupied his attention, adding to Pershing's sense of futility.

◖■◗

The battles that followed became increasingly difficult as Carranza dispatched more troops into the area in an attempt to push the Americans back over the other side of the border. Villa kept his men in hiding during most of the days and weeks that followed. While Pershing scoured the countryside looking for him, the main resistance he encountered was from the "Carrancistas," whom he was instructed not to go to war with but rather to just defend himself against when they attacked. Pershing felt that he was not being allowed to fight the kind of war he wanted to fight—the war he needed to fight in order to win. It was as though he were being unreasonably reined in by Washington every time he hatched a plan for victory.

Later generals in later wars would voice the same complaints, smoldering about the "armchair generals" in Washington who had never worn a uniform directing actions on the battlefield, more concerned about political than military strategy when men were getting killed and wounded in action. In May, Pershing ordered his units to reassemble in Colonia Dublán, which he regarded as a headquarters of sorts while he contemplated further action.

On May 14, Lieutenant George S. Patton, the future legendary general of World War II, was out buying some corn for his men near Chihuahua when he came across a ranch owned by a top Villista named Julio Cardenas. Patton assembled fifteen of his men, loaded them into three Dodge touring cars, and raided the ranch in America's first motorized military action. Patton and his men shot and killed Cardenas and two of his guerrillas, strapped each of them to the hoods of his cars, and drove them back to Pershing's headquarters in Colonia Dublán. Patton carved three notches into his rifle and earned the nickname "El Bandito," which was bestowed on him by Pershing. The Villistas got their revenge less than two weeks later, however, when they ambushed ten Americans out looking for cattle, killing one of them and wounding two others.

Reinforcements, including the Buffalo Soldiers of the Twenty-Fourth Infantry, marched south across the border and joined forces with Pershing and the men of the Tenth Cavalry. For the next month they rode and tramped for miles on end across the territory, fording one river seventy-one times in the space of a few miles as they followed any signs indicating that the Villistas were camped in the region. Mostly they came upon inhospitable locals who increasingly resented their presence on Mexican land. The paths the Americans traveled led to one dead end after another. At the end of June, Pershing thought he found the break he was looking for when he heard about a rebel entrenchment at the barrio of Villa Ahumada. If that were true, it would put Villa and his men in a good position to destroy Pershing's lines of communications with Columbus. Pershing sent a detachment of the Tenth, commanded by Captain Charles Boyd, an aide to Major Young, to reconnoiter the situation.

What happened next turned out to be a fateful encounter for Pershing and his forces, as well as a pivotal development in the entire Mexican punitive expedition. The precise details and the motives that set them in motion have become somewhat obscured in the great fog of politics and war. The official version is that Pershing's instructions to Boyd were clear: "A clash with Mexican troops would probably bring on war and for this reason was to be avoided."

More critical assessments have conjectured that a broader war between the two countries was exactly what Pershing—and, ironically enough, Pancho Villa—wanted, though for far different reasons. From that perspective, it would seem that Pershing had ordered Boyd to continue his advance on the Villista encampment, regardless of whether any Mexican army troops were in the area or not. Boyd carried out his superior's orders as he had interpreted them, believing that a clash with the Mexican army—if it came about—was what the general wanted. It appears less likely that Boyd would have taken the action he did on his own. Pershing, Boyd understood, thought that a show of American force would send the Carrancistas, despite their greater numbers, scurrying off into the bushes.

Boyd and his contingent of Buffalo Soldiers made camp at a ranch about thirty miles from their destination on the evening of June 20. They broke camp early the next morning and headed toward Villa Ahumada, but they never made it there. Before they completed the long march to the town where Villa was located, they spotted a large entrenchment of Carranza's troops well dug in near the barrio of Carrizal, about eight miles from camp and more than twenty miles closer than Villa Ahumada. Boyd moved his men to the edge of an open field lying between them and the Carrancistas, who were grouped along the far side.

The Buffalo Soldiers approached cautiously as the Mexicans formed a defensive perimeter. Boyd asked for permission from the Mexican commander, General Félix Gómez, to let his men proceed, but the general refused. At first, the enemy lineup did not appear to be that large in number, and Boyd decided to fight his way through. But as Boyd's men drew closer, they could see large contingents of Mexican troops filing out of the woods and flanking them on both sides. The Americans had walked into a trap. It was too late to back away now. Boyd sent their horses to the rear and urged his men to charge ahead. The Carrancistas fired first as the Buffalo Soldiers launched their attack.

The Buffalo Soldiers were badly outnumbered and, as a result, they paid a heavy price during the battle. Boyd paid the ultimate price, along with another officer, when Mexican bullets found their targets. "I am done for, boys," were the captain's last words as he fell on the battlefield. "All of our men were taking careful aim," a Buffalo Soldier wrote afterward, "and Mexicans and horses were falling in all directions. But the Mexican forces were too strong for us as they had between 400 and 500 and we only had 50 men on the firing line." So, even though the black troops were inflicting heavy damage on the enemy, the Mexicans outnumbered them to such a point that the Buffalo Soldiers were unable to stop them from advancing on their flanks.

Despite their smaller forces, the Buffalo Soldiers fought on for an hour and a half, holding off the Carrancistas as best they could as the enemy closed within thirty yards. Bullets fell like hot coals in all directions, taking a heavy toll on both sides of the conflict. As the battle raged on, the Tenth found itself running out of ammunition, and the men had no alternative except to escape from the trap sprung by the Mexicans. Some did get away, but the Carrancistas swarmed in and captured twenty-three of them, killed eleven enlisted men, and wounded ten others and a third officer. The Buffalo Soldiers had caused some serious damage of their own in return, killing Gómez, the Mexican commander who had refused to grant them safe passage, and forty-five of his soldiers, plus wounding forty-three others.

When Pershing received news of the defeat, he said that he was "surprised" and "chagrined" and was determined to revenge the loss of his men. War fever against Mexico was building in the United States, and Pershing wanted to seize the opportunity to launch a full-scale invasion of Chihuahua and wipe out the Villistas once and for all. President Wilson had other ideas, however, and refused to allow him to escalate the conflict. The punitive expedition to destroy Villa and his men was over as far as he was concerned.

A new war beckoned, and Wilson's attention had turned increasingly toward German aggression in Europe while much of his army was stampeding across the hills of northern Mexico. It was time, he thought, to pull the plug and salvage what remained of US relations with the Mexican government. Wilson gave the order to withdraw from the country without accomplishing his goal there after nine months of bloody warfare. The United States never did find Pancho Villa. It took an assassin's bullet to claim his life while he visited Parral on July 20, 1923, most likely with the approval of the Mexican government he was still so eager to topple.

Shortly after the Battle of Carrizal, the Mexican government shipped the bodies of the Buffalo Soldiers killed there back to the United States, where they received a heroes' welcome in El Paso, Texas. The War Department transported six of the fallen men, including Captain Boyd, to Washington, DC, for burial at Arlington National Cemetery. Crowds lined the entire route all the way from Union Station, across the Memorial Bridge, and out to the cemetery as the horse-drawn procession took the men to their final resting places.

In Mexico, there was little left for the troops to do except keep busy until each unit received its marching orders to head back north to the US side of the border. Pershing sent them out on tactical maneuvers, but he cut them short because of the hostility of the local population. They marked off makeshift baseball fields in the dirt, set up rings for boxing matches, and did calisthenics on the drilling field to stay in shape. On Thanksgiving Day, the

Buffalo Soldiers of the Tenth and Twenty-Fourth roasted turkeys in the adobe ovens scattered throughout the area and served up dinner complete with stuffing, potatoes, corn, cranberry sauce, pumpkin pie, and other trimmings. They topped it all off with cigars, local rum, wine, and brandy. Soon it would be time to head home—only to be sent off to the next war, which summoned them from the far side of the Atlantic Ocean.

All the American troops were back on US soil by February 5, 1917. They assembled in Columbus, New Mexico, the border town that had triggered the fruitless campaign to kill or capture Pancho Villa, and from there they departed to their new assignments, with the Tenth Cavalry and Twenty-Fourth Infantry ordered to protect the border dividing Mexico and the United States until the government decided where to station them next.

35

It wasn't long before the old racial prejudices resurfaced. Roosevelt had betrayed the Buffalo Soldiers after their service in Cuba, and now it was Pershing's turn to stigmatize them as virtual foreigners in their own country. The man who had earned the sobriquet Black Jack because of his high praise for the black troops he led in combat now labeled them a "constant menace" to American society in a directive he sent to the French Military Mission in Europe on August 17, 1918. "We must not eat with them, must not shake hands or seek to talk or meet with them outside the requirements of military service," he advised the French officers. "We must not commend too highly the black American troops, particularly in the presence of Americans. . . . Americans become greatly incensed at any public expression of intimacy between white women with black men."

It is difficult to believe that these words poured from Pershing's heart in light of his previous views about the Buffalo Soldiers with whom he served. Most likely his message was political, a reflection of the attitudes of the Wilson administration, which was initially opposed to admitting more blacks into the military, even as the

United States waded belatedly into the war that was supposed to end all wars. Pershing was a general who served his masters, and beyond his military acumen, he was a politician himself at the core, like most high-ranking military leaders. So, while his directive may not have emanated from what he felt in his heart, it issued forth from the soul of a man who was a politician first and foremost. Whatever the case, it was all the more disheartening coming from the pen of a man who may not have believed in his own hateful message.

The French responded to Pershing's missive with commendable Gallic disdain; they ordered copies of it burned. France itself was a battlefield on which one in twenty-eight of its citizens had lost their lives by the end of 1918, and its army boasted elite black officers, including two generals, who had served their country well during a four-year struggle against Germany. Senegalese, Algerian, and Moroccan troops had proved their loyalty and fighting spirit at the Battle of the Marne in 1914, which stopped the Germans cold just forty miles shy of the Champs-Élysées.

"It is because these soldiers are just as brave and just as devoted as white soldiers that they receive exactly the same treatment, every man being equal before the death which all soldiers face," read the official French reply.

France had long been a refuge for African Americans. The French welcomed their range of music and culture and accepted them as equals in a society that imposed no color barriers. It became a home away from home for many jazz musicians, performers, and writers who faced unrelenting bigotry at home. Black American warriors were no exception as they poured into a country that had already been ravaged by war for years before they arrived. At first, Wilson tried to minimize the presence of black soldiers in the military, but when he finally decided to involve the United States in the war in Europe, he realized he would need to beef up the ranks with whatever resources he had. He instituted a military draft in June 1917 that ensnared all able-bodied men between twenty-one and thirty-one years old—black men in disproportionate numbers to white men. Seven hundred thousand black citizens registered within a month, amounting to 13 percent of all draftees, even though the total number of blacks constituted less than 10 percent of the population at the time.

All in all, ten thousand African Americans manned the ranks of the US Army before the war ended, including the Buffalo Soldiers of the Ninth and Tenth Cavalries and the Twenty-Fourth and Twenty-Fifth Infantries. The Ninth boasted the presence of Lieutenant Benjamin O. Davis, the future first black general of the army, who had fought in the Philippines. Ten thousand more joined the National Guard in a growing number of states, and another ten thousand joined the US Navy. Wilson's need for manpower to flesh out his insatiable war machine induced him to create two additional black combat units: the Ninety-Second and Ninety-Third Divisions. Like the Buffalo Soldiers who had served in the Spanish-American War before them, the latest black warriors quickly earned the respect of both the enemy they fought against and the allies they fought beside.

Two white American aviators testified that, "While [the black troops] were captured at different points, and imprisoned at widely separate prisons," the first question German military intelligence asked was "How many colored troops the Americans had over here." The Germans were concerned that the Buffalo Soldiers, like the Senegalese and Algerians who fought with the French, were mighty warriors who took no prisoners.

The French were so impressed by the black Americans' fighting ability that they awarded the coveted Croix de Guerre to Sergeant Henry Johnson, the first American of any color to receive it. More than one hundred more would be given the honor or the even more prestigious Medaille Militaire. They came to be known among black

American civilians as the "Men of Bronze" and "Harlem's Own," while the Germans regarded them as "Hell Fighters." The French sympathized with the men's Class-B status by referring to them as Les Enfants Purdus—lost children, isolated within their home country.

⬤■➡

The war crushed Europe during a brutal four-year period, but US involvement lasted only nineteen months. Wilson claimed it was America's duty to make the world "safe for democracy," but there was little in the way of democracy at stake in Europe, which had been crippled by the turmoil of falling and rising empires, internecine monarchies, and a lust for other nations' territory over the centuries leading up to the First World War. "We have no selfish end to serve," Wilson declared in a speech. "We desire no conquest, no dominion. . . . We are but one of the champions of the rights of mankind."

While America's belated entry into the war did not exactly expand democratic freedoms across the Continent and elsewhere—Nazism and Communism would follow in the wake of the war—it did save the day for the beleaguered Allies. Italy was on the verge of surrendering to Austria, Britain and France were close to collapse, Germany was near triumphant, and the Russian Bolsheviks had used the opportunity to impose their own special brand of totalitarian hell over a vast spread of land from Europe through the frigid reaches of Siberia.

"We're finished forever with this filthy war!" read the lyrics of a popular French protest song of the period. The country's soldiers were deserting in droves, and England and France together had lost a million men plus countless civilians during the seemingly interminable onslaught. Germany was ready to declare victory in April 1918, when the landing of a million US troops on European soil turned the tide and disabused them of that notion. The German general Erich Ludendorff attributed his nation's "looming defeat" to "the sheer number of Americans arriving daily at the front." The Buffalo Soldiers were among the last US troops to hit the shores and were placed under the command of the French army. Afterward, an aide to Marshal Philippe Pétain praised the fighting spirit of both the black and white American soldiers who came to his country's rescue in a memo to Pétain: "The spectacle of these magnificent youths from overseas" symbolized "life coming in floods to reanimate the dying body of France," he wrote.

The Buffalo Soldiers suffered tremendous losses in the war to liberate Europe from German aggression, with the dead and wounded of the Ninety-Third alone totaling almost 50 percent of the division.

⬤■⬤

Within four months of their triumphal return to the United States, which included a ticker tape parade down Fifth Avenue in New York City, race riots exploded across the length and breadth of the country. The summer of 1919 was called the "Red Summer," a reference to the blood of black citizens that flowed through the streets of large cities and small towns in both the North and South. Seventy-eight black men—including several veterans in uniform— were strung up by the neck in the course of the year. The president of the United States defended the widespread racial antagonism in a book he had written in 1901, stating that "congressional leaders were determined to put the white south under the heel of the black south," and therefore whites were motivated by "the mere instinct of self-preservation." As president, Wilson institutionalized racism at the highest level of government.

This time around, however, African Americans were determined to give back as good as they got. "Like men we'll face the murderous, cowardly pack / Pressed to the wall, dying, but fighting back" was a call to rebellion penned by Jamaican American writer and poet Claude McKay in July 1919. African American civil rights activist and writer W. E. B. Du Bois followed that cry from the soul a month later with his own words: "They cheat us and mock us; they kill us and slay us; they deride our misery . . . TO YOUR TENTS, O ISRAEL! And FIGHT, FIGHT, FIGHT for freedom."

Black citizens in Chicago armed themselves with government-issued Springfield rifles and Browning automatic machine guns on the night of July 28, 1919, when a race riot broke out, the result of black residents fearing an invasion of their neighborhood by an Irish gang. Fortunately, the conflict never came off, since it would undoubtedly have ended in bloodshed and the loss of life for many participants. "Always I had been hot-tempered and never took any insults lying down," wrote black veteran Haywood Hall. "This was even more true after the war."

Republican congressman Hamilton Fish from New York, the son of the Rough Rider of the same name who had been killed in Cuba, spoke out in favor of a bill to make lynching a federal crime in 1922. "The colored man who went into war had in his heart the feeling that he was not only fighting to make the world safe for democracy but also to make this country safe for his own race." The bill was defeated with the help of President Warren G. Harding, who was elected in 1920. Harding was rumored to be part black himself; one of his ancestors may have "jumped the fence," the president admitted, with no trace of irony in his voice.

The aftermath of the war marked the beginning of the end of the Buffalo Soldiers as a group of tightly knit fighting units in the US military. Although the need for black warriors to help fight the country's battles never ended, when the United States began to downsize the armed services during the years following World War I, there is no question that African Americans were more adversely affected than whites; turned away from the military, they were left only the most menial jobs available in the mainstream economy.

The downsizing continued through the 1920s and into the 1930s, with the Ninth, Tenth, and other Buffalo Soldier units thinned out and all but obliterated as the Great Depression took hold. The cavalry and infantry divisions that survived continued to be segregated as they had been throughout the wars in Cuba, Puerto Rico, and the Philippines, and during the expedition into Mexico, and they were still under the command of mostly white officers. As late as 1941, there were still only five black officers in the army: Benjamin O. Davis, who became the first black general on October 25, 1940; his son Benjamin O. Davis Jr.; and three chaplains. Those who had served earlier had either been killed in battle or become ill and forced to retire—including Charles Young, who had fought valiantly in the Philippines and in Mexico and died an outcast in Nigeria in January 1922. He was buried there with full British military honors.

"They have left God out of the equation," Young had replied to a British officer who asked him just before he died what was wrong with white people in America. Young's remains were returned to his home country four months after his death, and he was interned with honors at Arlington National Cemetery. Assistant Secretary of the Navy Franklin D. Roosevelt had the final words on the way Young had been treated when he said, "No man ever more truly deserved the high repute in which he was held, for by sheer force of character, he overcame prejudices which would have discouraged many a lesser man."

36

Black Americans took up arms to combat the spread of Nazism and its twin brother Fascism across Europe and part of Africa in the 1930s. While much of Europe was still healing after the horrors of the First World War, Hitler grasped the opportunity to seize the Saarland region of Germany in 1935, and not to be out-done by the senior partner in the unholy alliance, Italian dictator Mussolini rained bombs on unprotected villages in Ethiopia later the same year. Most African Americans—and conscientious whites as well—considered the totalitarian juggernaut to be an exten-sion of the same kind of racist, economic, and political oppression that existed at home. White mercenaries poured into Ethiopia in response to a plea from Emperor Haile Selassie, and some black volunteers joined the tiny Ethiopian Air Force to help put down Mussolini's tragic push to establish a new Roman Empire.

Then Spain emerged as the major battleground for warring forces on the right and the left. The Spanish Civil War officially broke out on July 17, 1936, when a claque of army generals attempted a coup d'état against Spain's democratically elected coalition govern-ment. Paramount among the generals was Francisco Franco, whose forces were an amalgam of nationalists that included monarchists (or Carlists), fascists (or falangists), and Spanish, Algerian, Irish, German, and Italian soldiers of fortune. The unwieldy government coalition comprised a diverse group of anarchists, Stalinists, Trotskyites, syndicalists, various strains of socialists, and a ragtag contingent of international brigades fleshed out by volunteers from all over Europe and North America. Further complicating this ideological stew was a mix of separatists from Cataluna, Navarra, and Galicia, who wanted independence from Spain and self-rule for their own regions. Then there were trade and student unions that splintered into a mind-numbing array of more than forty different factions, each promoting its own political agenda.

When France, Britain, and the United States remained neutral and refused to supply arms to Spain's left-wing government, the republicans turned to Russia for support. Germany and Italy backed Franco and his nationalists. Trying to figure out which side to come down on was a devil's choice for most open-minded individuals, with Stalin in one camp and Hitler and Mussolini in the other. For African Americans, the war against racism and fascism was what mattered most. To them and most of the whites who decided to get involved, an alliance with the anti-Franco forces seemed like the right side to be on. Even Ernest Hemingway, who fought against Franco, said the Spanish Civil War was "a bad war in which nobody was right." But all that really mattered was to relieve the suffering of human beings, and Hemingway had good company in England's Winston Churchill, who claimed he would welcome the devil himself as an ally in a righteous cause to defeat his enemy. (It should be noted that the full extent of Stalin's crimes against his own people was not yet fully apparent.)

Journalist Milton Wolff said, "You had to be there to know what had happened. Basically, it was a war waged by the army and monarchists led by General Franco to reverse the 1936 election in which a leftist government of several parties was elected. It was called the Popular Front. Franco brought over Moorish mercenaries, a paid army, to destroy the elected government. . . . In the very first weeks of the war, long before Moscow decided to help the Spanish government, the republican side as they were called, Hitler and Mussolini were pouring in stuff to help Franco and the nationalists. The final factor was England putting the arm on France to close the border between France and Spain to cut off military aid to the republicans."

The international brigades that trooped into Spain were an unlikely mix of whites, blacks, and dark-skinned people from various economic and social backgrounds. They were a diverse group of idealists who made no racial distinctions and represented, by and large, a welcoming society for black Americans who had been ostracized and abused at home. As such, it held much appeal for black warriors looking to fight for a cause they believed was just. Many of them left the United States to fight against the Franco coalition alongside white volunteers from different nations.

One of the most popular among them was Eluard McDaniels, the adopted son of a white photographer from San Francisco named Consuelo Kanaga, whose ethnic background was Swiss despite her Hispanic-sounding first name. McDaniels had been a longshoreman, occasional art student, and baseball player who developed a reputation for "pitching" hand grenades with devastating accuracy at enemy forces. The Spaniards he fought beside regarded him as a comrade since his forebears had once been *enslavos*—slaves—which they considered themselves to be under fascism.

Vaughn Love and James Yates were among a group of five African Americans who sailed to Europe on the ocean liner *Île de France* on February 20, 1937. Their fellow volunteers numbered three hundred out of eight hundred passengers aboard, which included Hemingway, with whom they dined while crossing the ocean. Hemingway was already working on his novel about the war, *For*

Whom the Bell Tolls. Both Love and Yates wrote books of their own describing their experiences in Spain, Yates selling his on the streets of Greenwich Village a half century later, when he was in his eighties. "Although we talked with each other and played poker," Love wrote in his book about their experiences on the French ship, "we all kept our destination a secret." Both he and Yates crossed the Pyrenees with most of the other volunteers and saw action in several theaters of war in Spain.

The tide of war turned against the republican forces during the winter of 1937–38, the coldest in memory at the time, when they suffered a crushing defeat at the Battle of Teruel outside of Valencia. It was a loss the republicans would never recover from. More than fifteen thousand republican soldiers lost their lives there, and the volunteer brigades saw many of their own killed and wounded. Paul Robeson, the African American singer and civil rights activist, lent his voice and presence to the republican cause during a visit to the front. His business agent expressed concern about Robeson's political association with the left at a time when anti-Communist fervor was mounting in the United States, but the singer refused to be deterred. "The artist must take sides," he said. "I have made my choice. I have no alternative."

America's reluctance to get ensnared in another European war ended on December 7, 1941, when Japanese bombs dropped from the sky on a US military outpost in Hawaii's Pearl Harbor. The action caught the United States largely unprepared for another major conflict after nearly two decades of downsizing its military strength. The army alone was severely understaffed, with the white ranks thinned out and only four thousand remnants of the Buffalo Soldiers in uniform. Another three thousand black men served in the National Guard. Those numbers would soon change, however, with the inauguration of a new military draft that would pull blacks into all the military branches—the army, navy, army air corps, and marines—including positions they had never served in before. The government reestablished the old Buffalo Soldier units: the Ninety-Second and Ninety-Third Divisions, and the Ninth and Tenth Cavalry Regiments.

The eighteen hundred volunteers who had survived the war in Spain presented themselves to the US government as a single fighting unit in the war against the Axis powers. Had the government accepted them as such, the Spanish-American War veterans would have constituted the first racially integrated military entity in US history. But the government tagged them with being politically "red," as well as an unacceptable racial blend of white, black, and many shades in between. They were regarded as security risks because they had fought on the side that included known Communists and Communist sympathizers. Nevertheless, about six hundred of the volunteers managed to wangle their way into the armed services and the merchant marines. Some, including the writer Milton Wolff, were even accepted into the OSS, the predecessor to the CIA, which enlisted other writers into wartime service.

The black Spanish Civil War veterans also found a home in the military, fighting alongside the Buffalo Soldiers in several major European and North African campaigns. As soon as the United States entered the war after the bombing of Pearl Harbor, the NAACP sent a proposal to the army's chief of staff, General George C. Marshall, advocating the establishment of a division "open to all Americans irrespective of race, creed, color, or national origin," in the spirit of true democracy. Many whites endorsed the idea and volunteered to serve with black troops as enlisted men rather than as commanding officers. While FDR was open to the proposal largely on the advice of his wife, Eleanor, high-ranking members of the administration opposed it and were able to sway the president in their direction. Secretary of the Navy Frank Knox had fought beside Buffalo Soldiers in Cuba and said he had never seen "braver men" anywhere, but he invoked "tradition" as his reason for rejecting a racially integrated military. Eleanor Roosevelt was furious. "The nation cannot expect the colored people to feel that the US is worth defending if they continue to be treated as they are treated now," she lamented in a speech she made in the nation's capital shortly after the attack on Pearl Harbor. Yet defend it they did, even in the face of ongoing discrimination across all levels of society.

For the first time, black soldiers were fighting not just on the ground but in the air. The army accepted its first black pilots early in 1942 and sent them flying off into combat after eight months of training. Others flew with the navy and went into combat on the seas, earning the Navy Cross and other medals—albeit some of them belatedly, long after the war was over. A group of them earned the sobriquet the "Golden Thirteen," constituting the largest group of African American officers commissioned by the navy during World War II. The army shipped Buffalo Soldiers and black volunteers to fight in North Africa, Anzio, Omaha Beach, the Battle of the Bulge, and other critical battlefields in Europe and Asia, where many earned medals and other commendations for serving with distinction.

Then, not unexpectedly, when the war was all but won by the United States and its allies, the government started to deactivate the all-black combat divisions beginning in 1944, converting them to service units and relegating them to mop-up duty. In effect, the government relieved the black warriors of their military duties when their services were no longer needed and then transformed them into virtual orderlies, performing the only types of jobs that were available to them at home.

37

President Harry S. Truman wrote the last chapter in the long saga of the Buffalo Soldiers when he issued Executive Order 9981 on July 26, 1948. "It is hereby declared to be the policy of the President that there shall be equality of treatment and opportunity for all persons in the armed services without regard to race, color, religion, or national origin," the order read. "This policy shall be put into effect as rapidly as possible." Truman's order was partly political, since the Republican running against him that year, Governor Thomas E. Dewey of New York, was a moderate opposed to "the idea of racial segregation in the armed forces of the US." Within his own party, Truman had to walk a narrow line between progressives and liberals on the left, led by Henry Wallace, and racist "Dixiecrats" on the right, personified by Strom Thurmond. Truman scaled the divide and came down on the side of evolving history in the making.

In doing so, Truman declared that the age of segregation, in the military at least, was officially over. Thus began the slow process of integrating the black divisions that had fought for their country since the end of the Civil War into units that were formerly all white. Two of the old Buffalo Soldier divisions, the Twenty-Fourth and Twenty-Fifth Infantry, were officially disbanded in the years after World War II, when the country's need for such a large number of men in uniform had ended—for the time being—with the surrender of the Axis powers. It would not be long before a new war erupted—this one on a remote North Asian peninsula called Korea—so although the long saga of the Buffalo Soldiers sputtered to a close after Truman's historic action, black Americans would continue to answer their country's call to arms, as draftees and as volunteers, throughout the ensuing decades.

In early July 1950, several black combat units that had not yet been integrated were shipped to Korea with two companies of white soldiers. They were among the first to be sent abroad for what was expected to be a short "police action" before returning to their base in Japan a few weeks later. They brought with them their dress uniforms for the planned victory parade through the streets of Seoul. Instead, they would find themselves bogged down in a grinding war in extreme weather conditions that would last for two years, until Dwight D. Eisenhower brokered an uneasy peace soon after his election as president in 1952. The still-segregated troops of the Twenty-Fourth, which was soon to be dissolved, won the first ground victory on the peninsula and earned the first Medal of Honor bestowed in the conflict. A white officer with the group, Lieutenant Colonel John T. Corley, sang the praises of the black soldiers' performance in action, which was well received by the men he led on the battlefield.

"The 24th Infantry Regiment performed extremely well for Colonel Corley," wrote black combat pilot Charles Bussey. "Leadership seemed more important to him than skin color in determining success in battle." Later, however, Bussey altered his opinion of Corley when he learned that the colonel would have recommended Bussey and his men for even more medals had they been white. "I cannot allow you to become a hero, no matter how worthy," Corley admitted to Bussey. "I reduced the size of the battalion that you saved to a group, and I reduced the number of men you killed" out of fear, he said, that Bussey and other black warriors would "flaunt it." Blood brothers and drinking buddies they may have been in uniform, but the old racial bigotry resurfaced when they returned to peacetime life at home.

The Korean War gave birth to the nation's first black four-star general, Roscoe Robinson Jr., who graduated from West Point in 1951 and saw combat in Korea and Vietnam. He earned his fourth star in 1982 as the representative to NATO's Military Committee. The complete integration of the armed forces picked up steam during the Korean War as black volunteers poured heavily into recruiting offices. The post commander of the army training center in Fort Jackson, South Carolina, found it impossible to sort out the recruits along racial lines. He cast aside whatever personal reservations he may have had and simply assigned the incoming troops wherever they were needed most. The base quickly became a model for the only viable means of completing the process of integration—just bite the bullet and do it! The era of military segregation sputtered to a close. And as the full integration of the armed forces became a fait accompli, the curtain fell on the almost century-long drama of the Buffalo Soldiers and the role they played in the long, hard sweep of American history.

Colin Powell joined the army in 1959 after graduating from CCNY in New York City. As a cadet in the ROTC, Powell became a member of the crack Pershing Rifles drill team—named after General Black Jack Pershing—where Powell earned his bar as a second lieutenant when he graduated. It was a time between wars, with Korea now in the past and Vietnam still off in the future. Born in Harlem to Jamaican parents, Powell was sent to Germany where he quickly rose up the ranks. By the end of 1960, he became the first lieutenant in his battalion to command a company, a job ordinarily reserved for captains. He considered himself lucky that he was not personally subjected to racial discrimination, even from his white NCO from Alabama. "My color made no difference," Powell wrote. "I could have been black, white, or candy-striped for all he cared. I was his lieutenant, and his job was to break in new lieutenants and take care of them."

In 1981, Brigadier General Colin Powell jogged around a field at Fort Leavenworth, Kansas, the base where the first Buffalo Soldiers unit, the Tenth Cavalry Regiment, was established in 1867, 114 years earlier. Since that historic birthdate, some troops of the Tenth had been stationed there continuously through the end of World War II, but Powell noticed that there was little at the site to celebrate their presence; two alleys and two lonely graves bore the names of the Ninth and Tenth, and that was it. Powell vowed on the spot that, if he were ever in a position to rectify the situation, he would make sure the Buffalo Soldiers received the honor they deserved.

Powell fulfilled his promise ten years later. On July 25, 1992, more than ten thousand people arrived at Fort Leavenworth to witness the dedication of the Buffalo Soldiers Monument on the site. Senator Bob Dole addressed five hundred surviving veterans of the Ninth and Tenth, and General Powell stepped up to the microphone to deliver the keynote speech. He said the Buffalo Soldiers had made it possible for people like him to achieve their current positions. Without them, Powell would not be standing before them on that memorable July day. Powell pointed proudly at the towering statue of a Buffalo Soldier on horseback, created by sculptor Eddie Dixon, rifle in hand as he scouts the territory ahead in advance of his unit. The oldest Buffalo Soldiers in attendance were

110-year-old Jones Morgan of Richmond, Virginia, and 98-year-old William Harrington of Salina, Kansas. Another veteran, Elmer Robinson of Leavenworth, had summed up their emotions three years earlier when he heard that the statue was being built at Powell's urging: "After all these years, I didn't think anyone cared. Now I feel like a hero."

General Powell stated his own feelings poetically on the day of the dedication: "They are the wind beneath my wings." Indeed, they will be the wind beneath the wings of many generations to come.

38

The battlefields are in different places now, and many of the old ones have changed over the decades. The Civil War killing fields where the Buffalo Soldiers spilled their blood a century and a half ago are mostly national parks where Americans and foreign tourists can visit and get a rough idea of what special kind of hell the country lived through back then. The plains where the Buffalo Soldiers first got their name from the Comanche and Cheyenne warriors they battled in the late 1800s have been parceled into vast corporate ranches, upscale leisure communities, public parks, and reservations for the folks who first roamed the land. And the hills in Cuba, where the Buffalo Soldiers rescued Teddy Roosevelt and his colorful band of Rough Riders from almost certain annihilation, have changed most of all.

Today, the former Spanish stronghold at Santiago de Cuba is an industrial city on the harbor, replete with warehouses, factories, wharves, and other maritime facilities strewn along the water's edge. The historic center of town has been preserved much the way it looked in 1898 and has become a draw for tourists from around the globe. The San Juan Heights north of the city are dotted with residential developments that undulate across the rolling terrain to the top of San Juan and Kettle Hills and other peaks in the area. The original blockhouse at the crest of San Juan Hill where so many lives were lost no longer exists; the Cuban government ripped it down and built a replica that sits at the center of a park and museum, which were established twenty-five years after the war ended. The park contains well-preserved Spanish and US artillery pieces and other weapons used during the war, plus a plethora of statues and plaques commemorating the Cuban and American troops who together defeated the Spanish. Visitors can look out from the edges of the park and see the village of El Caney to the northeast and the peak of El Pozo to the east.

Perhaps the biggest eyesore in the area is the former Hotel Leningrad, more recently the Hotel San Juan, which was constructed by Soviet-era architects for Russian tourists in a clumsy attempt to capture the tropical splendor of the region. Fortunately, the grounds are covered with palm trees and other flora, which hide some of the monotonous outlines of the structure. Equally troubling are the size and location of the hotel, which cuts off views of the siege lines during the war. A zoo and amusement park also rest incongruously on the slopes. More appropriately, a hospital adorns the side of the hill, a vivid reminder of the carnage that took place there. The steepness of the slope leading to the crest of San Juan remains much in evidence, although some commercial and residential structures obscure the contours of near-lying Kettle Hill.

El Caney is much less recognizable as the quaint, historic battlefield village it once was, except for the church in the center of town, the main plaza, and the ruins of El Viso, which have been left standing. More modern and less imaginative developments engulf the winding, twisting streets and narrow passageways where much of the fighting occurred. Las Guasimas has been left largely intact, and both Siboney and Daiquiri are unaltered by the passage of time, except for a hotel compound that sits on the hill above the latter.

The memory of the Buffalo Soldiers lingers on in the hills of southeastern Cuba, as it does in other battle sites in the United States and abroad where they fought bravely for their country. The terrain and killing fields may look different these many years later, but the memory cannot be erased. What the Buffalo Soldiers accomplished during their long, remarkable history—which until now has remained a mere footnote in the pages of time—remains the wind beneath the wings of the black warriors who followed them into combat in later wars.

Acknowledgments

This book would not have seen the light of day were it not for my agent, Linda D. Konner, who encouraged me to move forward with it from the time I first mentioned it to her. No writer has ever had better representation. Many thanks go to my editor Jerry Pohlen. Ernest Hemingway once said that no good writers would need an editor if they had the leisure to wait five years from the time they finished until they published a book. But deadlines are rarely stretched out quite that far. Jerry served me well from the time I submitted the book until it was ready for publication, and I am indebted to him for that. Thanks also to Michelle Williams, Lisa Marietta, and the rest of the dedicated staff at Chicago Review Press, who ushered my manuscript from the typed page through the final stages of production and promotion.

I would like to thank General Colin L. Powell, who brought the Buffalo Soldiers to the forefront of the nation's consciousness by establishing the monument in their honor at Fort Leavenworth, Kansas, more than two decades ago. His stirring words on that occasion appear in the forefront and penultimate chapter of this book. His astonishing career is an inspiration to everyone who values military service as the ultimate guardian of liberty in a free society.

I also appreciate the help I received from the administrators, directors, and other personnel at the Library of Congress, the

National Archives and Records Administration, the National Park Service, the National Endowment for the Humanities, the National Gallery of Art, the Smithsonian Institution, the Association for the Study of African American Life and History, the Presidio Trust, the Spanish-American War Centennial Society, the US Army Garrison at Fort Leavenworth, the Chickamauga and Chattanooga National Military Park, and other organizations that provided me with pertinent information for this book. In particular, I would like to acknowledge the help and cooperation I received from National Park Service rangers Frederik Penn, Anthony Powell, and Shelton Johnson.

Many thanks go to my daughter Christine Tuccille Merry, proprietor of Merryhaus Design, who has been an emissary and surrogate for this project every step along the way. Her efforts in researching photographs and securing the rights for their inclusion in the book, promoting the project on social media and other venues, establishing a title-specific webpage, and helping in other ways have been invaluable to me.

Special thanks go to Don Holman who supplied me with an original research paper on the sinking of the *Maine* written by his father, Donald A. Holman. The information in it proved to be a valuable source of information unavailable anywhere else. I would like to thank Allen K. Boetig, whose knowledge of military operations was extremely helpful to me. Thanks go to Don Wimmer, who pointed me in the direction of his son Eric Wimmer, who went out of his way to do some legwork for me at the Presidio in San Francisco, the final resting place of 450 Buffalo Soldiers.

I owe a great deal to my wife of half a century, Marie Winkler Tuccille, who performed the first editorial review of the manuscript in progress and provided me with her usual incisive comments. Marie not only encouraged me to pick up the project after I temporarily put it aside, she also put up with my compulsive work schedule during the five or more years I researched and wrote the book.

Her patience and understanding mean more to me than I could ever express.

A complete list of source material appears in the bibliography following these pages. The list includes dozens of books, articles, monographs, previously published and unpublished documents, and detailed reports about the period covered in this book. There are too many to single out, but I would like to acknowledge my indebtedness to the writers who covered this subject in varying degrees of detail before me. Their own time and labor made it possible for me to complete my job.

If I have left anyone out who has been helpful to me, I apologize. I truly appreciate all contributions and take full responsibility for any errors that may have found their way into the final printed pages of *The Roughest Riders*.

Bibliography

Books

Abbott, Lawrence F. *Impressions of Theodore Roosevelt.* New York: Doubleday, Page and Company, 1919.

Alger, R. A. *The Spanish-American War.* New York: Harper and Brothers,
1901.

Atkins, Edwin F. *Sixty Years in Cuba.* New York: Arno Press, 1980.

Atkins, John Black. *The War in Cuba: The Experiences of an Englishman with
the United States Army.* London: Smith, Elder and Company, 1899.

Azoy, A. C. M. *Charge! The Story of the Battle of San Juan Hill.* New York:
Longmans, Green and Company, 1961.

Berryman, John. *Stephen Crane: A Critical Biography.* New York: Cooper
Square Press, 1950.

Bigelow, John Jr. *Reminiscences of the Santiago Campaign.* New York:
Harper and Brothers, 1899.

Bonehill, Ralph. *When Santiago Fell.* Rahway, NJ: Mershon Company,
1899.

Brands, H. W. *The Reckless Decade: America in the 1980s.* Chicago and
London: University of Chicago Press, 1995.

Brooks, Elbridge S. *The Story of Our War with Spain.* Boston: Northrop
Publishing Company, 1899.

Brown, Charles H. *The Correspondents' War.* New York: Charles Scribner's
Sons, 1967.

Buckley, Gail. *American Patriots: The Story of Blacks in the Military from the
Revolution to Desert Storm.* New York: Random House, 2001.

Carlson, Paul. *Pecos Bill: A Military Biography of William R. Shafter.* College
Station: Texas A&M University Press, 1989.

Carter, William H. *The Life of Lieutenant General Chaffee.* Chicago: University of Chicago Press, 1917.

Cashin, Herschel V. *Under Fire with the Tenth US Cavalry.* New York: F. Tennyson Neely, 1899.

Chesnutt, Charles W. *The Marrow of Tradition.* New York: Penguin Classics, 1993.

Chidsey, Donald Barr. *The Spanish-American War.* New York: Crown Publishers, 1971.

Davis, Charles Belmont, ed. *Adventures and Letters of Richard Harding Davis.* New York: Charles Scribner's Sons, 1917.

Davis, Richard Harding. *Cuba in War Time.* New York: R. H. Russell, 1899.

———. *Notes of a War Correspondent.* New York: Charles Scribner's Sons, 1912.

Dawes, Charles G. *A Journal of the McKinley Years.* Chicago: The Lakeside Press, 1950.

Dickman, J. T., ed. *The Santiago Campaign: Reminiscences of the Operations for the Capture of Santiago de Cuba in the Spanish-American War, June and July, 1898.* Richmond, VA: Williams Printing Company, 1927.

Dolan, Edward F. *The Spanish-American War.* Brookfield, CT: The Millbrook Press, 2001.

Draper, Andrew S. *The Rescue of Cuba.* Boston: Silver, Burdett and Company, 1899.

Dyer, John P. *"Fightin' Joe" Wheeler.* Baton Rouge: Louisiana State University Press, 1941.

Egli, Ida Rae, ed. *No Rooms of Their Own: Women Writers of Early California, 1849–1869.* Berkeley, CA: Heyday Books, 1992.

Eicher, David J. *The Longest Night: A Military History of the Civil War.* New York: Simon & Schuster, 2001.

Fletcher, Marvin. *The Black Soldier and Officer in the United States Army: 1891–1917.* Columbia: University of Missouri Press, 1974.

———. *America's First Black General: Benjamin O. Davis, Sr., 1880–1970.* Lawrence: University Press of Kansas, 1989.

Foner, Philip S. *The Spanish-Cuban-American War.* New York: Monthly Review Press, 1972.

Gatewood, Willard B. Jr. *"Smoked Yankees" and the Struggle for Empire: Letters from Negro Soldiers 1898–1902.* Urbana, Chicago, and London: University of Illinois Press, 1971.

Gould, Lewis L. *The Spanish-American War and President McKinley.* Lawrence: University Press of Kansas, 1950.

Halstead, Murat. *Full Official History of the War with Spain.* Chicago: Dominion Company, 1899.

Hill, Henry. *San Juan Hill.* New York: Dorchester Publishing Company, 1996.

Johnson, Edward A. *History of Negro Soldiers in the Spanish-American War.* Raleigh, NC: Capital Printing Company, 1899.

Katz, Friedrich. *The Life and Times of Pancho Villa.* Stanford, CA: Stanford University Press, 1998.

Keithley, Ralph. *Buckey O'Neill.* Caldwell, ID: Caxton Printers, 1949.

Konstam, Angus. *San Juan Hill 1898: America's Emergence as a World Power.* Chapel Way, Botley, Oxford, UK: Osprey Publishing, 1998.

Lane, Ann J. *The Brownsville Affair: National Crisis and Black Reaction.* Port Washington, NY: Kennikat Press, 1971.

Longacre, Edward G. *A Soldier to the Last: Major General Joseph Wheeler in Blue and Gray.* Washington, DC: Potomac Books, 2006.

Lynk, Miles V. *The Black Troopers.* New York: AMS Press, 1971.

Mahan, Alfred T. *Lessons of the War with Spain.* Boston: Little, Brown, and Company, 1899.

Millard, Candice. *Destiny of the Republic: A Tale of Madness, Medicine and the Murder of a President.* New York: Anchor, 2012.

Millet, Frank D. *The Expedition to the Philippines.* New York: Harper and Brothers, 1899.

Morris, Charles. *The War with Spain.* Philadelphia: J. B. Lippincott Company, 1899.

Moss, James A. *Memories of the Campaign of Santiago.* San Francisco: Mysell-Rollins Company, 1899.

Munroe, Kirk. *Forward March: A Tale of the Spanish-American War.* London: Forgotten Books, 2012.

Norris, Frank. *The Surrender of Santiago.* San Francisco: Paul Elder and Company, 1917.

O'Toole, G. J. A. *The Spanish War: An American Epic 1898.* New York and London: W. W. Norton & Company, 1984.

Quesada, Alejandro. *The Hunt for Pancho Villa: The Columbus Raid and Pershing's Punitive Expedition 1916–17.* Chapel Way, Botley, Oxford, UK: Osprey Publishing, 2012.

Rickover, H. G. *How the Battleship Maine Was Destroyed.* Washington, DC: US Department of the Navy, 1976.

Roosevelt, Theodore. *The Rough Riders.* New York: Charles Scribner's Sons, 1899.

Samuels, Peggy, and Harold Samuels. *Teddy Roosevelt at San Juan: The Making of a President.* College Station: Texas A&M University Press, 1997.

Sears, Joseph Hamblen. *The Career of Leonard Wood.* New York: D. Appleton and Company, 1919.

Sinkler, George. *The Racial Attitudes of American Presidents.* Garden City, NY: Doubleday and Company, 1971.

⅃Stewart, T. G. *Buffalo Soldiers: Colored Regulars in the United States Army.*
Philadelphia: A. M. E. Book Concern, 1904; reprinted by Humanity
Books, 2003.

Various authors. *The Spanish-American War: The Events of the War
Described by Eye Witnesses.* Chicago and New York: Herbert S. Stone &
Company, 1899.

Wells, Ida B., and Alfreda M. Duster. *Crusade for Justice: The Autobiography
of Ida B. Wells.* Chicago: University of Chicago Press, 1991.

Wells, Ida B., and Jacqueline Jones. *Southern Horrors and Other Writings:
The Anti-Lynching Campaign of Ida B. Wells, 1892–1900.* New York:
Bedford/St. Martin's, 1996.

Wolff, Leon. *Little Brown Brother: How the United States Purchased and Paci-
fied the Philippines.* New York: Oxford University Press USA, 1992.

Articles

Addeo, Alicia. "Tampa Is a Bum Place: The Letters of First Sergeant
Henry A. Dobson in 1898." *Tampa Bay History,* Spring/Summer
1998.

Allen, Thomas B. "Remember the *Maine?*" *National Geographic,* February
1998.

Cook, Roy. "Plains Indian View of the 'Buffalo' Soldier." American
indiansource.com. http://americanindiansource.com/buffalo%20
soldiers/buffalosoldiers.html.

Covington, James W. "The Rough Riders in Tampa." *Tampa Bay History,*
Spring/Summer 1998.

Draffen, Duayne. "Roosevelt's Rough Ride Led to Montauk." *New York
Times,* May 17, 1998.

Dumindin, Arnaldo. "Philippine-American War, 1899–1902." Philippine
americanwar.webs.com. http://philippineamericanwar.webs.com/
emilioaguinaldoreturns.htm.

Gatewood, Willard B. "Black Troops in Florida during the Spanish-
American War." *Tampa Bay History,* Spring/Summer 1998.

Hicks, George III, and Carmen Weaver Hicks. "Kansas City, Missouri,
and Fort Leavenworth, Kansas." Buffalo Soldiers Research Museum,
February 2005.

Hillestad, James H. "Up, Up and Away!" Toy Soldiers Museum and Shop,
Cresco, PA.

Holman, Donald A. "The Destruction of the *Maine,* February 15, 1898."
Quarterly Review, Autumn 1953.

Hubener, Hal. "Army Life in Lakeland, Florida, during the Spanish-
American War." *Tampa Bay History,* Spring/Summer 1998.

Hymel, Kevin. "Black Jack in Cuba: General John J. Pershing's Service in the Spanish-American War." *On Point*, Winter 1998.

Kite-Powell, Rodney. "All Eyes Were on Tampa in 1898." *Tampa Tribune*, August 26, 2012.

Lorenzen, William A. IV. "The Rocking Chair War: Views of Tampa in the New York Press during 1898." *Tampa Bay History*, Spring/Summer 1998.

McSherry, Patrick. "A Brief History of the 2nd US Artillery, Battery A." Spanish-American War Centennial Website. www.spanamwar.com /3rd%20Alabamahistory.html.

O'Malley, Michael. "A Blood Red Record: The 1890s and American Apartheid." http://chnm.gmu.edu/exploring/19thcentury/empire /lecture.html.

Plant, Trevor K. "Researching Service in the US Army during the Philippine Insurrection." National Archives and Records Administration.

Pohanka, Brian C. "Fort Wagner and the 54th Massachusetts Volunteer Infantry." *America's Civil War Magazine*, July 18, 1863.

Powell, Anthony L. "Black Participation in the Spanish-American War." Spanish-American War Centennial Website. www.spanamwar.com /AfroAmericans.htm.

Rattiner, Dan. "Teddy Roosevelt's Montauk Summer Vacation in 1898 with the Rough Riders." *Dan's Papers*, January 26, 2012.

Rau, R. "Henry Ware Lawton: Forgotten Warrior." Library of Congress, 1998.

Rosenberg, Jennifer. "Pancho Villa." About.com. http://history1900s .about.com/cs/panchovilla/p/panchovilla.htm.

Schellings, William J. "Key West and the Spanish American War." University of Florida, 1958.

Tessman, Norm. "Captain William Owen 'Buckey' O'Neill (1860–1898)." Spanish-American War Centennial Website. www.spanamwar.com /Oneill.htm.

Select Monographs and Online Postings

"African-American Civil War Soldiers." Kansas Historical Society, January 2010. www.kshs.org/kansapedia/african-american-civil-war -soldiers/15122.

"African-American Milestones in Naval History." Naval History and Heritage Command. www.history.navy.mil/search.html?q=african+ american+milestones+in+american+history.

"African-Americans and the US Navy: The Golden Thirteen." Naval History and Heritage Command. www.history.navy.mil/our-collections /photography/us-people/s/sublett-frank-e/nh-95624.html.

"Battle of Carrizal (1916)." BlackPast.org. www.blackpast.org/aah /battle-carrizal-1916.

"Black Americans in the US Military from the American Revolution to the Korean War." New York State Military Museum and Veterans Research Center, NYS Division of Military and Naval Affairs. http://dmna.ny.gov/historic/articles/blacksMilitary/Blacks MilitaryWW1.htm.

"The Brownsville Incident: A War at Home." New York State Military Museum and Veterans Research Center, NYS Division of Military and Naval Affairs. http://dmna.ny.gov/historic/articles/blacks Military/BlacksMilitaryBrownsville.htm.

"Buffalo Soldier Memorial Park." Garrison.leavenworth.army.mil.com. http://garrison.leavenworth.army.mil/Newcomers---Visitors /Attractions/Buffalo-Soldiers.aspx

"The Buffalo Soldier Monument: Its Meaning and Significance." *Military Review*, August 1990.

"The Buffalo Soldiers." National Park Service, US Department of the Interior.

"Buffalo Soldiers and the Spanish-American War." National Park Service, US Department of the Interior.

"Calixto García's Letter to General William R. Shafter (July 17, 1898)." Historyisaweapon.com. www.historyisaweapon.com/defcon1 /calixtocuba.html.

"Charles Trumbull Boyd, Captain United States Army." Arlington National Cemetery Website. www.arlingtoncemetery.net/ctboyd .htm.

"Col. Charles Augustus Wikoff: Commanding Officer 22nd Infantry, January 28, 1897–June 20, 1898." 1st Battalion Website. http:// 1-22infantry.org/commanders/wikoffpers.htm.

"Colonel Miles Report to the War Department." War Department Reports, July 5, 1898.

"The Destruction of the USS *Maine*." Department of the Navy—Naval History and Heritage Command. www.history.navy.mil/browse-by -topic/disasters-and-phenomena/destruction-of-uss-maine.html.

"El Caney." Cuban Battlefields of the Spanish-Cuban-American War. http://cubanbattlefields.unl.edu/battlefields/El_Caney.php.

"The Final Years." National Park Service, US Department of the Interior.

"General Lawton the Victim of a Filipino Bullet." *The Call*, December 20, 1899.

"The History of Mexican Independence." Mexonline.com. www.mex online.com/mexican-independence.htm.

"Joaquín Vara del Rey y Rubio." Spanish-American War Centennial Website. www.spanamwar.com/delreydeath.htm.

"Las Guasimas." Cuban Battlefields of the Spanish-Cuban-American War. http://cubanbattlefields.unl.edu/battlefields/Las_Guasimas .php.

"Lieutenant-Colonel A. S. Daggett's Letter to Adjutant-General, Second Brigade, Second Division, Fifth Corps." July 5, 1898. www.history .army.mil/documents/spanam/BSSJH/25Inf.htm.

"Pancho Villa Raids US." History.com. www.history.com/this-day-in -history/pancho-villa-raids-us.

"The Philippine War: A Conflict of Conscience for African-Americans." National Park Service, US Department of the Interior.

"Presidio Garrison." National Park Service, US Department of the Interior.

"Pursuing Pancho Villa." National Park Service, US Department of the Interior.

"San Juan Heights." University of Nebraska–Lincoln, 2007–2008.

"The Santiago Campaign." University of Nebraska–Lincoln, 2007–2008.

"Second Lieutenant Henry O. Flipper: First Black Graduate of West Point." National Park Service, US Department of the Interior.

"Teddy Roosevelt and the Rough Riders." *Montauk Life*, 2004.

"Trouble at Key West: Negro Soldiers Create a Stir in the Island City." *Miami Metropolis*, April 22, 1898.

"25th Infantry Bicycle Corps." Historical Museum at Fort Missoula, Missoula, MT.

"The War in 1900–1901: African Americans in the Fil-Am War." Philippineamericanwar.webs.com. www.mikelatrinadedivulgacao .blogspot.com/2011/09/war-in-1900-1901-african-americans -in.html.

"William Shafter." Library of Congress.

"The World of 1898: The Spanish-American War." US Department of State: Office of the Historian. http://history.state.gov/milestones /1866-1898/spanish-american-war.

"World War I and the Buffalo Soldiers." National Park Service, US Department of the Interior.

"Yauco." *Puerto Rico Encyclopedia*. www.isnare.com/encyclopedia /Yauco,_Puerto_Rico.

Index